MW01127042

THE TECHNE OF GIVING

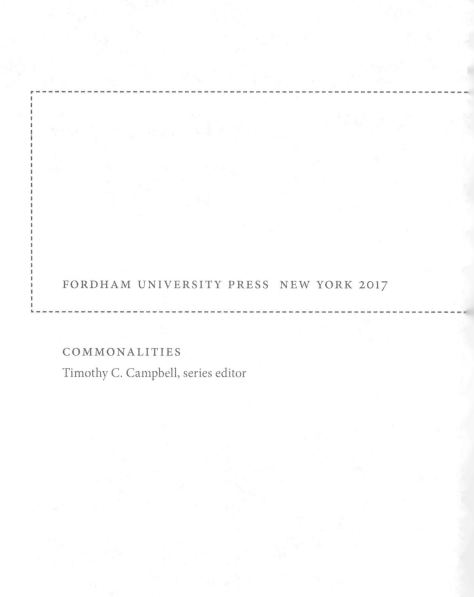

FORDHAM UNIVERSITY PRESS   NEW YORK 2017

COMMONALITIES

Timothy C. Campbell, series editor

THE TECHNE OF GIVING

Cinema and the Generous Form of Life

TIMOTHY C. CAMPBELL

Fordham University Press has no responsibility for the persistence or accuracy of URLs for external or third-party Internet websites referred to in this publication and does not guarantee that any content on such websites is, or will remain, accurate or appropriate.

Fordham University Press also publishes its books in a variety of electronic formats. Some content that appears in print may not be available in electronic books.

Visit us online at www.fordhampress.com.

Library of Congress Cataloging-in-Publication Data

Names: Campbell, Timothy C., author.
Title: The techne of giving : cinema and the generous form of life / Timothy
    C. Campbell.
Description: First edition. | New York : Fordham University Press, 2017. |
    Series: Commonalities | Includes bibliographical references and index.
Identifiers: LCCN 2016013978 | ISBN 9780823273256 (hardback) | ISBN
    9780823273263 (paper)
Subjects: LCSH: Motion pictures—Italy—History. | Motion pictures—Moral and
    ethical aspects. | Motion pictures—Philosophy. | BISAC: POLITICAL SCIENCE
    / History & Theory. | PHILOSOPHY / Political.
Classification: LCC PN1993.5.I88 C24625 2017 | DDC 791.430945—dc23
LC record available at https://lccn.loc.gov/2016013978

Printed in the United States of America

19 18 17   5 4 3 2 1

First edition

CONTENTS

Preface: Uncommon Grips vii

1 Forms of Life in a Milieu of Biopower   1

2 Freeing the Apparatus 42

3 "Dead Weight": Visconti
and Forms of Life 61

4 Playful Falls in a Milieu of Contagion 91

5 The Tender Lives of Vitti/Vittoria 117

Conclusion: Attention, Not Autopsy 161

Acknowledgments 167

Notes 169

Index 215

PREFACE: UNCOMMON GRIPS

This book began as a reflection on the possible relation between Italian cinema and contemporary reflections on biopolitics. Sensing a connection, I wondered if a number of classic Italian films might tell us something about contemporary life in both its political and less political forms. Surely, I thought, if philosophical genealogies of biopolitics were possible, then just as surely, a reading of biopolitics and cinema was there for the taking as well.

After some time, my perspective on cinema and biopolitics changed. I concluded that if films such as Luchino Visconti's *The Earth Trembles*, Roberto Rossellini's *Germany Year Zero*, and Michelangelo Antonioni's *Eclipse* were indeed reflections on the relation of (bio)power to life, then they were also ethical enterprises. These films continually show us how important it is to extend the meaning of holding, be it of ourselves, our ideas, or each other. Yes, these directors visualize the political conditions of their time, and yes, for some of that time, it makes sense to frame those conditions biopolitically. I came to understand, however, that just as important is noting how Visconti, Rossellini, and Antonioni model modes of spectatorship that, when taken together, constitute a heretofore ignored ethical horizon for postwar Italian cinema, that if I was going to write about a number of films from Italy that I love, I would have to propose something resembling an ethic of grips: an ethic of how we hold and how we let go. My hunch was that the commonalities among the films could be summed up in a series of questions. What is the relation of gratitude to fear in the films? How does the holding of one's body, self, or objects in and outside the frame allow occasions for reciprocity to become visible? And finally, how might we link these forms of holding (and letting go) to potential forms of life that could offer a response to contemporary biopower?

As I say, I began to describe the films as biopolitical enterprises, but not in the traditional sense with which we understand the term—as a conjunction between *bios* and *politikos* that Michel Foucault, among others, first saw as one of the defining biological thresholds modernity crosses at the end of the eighteenth century. For Foucault, and then more recently Giorgio Agamben, biopolitics has named what happens after notions of the political drift away from the ideological. No longer based simply on friend/enemy distinctions à la Carl Schmitt, biopolitics and with it biopower name two contemporary movements in which the political grows increasingly concerned with biology, health, populations, and how best to secure them. As my research here suggests, as important as the rise of biopower is, so too is the notion of grip and more broadly holding, which, if we follow an etymological line, allows us to link holding to having, to possessing. Indeed, the impression that forced itself upon me was simply that if biopower involved a kind of grip of biology over power, or for that matter the reverse, then one could just as easily imagine another response, this one based in reciprocity, forms of letting go, or what Émile Benveniste refers to as the circuit of generosity.

It was here that D. W. Winnicott's insights into "transitional objects" became decisive as they made it possible to pose a series of questions about cinema and biopolitics that otherwise might have gone unasked.[1] What happens when we center individual and collective forms of life on degrees of possession? How might the proliferation of "transitional objects" change our reading of a number of films and so point us in the direction of an ethical response to the unceasing search for objects possessed and expertise mastered. It is this search, to lay my cards squarely on the table, that anchors how I understand biopower. Thus, could these films provide us with modes of viewing more open to the non-possession and non-knowledge of what we see onscreen?[2] If so, how might we spell out the relation among viewership, forms of reciprocity, and forms of life? Clearly, to do so would require paying attention to those moments when grip becomes possession onscreen and off because it is then that possession functions as a lever for power to capture life.

Visconti, Rossellini, and Antonioni offer the following instruction: What counts more than anything else when viewing a film is the commonality that we as viewers have with the protagonists onscreen both in terms of how we hold things and how we hold ourselves. They do so by asking the spectator to pay attention to how actors hold, sway, or drift in the frame; how characters interact differently with landscapes made mobile by the cinematic apparatus; how hands and the bodies they stand in for receive and hold; and finally how bodies with hands learn how to take lightly and to release. In such a constellation of different forms of holding, we are asked to imagine different forms of reciprocity and to participate in making visible other possible social forms of life. In the alternately tight or loose grip of holding things, possible forms of life and possibly different futures emerge. It is thanks to that possibility that responses to contemporary biopower and its one-dimensional view on possession can be fashioned.

The adjective "generous" may raise eyebrows as it often appears far removed from the theoretical arsenal that many of us have at our disposal. Slight and seemingly ineffective, generosity fails to conjure up anything like power, multitudes, or force. In a world that would, if some are to be believed, consist solely of dispositifs, captured humanity, and the longed-for event, questions of how to imagine generosity, gratitude, and its off-shoots as offering any counter-dispositifs worthy of the name have often been met with silence.

While not yet speaking in the tongue of apparatuses, Friedrich Nietzsche did point out the importance of generosity. In the section "Learning to Do Homage" in *The Gay Science*, he lays out the bodily conditions for expressing thanks:

> Whoever goes in new paths and has led many persons therein, discovers with astonishment how awkward and incompetent all of them are in the expression of their gratitude, and indeed how rarely gratitude is able even to express itself. It is always as if something comes into people's throats when their gratitude wants to speak, so that it only hems and haws, and becomes silent again. The way in which a thinker succeeds in tracing the effect of his thoughts, and their transforming and convulsing power, is almost a comedy.[3]

With Nietzsche's focus on silence and gratitude in mind, I return across the following pages to the relation of gratitude to letting go, be it of objects and of words stuck in the throat, and also the I, the ego, and the self. The films that I discuss can help us pinpoint the ways we attend to our sense of self, identity, and giving when watching a film, and how doing so transforms things into objects, leading in many cases to how we as viewers may come to dispossess ourselves of these objects and identities.

But why even choose to make such a move? One response would be to see the films as fundamentally ethical—not ethical in the sense of rules to be followed, but in the pragmatic sense of how the films attempt to convince us of the advantages and perils of giving and receiving. A consequence is to invite us to speak differently about giving. Admittedly, I was also taken by the chance to update a political lexicon when discussing these films, all of them classics of twentieth century Italian cinema, a lexicon that to me at times feels to be deeply out of step with contemporary philosophical discussions. The study became a way of inserting discussions of some seminal Italian films into contemporary paradigms to better understand the political grouped around the rubric of the biopolitical. To return to Schmitt's friend/enemy distinction I mentioned earlier—that binary, if anything, has grown more persistent over the last decade as a way of understanding the political. It certainly has come to characterize a certain way of understanding biopolitics more properly as a thanatopolitics. And yet, biopolitics need not be read tragically. The following work resides squarely within an affirmative biopolitics, one that offers, for those willing, the chance to short-circuit the binary of friend and enemy.

You might well respond that this is an awful lot to ask of a film or, for that matter, a national cinema. And of course you would be right. Watching *The Earth Trembles* and *The Night* isn't going to change your life (or if it does, it won't be after just one viewing). Yet these films ask us to reflect without judgment on the relation between holding oneself and possible forms of life, to consider the possibility of a cinema of non-possession and the attending that is required of the spectator and then to consider with what effects. In one sense, this simply extends André Bazin's perspective on neo-realism as a phenomenology of holding to contemporary philosophical readings of violence and biopolitics.[4]

My perspective on a phenomenology of holding in the following pages breaks into two parts. In the first, I introduce a reading of gratitude that moves across a number of thinkers. The names will be known to everyone, and of course I will plead guilty to having drawn out those passages in which forms of reciprocity take on greater importance than in others. I follow up Chapter 1 with a reading of the cinematic apparatus in which I highlight its ability to construct reciprocity, a feature that sets it apart precisely from other apparatuses. It is here that the ground for a different reading of apparatus, and with it politics, begins to come into focus. In the later chapters, I put forward a number of films from Visconti, Rossellini, and especially Antonioni as extensions of some of the insights on gratitude from Chapter 1 that authors such as Adorno, Benjamin, Bataille, and Benveniste offer. Bringing a certain strand of contemporary thought and Italian postwar cinema together constitutes a wager: If new forms of political life are to take shape, then how might cinema, Italian cinema in particular, become the catalyst for creatively imagining what those forms of life may look like?

This raises further questions. How do these films make the case to the spectator that expressing gratitude leads to greater reciprocity? And, as long as we are still comfortable with these questions and their possibly uncomfortable answers, there is also this: What about the cinematic apparatus provides a counterweight to so much of what ails the self, the subject, our relations with others in our global society of the spectacle? To pick up on the title of the series of which this book is a part, what kind of commonality emerges in the interval between forms of life on film and the potential forms of life among spectators?

THE TECHNE OF GIVING

1

FORMS OF LIFE IN A MILIEU
OF BIOPOWER

Is there such a thing as biopower and if there truly is, how do we experience it? To frame the question in this way, without immediately having an answer at hand, moves us toward the often inscrutable features of biology crossed with power to the impact bodies experience when power and its subset, biopower, alter not only perceptions, and senses, but relations with others. The impression, Heideggerean at its root, has it that biopower is standardizing how we live bodily existences and that biopower normalizes thanks to the intensity with which biology allows power to target bodies.[1]

Over the last decade, a number of thinkers and activists, taking a page (admittedly, often the same page) from Michel Foucault, have constructed genealogies and archaeologies of biopower, as they attempt to fill the void that Foucault's death thirty years ago created in our understanding of biopower as category and threat. In particular, a number of philosophers from Italy, writing in the wake of what often feels like a second "Foucault Effect," have spelled out where they think biopower begins and where, if at all, it might end. For Toni Negri, contemporary biopower is founded on the increasing appropriation of labor power; for Roberto Esposito, biopower cannot be separated from the increasing immunization brought forward by globalization; while, lastly for Giorgio Agamben, biopower is part of a continuum that runs from *oikonomia*, in a not so distant past, to the emptied subjectivity known as bare life or *zoē* today.[2] All these accounts continue to dominate discussions of biopolitics, but because Agamben's account remains the most influential, with glosses on *homo sacer* spun off with great regularity, it is to his account that I want to turn at least initially in the pages that follow. To be clear at the outset, my engagement with Agamben's reading of biopolitics is meant to open a space in which other perspectives on life framed through reciprocity and generosity may become more available to us.

Much has already been written about Agamben's perspective on bare life and *homo sacer*.[3] Many have noted the effects of substituting biopower with a transformative reading of sovereignty as Agamben often does; many have focused on what happens when past and present merge in Agamben's biopolitical paradigm.[4] It is tempting, of course, to launch immediately into a discussion of the numerous insights of *Homo Sacer* across all of its volumes, or to choose from among the number of rich perspectives available on them. And yet let's put down these possible readings and take up instead a perspective on biopower, not as the force responsible for bare life, but rather biopower as a form of mythic violence intricately linked to fear. By registering how deeply mythic violence and its contemporary form in fear agitate in our understanding of biopower, we can, I believe, begin to sense how deeply the experience of fear runs across contemporary reflections of the human, our common future or lack thereof, and the biopolitical reasons for it. In my view, it is fear that often is driving our reading of biopower and in so doing reinforces it. Indeed, it is fear that often drives the tragic and negative readings of biopolitics that have come to characterize our understanding of the term. Can we imagine readings of biopower that would not immediately and inexorably lead to bare life? Is there another narrative concerning power, apparatus, and life more in line with the kinds of generous acts that may, if I may say so at this early stage, be more consistent with forms of life not linked only to subject, object, and self? These questions are the stepping stones to what lies at the heart of this book, namely gratitude as an antidote to fear and non-mastery as a response to biopower.

As Walter Benjamin's essay, "Critique of Violence," continues to underpin many readings of biopower, Agamben's included, it is the natural place to introduce the reading of biopower that continues to be featured in how we make sense of contemporary life.[5] Typically, glosses of the essay focus on the distinction between mythic and divine violence that Benjamin draws out in the essay, with attention frequently hovering over the latter term. My reading differs little initially since I, too, want to examine how Benjamin's two forms of violence relate to power and, in particular, the law. The reason for doing so will become clear soon enough to the reader because it concerns the relation of the law to uncertainty, fear, and violence. At the same time, let me repeat that the path leading through mythic violence, fear, and biopower is not intended to bring us once again to the tragedy of a negative biopolitics in which responses to biopower are impossible, nor is it meant to land us once again in a full-blown thanatopolitics. Rather, what lies on the other side of these negative readings is a more affirmative perspective that forgoes mastery and holding in favor of non-possession and something approaching generosity.

IMPROPER VIOLENCE

In a number of well-known passages from the essay, Benjamin sketches the relation of mythic and divine violence to law. Here is the first:

> If mythic violence is lawmaking, divine violence is law-destroying; if the former sets boundaries, the latter boundlessly destroys them; if mythic violence brings at once guilt and retribution, divine power only expiates; if the former threatens, the latter strikes; if the former is bloody, the latter is lethal without spilling blood.[6]

All mythic, lawmaking violence, which we might call "executive," is pernicious. Pernicious, too, is the law-preserving, "administrative" violence (*die verwaltete Gewalt*) that serves it. Divine violence as the sign and seal but never the means of sacred execution will be referred to as sovereign violence (*die waltende Gewalt*).[7]

Accordingly, the divine can have no truck with lawmaking violence. God, who slips in the essay to the divine, refuses a relation not with lawmaking but with the violence that is the condition for law-making. For its part, mythic violence arrives in two forms: executive and administrative. Administrative violence preserves and maintains the law and is political to the degree that it enforces, executes, and administers. Let's not wait too long before noting the close relation between administration and preservation: In order to protect, administration of the law is required, which preserves the law through its execution. Pushing further, we can conclude that an un-administered law is one bound for the dust heap.

Consider, too, how "verwaltete Gewalt" slides in the second passage from "die verwaltete Gewalt" to "die waltende Gewalt." Sovereign may not be the most appropriate translation of "waltende" in this instance as it fails to make clear what distinguishes "waltende Gewalt" from a "verwaltete Gewalt." Observe, in fact, how the prefix "ver" both intensifies "walten," and thus governing; "verwalten" augments violence, signaling greater power.[8]

Another passage from the essay confirms this reading:

> For blood is the symbol of mere life . . . For with mere life, the rule of the law over the living ceases. Mythic violence is bloody power [Blutgewalt] over mere life for its own sake [um ihrer selbst]; divine violence [die göttliche reine Gewalt] is pure power over all life for the sake of the living. The first demands sacrifice; the second accepts it [die erste fordert Opfer, die zweite nimmt sie an].[9]

Agamben will, in his readings of Benjamin, link mere life to the ending of the rule of the law over the living, which in turn he associates with Foucault's notion of a normalizing power.[10] The normalizing features of biopower that Foucault spelled out in Part III of volume 1 of *The History of Sexuality* are in Agamben's reading of Benjamin linked to the ceasing of the law to function over the living.[11] A bloody power linked to mythic violence is possible when the "verwaltete" features of mythic violence turn toward the living, with blood marking the greater violence of the mythic. Leaving aside this appropriation of mythic violence from Benjamin for one perspective on biopower, let's consider for now simply the conflation of mythic violence with blood, the body, and the emphasis on the "the living" over which the law no longer rules. Some of this is brought on again by *ver* preceding "walten." The dominion of the rule of law over the living intensifies under mythic violence to such an extent that a feedback loop results. The result is that these entities begin to inhabit a zone of lawlessness of captured humanity that merely lives. Implicit here then is a sense that divine violence is boundless, including as it does "power over all life."

One of the most important boundaries constructed by the law will be found between guilt and innocence. No one is seen as more guilty according to Benjamin than the living.[12] Indeed, for Benjamin the nexus between guilt and the living is precisely what he contests in another essay that deserves our attention, "Fate and Character."

Fate shows itself, therefore, in the view of life, as condemned, as having essentially first been condemned [*verurteilten*] and then become guilty [*schuldig*]. Goethe summarizes both phases in the words "the poor man you let become guilty." Law condemns not to punishment but to guilt. Fate is the guilt context of the living. It corresponds to the natural condition of the living—that semblance [*Schein*], not yet wholly dispelled, from which man is so far removed that, under its rule, he was never wholly immersed in it but only invisible in his best part. It is not therefore really man who has a fate; rather, the subject of fate is indeterminable.[13]

To live is to live with guilt. Moreover, it is this condemning—"verurteilen"—which intensifies judgment, linking it once again to the law. It is the law that enjoys a relation with guilt through fate: "Schicksal ist der Schuldzusammenhang des Lebendigen." It is the fate of man to live and die that makes man guilty. Yet this primacy of guilt should not blind us to a preceding moment in the essay in which living bare life (*bloßes Leben*), the indeterminable subject of fate, is condemned as guilty.

How are we to hold together the strands of Benjamin's reading of fate with mythic violence? We have mythic violence deeply enmeshed with fate so as to increase guilt and retribution. The suggestion is that for mythic violence to be extended, its mechanism depends upon "bringing guilt and retribution," where guilt and bare life are made homologous. Mythic violence works by placing fate front and center in its extension of guilt to the living. Fated to be guilty is what mythic violence employs as both its cause and its effect.

If that is the case, then we can see how mythic violence works across a number of areas today. Whenever a moment arises in which a subject cannot be determined and is, as a result, ignored, fate enters. Any strategy or event that moves the subject along the path to guilt will be intimately involved with mythic violence. Mythic violence, in other words, depends upon the law's condemnation of you; you should have known better or, more broadly, "a loser is a loser" in David Mamet's unforgettable phrase.[14] From pharmaceutical companies to drone attacks, mythic violence is premised on condemning before announcing guilt. Vast areas of the world are given over to natural and mere life and the subject is indeterminate of fate because there is no way of qualifying the subject of that intense judgment beyond ontological guilt. What else are drone strikes if not simply judgment by proximity to the guilty? My point in raising mythic violence in the wider context of the living and gratitude is simply that mythic violence depends upon a reading of fate and judgment in which the latter enjoys no relation to the particular attributes of the individual.

Benjamin's response to mythic violence is often found in the divine violence expressed by and in the general strike. "Fate and Character" offers another response and it is one that we may find surprising. Speaking of Nietzsche and the eternal return, Benjamin writes, "If a man has character, his fate is essentially constant. Admittedly, it also means: he has no fate—a conclusion drawn by the Stoics."[15] In order for this form of fate to be possible, something similar must happen to character. It needs to be related "to a natural sphere and to have no more to do with ethics or morality."[16] Continuing, he observes:

> On the other hand, the concept of character will have to be divested of those features that constitute its erroneous connection to that of fate. This connection is effected by the idea of a network that knowledge can tighten at will into a dense fabric.[17]

We know a person's character through those qualities that "indicate character traits that cannot be abstracted from moral evaluation."[18] Here Benjamin introduces the genre of comedy in relation to character because it is only in comedy that the character's actions do *not* lead to knowledge of the character of the individual—he or she is not a scoundrel (*Schurken*) in the comedy on stage, is not the "subject of moral condemnation [*Verurteiling*] but of high amusement [*Heiterkeit*]."

Heiterkeit merits a paragraph. The word originates in Sanskrit and signifies "glittering bright," which in turn in a contemporary sense has come to mean "serene" and "serenity" in addition to amusement.[19] If we take *Heiterkeit* not only as what names amusement and with it serenity, then the comedic character is not the indeterminate subject of fate, natural man, *blosses Leben*, but rather an individual whose actions reflect "the light of character." To be clear, with such a character, the moral effect of his or her actions will be nil. Indeed "his deeds are interesting" only insofar as they reflect that light.[20] The comedic character for Benjamin will naturally be sublime, which rests on an "anonymity of man and his morality, alongside the utmost development of individuality through its exclusive character trait."[21] Another name for such a development is "genius."[22]

COMEDY, CAPRICE, CHARACTER

Where does this brief foray into comedy and character lead? In two directions I think. First, the distinction between mythic and divine violence, and the ease with which divine violence is ceaselessly folded into thinking a certain form of biopolitics—the divine violence of the multitude in Negri and Hardt, for instance—implicitly suggests an acceptance of mythic violence's relation to biopower,[23] with divine violence moving to the labor power located in the multitude.[24] Yet if we connect the dots between Benjamin's reading of fate and mythic violence to character and the comedic, another possibility emerges, one to be found in opposing *Verurteiling* to *Heiterkeit*, that is the condemnation of natural life in opposition to the orientation to serenity. Indeed, if we take *Heiterkeit* as the serenity that results from seeing how deeds "reflect the light of character," then an interval might open, allowing us to oppose the mythic violence of biopower by turning to individual character. Furthermore, raising the possibility of the comedic in a moment of biopower requires that we find out whether a reading of the comic might offer an alternative to the tragic readings surrounding conflict, bare life, and biopower. In other words, Benjamin gestures to the possibility of separating character from fate and so short-circuiting the violence associated with myth.

The context of violence in light of comedy and serenity will be the bridge to a series of analyses of films from Italy that appear later, and I will have much more to say then apropos of how Antonioni, Visconti, and Rossellini imagine characters de-anchored from fate and thus from the "indeterminacy" of Benjamin's natural life. Admittedly, some readers may feel put off by a reading that highlights the comic features of these films, but please bear with me as I sketch how these films can help us fashion different responses to mythic violence based in gratitude and the different sense of reciprocity that it brings. These directors in my view are asking important questions in their films: What kind of reciprocity does one find in comedy? Is there a mode of reciprocity in comedy different from that of tragedy, one perhaps to be thought together with what Hegel disparagingly called "subjective caprice"?[25] Is there any room today to rehabilitate "subjective caprice" as response to mythic violence? It behooves us at least to consider how comedy might be employed when our frame moves to the violence of biopower premised on fear.

To be clear, we wouldn't have to turn to the comic if it weren't for the stunning inflation associated with the tragic in accounts of biopower. Some of the difficulty in locating an affirmative potential in tragic readings of biopower and biopolitics results from tragedy's enmeshment in mastery, and so the inability to see where individuation and the comic meet. *Pace* Agamben, this wouldn't necessarily be found only in genius. The reason for this is associated with the comic's undercutting of mastery, which an emphasis, even on the impersonal, only blurs.

GRATITUDE AND INVARIANCE—A FIRST TAKE

With these questions still lingering, let me propose a possible antidote to mythic violence and fear in the notion of gratitude. I want to begin with a reading from an unlikely source: Adorno and his 1956 *Notes to Literature*.[26] *Notes* contains some of Adorno's pithiest writings on a host of themes, not the least of which is literature's relation to the quotidian. One essay, in particular, stands out in a context of biopower and the living: "Parataxis: On Hölderlin's Late Poetry." Here Adorno examines two categories that Benjamin had written of in "Critique of Violence" and "Fate and Character," namely the mythic and fate.[27] Where Benjamin focused on violence and myth, Adorno surprisingly centers his reading on gratitude, especially as it emerges in Hölderlin's poem "Friedensfeier." After noting how intimately Hölderlin's poetry aligns itself with myth, Adorno notices something appearing to slip out of the poet's grasp: how powerfully language, "used poetically, shoots out beyond the mere subjective intention of the poet." Adorno names this configuration of moments "Dank" (gratitude). Quoting the following lines from the poem:

> For sparing, at all times sure of the measure,
> For a moment only a god
> Touches the houses of mean,
> Unforeseen, and no one knows it, who?
> And on it all manner of insolence may tread

And to the holy place the savage must come,
Ignorant of ends, and creduly feeling it, proves
His delusion and thereby strikes a fate,
but never at once does gratitude [Dank] follow such gifts.[28]

Adorno observes how the linguistic configuration of the poem leads the reader to conclude that gratitude is "the antithesis of fear, or, in Hegelian terms, as the qualitative leap that in responding to fate leads out of it."

> In its content, gratitude is purely and simply anti-mythological; it is what is expressed at the moment when eternal invariance is suspended. While the poet praises fate, the poetry, on the basis of its own momentum, opposes gratitude to fate, without the poet having necessarily intended this.[29]

Are there more beautiful lines to be found in Adorno's writings? Insights for which we respond, in turn, with gratitude? To express our gratitude, let's first note the none-too-obvious lining up of fear, fate, and myth. According to Adorno, fate drives fear, the former understood as eternal invariance, a future or futures that cannot be evaded. Where there is fate, fear is nearby. Gratitude arises exactly at the moment when Hölderlin, praising fate, sets in motion the impetus for a series of moments "that taken together signify more than the structure intends." Adorno collects these moments under the title of gratitude, finding that the anti-mythological features of the poem coalesce around those instances able to block invariance, though not through any specific and localizable "content" of the poem. This occurs instead thanks to a connection of moments that together evoke a structural response to fate. Fear necessarily will hold sway for as long as we fail to name exactly its antithesis in gratitude. Hegel's appearance confirms this; the "qualitative leap" of gratitude out of fear, one that bravery or courage or any of those near cousins to fear cannot match. The reason is clear. Those terms remain inscribed in the register of fear and cannot constitute a "leap" of the sort that gratitude does. They don't lead out of fate, out of the tragic, or out of the negative.

The passage stands out for another reason. The content of gratitude "is purely and simply anti-mythological" to the degree that it announces a suspension of eternal invariance. This doesn't mean that gratitude itself somehow suspends eternal invariance, but rather that such a suspension is linked to its impact on the poem's content. And that impact is measured in the degree to which the fog of myth and fear clears. Furthermore, the break in invariance doesn't actually concern how the void of myth is filled, but rather only how one ought to hold open such a void. Holding open the interval allows for momentum to arise, where interval names the distance "between the extended and the unextended," and the possibility of marking the tension without which extension and dis-tension would have no meaning. Lastly, let's make a note of the contrasting terms Adorno employs: on one hand, invariance and fate, and on the other, the "suspension" of invariance and its result, gratitude. Too often, we understand fate as merely invariance, which renders fear nothing other than the daily (and ultimately useless fight) against that which never changes.

The foray into Adorno and myth opens a window from which to observe how gratitude relates to poetic form. The question to be asked, according to Adorno, is this: "What form itself, as sedimented content, does. Only when one asks this does one notice that the language creates distance."[30] The sedimented content that together spells the moments that exceed fate is another name for form: the form of the poem, or more specifically parataxis. Parataxis suspends invariance. Here the stakes of Adorno's reading of Hölderlin for a discussion of fear and biopower become clearer. Parataxis interrupts, prying away fear from fate, the consequence of which will be to replace myth with gratitude. Parataxis rhetorically refuses the hypostasis of fate and with it the readings that only promote the negative.

Cutting to the chase—is there a way of translating parataxis from a rhetorical lexicon to a biopolitical one? Might the form of the poem that impedes myth and violence be made to work biopolitically? Certainly, others writing after Adorno recognized the power of parataxis. Roland Barthes saw its power clearly, locating it in a "circularity in which no one (not even the author) has an advantage over anyone else."[31] When one considers how thoroughly real, communal connections among people, animals, and worlds have become unmoored, a tactics of parataxis might be able to undercut the continued creation of hypostatic forms of life in which a few lives dominate over many others; in which a few languages dominate over others. This would be a practice in which the notion of form resists the power of the I to consider itself as everything.

In such a situation, parataxis promises to arrange forms of life next to one another without regard to rank. Today, in a moment of community breakdown and an increasingly dominant narrative of the impossibility of community coming into being (or for that matter coming back), we face hypostasis at every corner: the ordering of lives according to logical schema and with it the creation and maintenance of hierarchies. This isn't surprising given how deeply affiliated hypostasis is with mastery, logic, and fate. This follows this, and then this, all bent on coordinating the lower (the Greek *ipo* signifies "under" and "below"): subordinate clauses, subordinate lives. But rather than accepting hypostasis as the only reality in a contemporary ontology of actuality, it makes more sense to highlight *tassein*, that is arrangements and tactics that "set aright." Adorno says as much when he notes the possibility of elaborating a *tatikos techne*, which is an art of arranging. The question will be how to think this tactical techne through a powerful enough parataxis capable of breaking free of mythic violence.

TAKE TWO—BENVENISTE, EXCHANGE, GRACE

Moving along in an itinerary from gratitude to a tactics of reciprocity, the moment has arrived to introduce Émile Benveniste's reading of gratitude and exchange as he draws it in his *Indo-European Language and Society*. It is here that we can begin to flesh out what a tactics of generosity might actually look like. Near the conclusion of the entry on grace, and after noting that in a money-based civilization to "show grace" means to suspend an obligation to pay for the service received,"[32] Benveniste writes:

> Yet the reciprocal process of supply and demand can be interrupted voluntarily: here intervene services without return, offerings "by grace and favor," pure acts of "grace," which are the starting points of a new kind of reciprocity. Above the normal circuit of exchange—where one gives in order to obtain—there is a second circuit, that of benefice and gratefulness, what is given without thought of return, what is offered in thankfulness.[33]

For Benveniste, new forms of reciprocity begin when one does not give in order to have but instead gives with no consideration of receiving something in return. Where Adorno finds in parataxis a momentum of moments that propel form into content so as to empty content of myth, Benveniste notes something else, less a horizontal relation than a vertical one, which is captured in Benveniste's description "above the normal circuit of exchange" and with it the distance between one circuit and another. Thought marks the distance between them—one gives and no thought arises of return, whereas in the "normal" circuit, a giving is accompanied by the thought of what one will obtain. On one hand, there is the thought that takes. On the other hand, there is the non-thought that lies above.

A further affinity suggests itself between Benveniste's distinction of two economic circuits and the myth that anchors Adorno's reading of Hölderlin. In Benveniste's first circuit of giving to obtain, we have something that resembles the calculus of giving characterizing the law as well as myth, especially with regard to the market. Consider the meaning of "obtain" in this regard, especially in the "normal circuit" and the opposition between obtaining (from the Latin *ob* and *tenere*, to hold, keep), and offering (from the Latin, *offerre*, to bestow). Obtaining marks a kind of possession in which giving equals receiving, which rhymes with how *Black's Law Dictionary* envisions the relation among holding, having, and possessing. The entry for "have" on this score merits a look: "In the civil law, to have. Sometimes distinguished from *tenere* (to hold), and *possidere* (to possess); *habere* referring to the right, tenere to the fact, and *possidere* to both."[34] Now consider the entry for "*tenere*":

> Lat. In the civil law. To hold; to hold fast; to have in possession; to retain. In relation to the doctrine of possession, this term expresses merely the fact of manual detention, or the corporal possession of any object, without involving the question of title; while *habere* (and especially *possidere*) denotes the maintenance of possession by a lawful claim; i. e., civil possession, as distinguished from mere natural possession.[35]

To see holding as having in possession—and not as having title to—implies the existence of a weaker form of possession and having.[36] It will continue to be thought of as calling forth a corporeal possession of an object. The possibility hinted at is that the holding will come to an end either when holding completely ceases or when the holding intensifies and so moves to a maintenance of possession. To complicate matters, however, maintenance etymologically recalls a holding in the hand, which in turn suggests that the corporeal possession of the object differs from the holding in the hand, which "denotes the maintenance of possession." Possession is taken to mean the "detaining" of an object by the hand for some time, but *not* the extended "holding" in the hand of the object. It is the difference between detaining and holding.

The "doctrine of possession" towers over our understanding of holding and so one would want to consider the role of possession and its changing role in relation to labor in the work of Kant and Locke, among many others.[37] For now, we might see the distinction between holding and possession this way: Possession names a powerful mode of holding. The mode of holding (or *tenere*) involves a form of manual detention linked to the question of title. Maintaining possession over time then becomes the mark of the difference in degrees of holding. One holds the title and the object longer than one does by merely holding the object. Eventually this will come to mark the difference between civil and natural possession.[38]

How are we then to understand the new circuit of reciprocity that Benveniste superimposes over the "normal" circuit of giving to obtain with the form(s) of *tenere*? The answer lies in translating "what is given without thought of return" in Benveniste's phrase into the terms of natural possession—that is, into a kind of less intense corporeal possession that does not involve title. There is a kind of holding when we project ourselves into the future with the thought of receiving another object in return. It is the thought that possesses, which is to say, that marks the potential for a future having. Implicit in this reading is possession as virtuality; of giving and receiving based upon maintaining a future object, one held virtually in the mind, and with it the possibility for holding in return. Memory provides the continuity over time that a literal maintaining in the hand does not. The point of such virtual possession is simply that holding a future object in the hand creates a sense of having which in turn can become the basis for a title. The giving to obtain is premised on a function of memory, that is on the possession of a future object of thought.

Giving without consideration of receiving for Benveniste ("what is given without thought of return") short-circuits the form of holding as possession precisely because there is no projection into the future of a possible response. There is no "hope," which also means that there is no fear at the prospect of no future receiving. Now some may say that such a form of giving with no link to the future or the past offers so little in terms of reward or payoff that any chance of the second circuit operating above the "normal" circuit is bound to fail. Leaving such a judgment aside for the moment, we might simply acknowledge that the form of giving from which some future receiving has been subtracted enjoys a relation to that same subject though it may, however, make more sense in such a context of privation to speak less of subjects than another category that signals in ways that subject does not a constitutive openness to the other through non-reception.

AFFECT AND FATE

The relation of future reception to giving brings us back to the earlier context of fate and myth. Benveniste's etymology of grace and reciprocity—alongside the juridical meaning of natural holding (*tenere*) as non-possession—involves how one imagines the future and holds it to be likely. With that belief comes the potential to hold (or not) and so to possess (or not) in the future. Ultimately, the fate of possessing is at issue here—the fate that our holding in the present moment becomes possession when projected into the future. Fate read through Benveniste, Benjamin, and Adorno revolves around a future potential for owning, a supply and demand of objects given and objects potentially received that forms the myth of normal circuits of reciprocity. If we were to speak of a will to power in terms of gratitude, it would be a will to constitutive openness that comes when no gift has been given or received. Here I have in mind the gloss that Gilles Deleuze provides of active and reactive forces in Nietzsche's conception of will to power, especially the translation of will to power "as a capacity for being affected."[39]

> Similarly, for Nietzsche, the capacity for being affected is not necessarily a passivity but an *affectivity*, a sensibility, a sensation. It is in this sense that Nietzsche, even before elaborating the concept of the will to power and giving it its full significance, was already speaking of a feeling of power . . . This is why Nietzsche always says that the will to power is 'the primitive affective form" from which all other feelings derive.[40]

With "primitive affective form" in mind, the notion of form of life offers itself as a more helpful term when thinking the relation of gratitude to mythic violence. Although I will have much more to say about the value added of using the term "forms of life," I would like at this juncture simply to note that the term "subject" often appears to be less constitutive of gratitude than form of life, where the latter marks that "primitive affectivity" or sensibility that attends to sensations while foregoing the "normal" circuit of giving and receiving. Form of life names an entity that gives attention, that attends to those sensations in such a way that reception (or reaction) does not necessarily follow.[41] The term form of life operates here as what Kenneth Burke describes as a "terministic screen" in ways fundamentally different from subject.[42] Form of life bridges between will to power and affectivity in such a way as to highlight the missing place generosity has in our contemporary understanding of subject. Another way of saying this is that by emphasizing forms of life, we move closer to modes of affectivity and away from the fatedness and mastery that often characterizes subject or self for that matter.

What Benveniste and Adorno share in their notions of gratitude and grace is the role precisely played by parataxis. For Benveniste, the second circuit of exchange is premised on the notion of "services without a return" and "what is given without thought of return." The emphasis on no return is remarkable. There is no thought of return, no hypostasis that would weigh giving more than receiving, or vice-versa. Instead, we find a placing side by side without coordination while attending to sensory perception in such a way that the subject of parataxis com-poses (to place next to) the objects of sense perception. Here the earlier difficulty of translating parataxis biopolitically appears easier to manage: Parataxis would name the practice of being in the world that arranges without creating hierarchies among what we see, sense, think about, and judge. In other words, parataxis as a practice seems particularly suited for forms of life to the degree that the form that practices parataxis is the one capable of holding a number of sensations without simultaneously identifying with them, without hypostasizing forms of life. Benveniste's second circuit of exchange also suggests a mode of Deleuze's "affective openness" to the future held in a present suspension of inevitability. In Benveniste's reading, no connection exists between a gift or giving and a future moment of receiving. This is precisely what Adorno and Benveniste share in their perspectives on gratitude, namely that the second circuit delinks giving to consequence and so lessens calculation.[43]

And yet not all receptions involve the same degree of holding and having, touching and grasping. Some receptions reinforce possession less than others. Indeed, we might read the suspension of inevitability as delaying more closed, more powerful moments of grasping. That no one kind of holding is valid for all, be it material holding or the holding of thoughts, beliefs, or even the sense of self. Indeed some forms of holding are more likely to lead to openness and affect than others. Parataxis will name the practice that leads to the suspension of the inevitability of receiving, acknowledging that not all giving reciprocally calls forth the same kind of receiving. This represents a key moment for moving toward forms of life that are more open to possible futures.

Before leaving Adorno and Benveniste, two other points are worth noting even though a full discussion is beyond the scope of this book. The first concerns the relation between possession and community. In the previous passage I cited on *tenere* and possession, Carol Rose quotes the judgment in the case of *Slatin's Properties, Inc. v. Hassler*: "Possession" means acts that "'apprise the community[,] . . arrest attention, and put others claiming title upon inquiry.'"[44] Possession apparently serves to break into attention and so doing to "apprise" the community. Said slightly differently, possession when thought communally functions both to distract and capture community and its members who may themselves want to claim a title. Note that in such a perspective, attention is constitutive of community; that community may be thought of as the attention that precedes possession or that which comes before a determination of what is mine and what is ours. If we translate into terms of holding and gratitude, community preceding possession is that entity in which objects, things, our bodies, and our selves are held in attention without moving to ownership or to identification. In this perspective, community represents a form of *tenere* characterized by the gratitude that is experienced when no thought of receiving some thing in return for having given occurs. Such a giving ought to be joined to the attention of a community with no demands made on how the community's members attend without possessing.

This kind of perspective on possession and holding responds powerfully to neo-liberalism. When biopower turns to the biology of individual members of the community, offering them the possibility (which is nearly akin to the likelihood) that they can mine their own bodies because they possess a title to them, other members are put on notice that they, too, have title to their bodies (this is because possession is premised on a series of divisions—of self from self, body from other bodies, limbs from body or bodies). If possession represents a kind of grip with a title, then holding without possession may well escape the neoliberal fatedness of ownership. Neo-liberalism is a way of taking those things that contribute to community, namely attention without identification or title to what one sees or feels. It works against primitive affective forms by continually positing that every gift be received and every reception be taken for something given. Such moments of no returns are precisely what capitalism and its hyper form, neo-liberalism, cannot fathom: the possibility of a reciprocity not founded on return.

PROPER AND IMPROPER GIFTS

We should not underestimate the importance of this insight. It is what Jacques Derrida in a not so different context spoke of as "given time" and the impossible gift that is neither given nor received. Understanding the importance of how to give and what to give as well as receive goes to the heart of what is and what remains one of the most pressing questions of our lives. How are we to imagine a notion of the common that doesn't call forth what Roberto Esposito calls the immunitary *dispositif*?[45] If community names a gift that individual members of the community cannot refuse (to give), then the only option for not giving or receiving will be refusing the gift of *munus* by those who are immune (and why would they chose to forego immunity?). Yet this brief tour of gratitude through Benveniste and Adorno suggests another possibility. We can hold in attention what is given and received for as long as possible, allowing the interval to create momentum to allow for gratitude to appear.

Such a reading of attention as a holding that is not a having is implicitly contained in Derrida's reading of the gift. Let's recall those stunning passages on the circle and the impossibility of the gift in *Given Time*:

If the other gives me back or owes me or ought to give me back what I give him or her, there will not have been a gift, whether this restitution is immediate or whether it is programmed by a complex calculation of a long-term deferral or, if you like, différance. This is all too obvious if the other, the donee, gives me back immediately the same thing.

He adds:

It may, moreover, be a matter of a good thing or a bad thing. Here we are anticipating another dimension of the problem, namely, that if giving is spontaneously evaluated as good (it is well and good to give and what one gives, the present, the cadeau, the gift, is a good), it remains the case that this good can easily be reversed. We know that as good, it can also be bad, poisonous (Gift, gift), and this is true from the moment the gift puts the other in debt, so that giving comes down to hurting, to doing bad; here one need hardly mention the fact that in certain languages, for example in French, one may say as readily "to give a gift" as "to give a blow" [*donner un coup*], "to give life" as "to give death" [*donner la mort*], thereby either dissociating and opposing them or identifying them.

A stunning conclusion follows:

> Even though all the anthropologies, indeed the metaphysics of the gift have, quite rightly and justifiably, treated together, as a system, the gift and the debt, the gift and the cycle of restitution, the gift and the loan, the gift and credit, the gift and the countergift, we are here departing, in a peremptory and distinct fashion, from this tradition. That is to say, from tradition itself. We will take our point of departure in the dissociation, in the overwhelming evidence of this other axiom: There is gift, if there is any, only in what interrupts the system as well as the symbol, in a partition without return and without division [*repartition*], without being-with-self of the gift-countergift.[46]

An interruption in the system of gift and debt, loan or cycle of restitution signals that a gift has been given.[47] Symbol and system, the cycle of giving of intentions, things, is interrupted and with it division follows. At one moment, a mode of being appears: It is one Derrida refers to as the "without being-with-self" of the circle of gift-countergift. The phrase is difficult to understand, and so perhaps reversing the final sentence may prove helpful. When there is a gift—we note Derrida's avoidance of reception throughout—a break in the dialectic of gift-countergift is registered in the appearance of a being that enjoys a different relation to self. It is not a being *with* self because being with self is the proof that a gift has been received and is not simply present ontologically.

What is the nature of the interruption that breaks the circle, circulation, and calculation of gift-countergift? It is the gift that cannot be named as such. Indeed, Derrida's deconstruction of gift is intended to show that there is no such thing as a proper gift, but only improper ones that circulate thanks to their own impropriety. As a result, we come face to face with the aporia of the gift and with it the key relation between indebtedness and the exchange of gift-countergift. One of the only recourses would appear to reside in refusing to name what has been given as a gift, or to acknowledge the impossibility of appropriation.[48]

Yet what if interruptions in the circulation of improper gifts aren't isolated; what if the circle that joins giving and receiving isn't to be thought only in terms of the object of giving or taking, but is seen as an instance not understood in terms of one object? In other words, what would an intransitive giving look like? Giving without object would bring in its wake a mode of being that no longer is supplemented with the self that arises out of the movement of exchange, what Derrida calls the gift-countergift. What would distinguish this mode or form—to pick up on the relationality of event and form—from the subject constituted by the impropriety of the gift identified as gift? I return often to these important questions in later chapters when I look for instances of generosity in a number of films, but for now let me observe that attention might well be a practice that avoids the giving of improper gifts if not completely then perhaps initially.[49]

"GIVING AWAY"

Thanks to Roberto Esposito, we know how deeply community and giving are enmeshed. The *munus* in his reading emerges as the gift that cannot be refused, bringing in its wake the co-*munus* or community. Yet I wonder in this relation between giving and community, if another, attenuated form of community is possible, one that is less indebted to *munus* as gift and hence to the giving of gifts.

Few more than Georges Bataille thought and lived more intimately or more corporeally this relation between community and the gift. At the same time, Bataille's work raises further questions that will prove helpful when turning to the individual and collective forms of life that appear across a number of films. For Bataille as well as for Rossellini and Antonioni, it becomes possible to arrest the inevitability of possession and identification through attention, so that attention becomes the impetus for imagining and living other forms of life. A number of questions guide my discussion of Bataille. How does Bataille offer a response to Derrida's reading of gift such that we can consider ways of giving and receiving a thing without naming it as a gift (where gift suggests more an object that changes hands and less a thing)? What can we call gifts that are not objects? Are there things we receive that are not received as gifts, ones that we can receive differently to the degree we alter the way we hold, have, and possess them? And finally, can we receive things without making them our own?

These questions emerge nearly fully formed in a number of Bataille's texts, but especially in "The Gift of Rivalry: Potlatch." Here, not surprisingly, Bataille, too, notes the importance of the economic in gift giving:

> If there is within us, running through the space we inhabit, a movement of energy that we use, but that is not reducible to its utility (which we are impelled by reason to seek), we can disregard it, but we can also adapt our activity to its completion outside us. The solution of the problem thus posed calls for an action in two contrary directions: We need on the one hand to go beyond the narrow limits within which we ordinarily remain, and on the other hand somehow bring our going-beyond back within our limits.[50]

The issue for Bataille concerns the relation of gift to surplus:

> The problem posed is the expenditure of the surplus. We need to give away, lose or destroy. But the gift would be senseless if it didn't take on the meaning of an acquisition. Hence giving must be acquiring a power. Gift-giving has the virtue of a surpassing of the subject who gives, but in exchange for the object given, the subject appropriates the passing. He regards his virtue, that which had the capacity for, as an asset, as a power that he now possesses.[51]

For Bataille, one gives in order to receive and thus to acquire a power. Is this true of all giving or are there gifts given that remain things unhindered by possession? An initial approach is to ask how an object might be opposed to what one gives away ("object" is Bataille's preferred choice rather than "thing"). It is this giving away of an object that enmeshes the giver in power relations, that makes giving about exchange and thus about power. For Bataille, the question of giving cannot be separated from a movement of energy outside of utility—indeed the narrative of the entire essay is one from non-utilitarian energy to the adaptation of that energy outside of us. It is the dual movement of inside and outside and the desperate "somehow" when bringing "our going back" within a limit that lingers. Energy is conceived as surplus expended in such a movement of going-beyond and remaining. The difficulty of the passage is that such an expenditure of surplus energy relates to the action of giving, and that in giving, we give to get, an action Benveniste and Derrida both see as constituent of ungenerous forms of exchange.

Yet the "going beyond" needs to be thought in terms of the act of giving, which accounts for Bataille's suggestion that we reverse how we traditionally understand exchange. "We need to give away," he writes and the obvious question is give away what? For Bataille, the answer is simply that it does not matter. What we give has less power than the simple act of giving away: the intransitive versus the transitive. Here, then, we return to the earlier moment of giving and the power that giving bestows on the giver. What is the nature of the power that runs to the giver? For Bataille, it is power based on the appropriation of "the passing," which is to say of making the passing more properly the giver's own. It is also the power of believing oneself to possess a virtue, to grab hold of that virtue and thus to gain title to it. This is, of course, how giving is understood in liberal and neoliberal terms, where the appropriation of gift-giving by the individual involves as well that portion of giving of what before was held to be a commonly held thing. The gift held in common is the one that can be given without sense of reward or virtue gained because it does not belong to, nor can it be appropriated by an individual. The phrase *Timeo danaos et dona ferentes* is borne out of this attempt to appropriate "passing."

Note as well how deeply Bataille's perspective on gift-giving and virtue is premised on giving so as to acquire something in return. It still retains the stamp of giving to receive, which differs from the other circuit of generosity based around a *tenere* without having. We can conclude that Bataille's surplus of energy and virtuous power fails to register the possibility of a holding that does not bring with it power, mastery, or virtue.

Bataille senses this when the topic turns to potlatch and the revolutionary potential therein. Under the title "The Apparent Absurdity of Gifts," he writes:

> But "you can't have your cake and eat it too," the saying goes. It is contradictory to try to be unlimited and limited at the same time, and the result is comedy: The gift does not mean anything from the standpoint of general economy; there is dissipation only for the giver. Moreover, it turns out that the giver has only apparently lost.[52]

His conclusion?

> Thus the gift is the opposite of what it seemed to be: To give is obviously to lose, but the loss apparently brings a profit to the one who sustains

it . . . Actually as I have said, the ideal would be that a potlatch could not be repaid. The benefit in no way corresponds to the desire for gain. On the contrary, receiving prompts one—and obliges one—to give more, for it is necessary to remove the resulting obligation.[53]

What is required is a giving and receiving that does not bring in its wake an obligation of future gift-giving. Is there a way of imagining reciprocity that doesn't move to mutual obligation, that is a receiving that dissipates the power that accrues to the giver of a gift (since clearly the issue for Bataille about gift-giving, even in potlatch, is that the giver comes to possess a power and appropriate a virtue)? Following this out further leads us back to the question Derrida posed. In order for gift-giving not to count as power, an ontological mode of not-being there for the reception of the gift is required, or concurrently, a mode of non-appropriation of the passing of the gift as one's own. This would be a form of reciprocity that fails to set in motion the circuit of exchange.

Can one accept a gift without at the same time being prompted to feel an obligation?[54] Would such a view presuppose that for such a circuit of exchange to be possible, a subject as giver and receiver must be present? If so, it begs the question of an opening to a form of subjectivity that is not-present. Both questions are important and the instinct is to rush ahead. Yet let's hasten slowly and focus on the insight that not all gifts must be received. Not everything that is received as a gift need necessarily qualify as a gift in a system of obligation associated with potlatch. And, as contradictory as this may sound in a chapter devoted to gifts and giving, perhaps what needs to be combated is precisely the inflation around gifts and giving—moving away from a perspective that totalizes all giving and receiving as involving an object known as a gift.

This is the context surrounding Bataille's phrase "intimacy with things." Writing on the relation between thing, holding, and object, he observes:

Intimacy is expressed only under one condition by the thing (la chose); that this thing fundamentally be the opposite of a thing, the opposite of a product, of merchandise, a burn-off (consummation) and a sacrifice. Since intimate feeling is a burn-off, it is burning-off that expresses it, not the thing, which is its negation.[55]

Bataille uncovers two regimes of thing (*la chose*) that cross the heart of intimacy. Only on the near side of the thing, as *la chose* and not product (merchandise, burn-off, and sacrifice), does intimacy arise. Product negates an intimacy with things to the degree that the produced thing is consumed and as such stands in for a consummation that would formerly have been the purview of an intimacy with *la chose*. Translating the passage into the key terms of holding and gratitude, we might say that a certain kind of grip characterizes the relation with *la chose* as non-product or non-merchandise, and that the name to be given to it is intimacy, a grip that makes possible a consummation and not consumption.[56] In other words, the way that one holds a thing expresses a kind of intimacy with it that is the predecessor to consummation and sacrifice. The thing remains apart as the negation of the burning off.

Clearly, Bataille is speaking of the ways in which things remain as things and not as products, merchandise, and possessions and so helps push forward our understanding of gratitude into areas often seen as far removed from it. Consider this. To the degree that one names something, intimacy is less likely. In an increasingly filled-up world of products, objects, and names, Bataille suggests that our current situation is premised on a proximity to things that makes the consumption of them infinitely easier but at a huge cost to proper intimacy, to borrow the language of neo-liberalism. The product as the negated negation dooms intimacy.

In terms of generosity, here and across volume 1 of *The Accursed Share*, Bataille allows us to see how intimacy with things precludes certain forms of holding. We might go further and say that the difficulty with the gift is precisely its enmeshment with the product. The way one holds the gift as thing will express an intimacy that precludes other forms of holding. Circling back to Benveniste's earlier circuit, gratitude concerns the mode of receiving things but not gifts, which is to say, receiving things without consuming them or choosing to linger over a secondary burn-off. The giving of a gift sets in motion a circuit of exchange and hence of power—the power that comes to the one who gives and the obligation to the one who receives. If one gives, however, without thought of return (of future consequence, of virtue), then we cannot give what we do not possess, or for that matter, we cannot give what we are not intimate with. We cannot receive what has been given intimately as it precludes ownership, mastery, and possession.

Armed with a perspective on the relation of holding to intimacy, we can now return to forms of life as terministic screen. To speak of a non-intimacy with things requires a different name for the being that handles things without consuming them. Subject and self, individual and entity, too often appear bound up with burn-off and sacrifice. The term form of life captures better the possibility of avoiding a mere intimacy with things as consumption for two reasons. First, it is difficult to speak of possessing a form of life. Constitutive of the notion of form of life, rather, is precisely non-possession that allows movement from one form to another. Such a movement frequently goes missing when our focus shifts to subject. "You must change your life," commands Peter Sloterdijk, by which he means your form of life, but it isn't clear how one might change one's subject. The reason will be found in the missing possessive in form of life: my form of life, your form of life, our form of life,[57] Second, form of life makes tactical sense—in Adorno's earlier formulation—given the relation between mythic violence and biopower, which is to say that by foregoing the fixedness of self and subject, it may be easier to recuperate gratitude as an important experience of intimacy whose momentum can respond to mythic violence. Foucault believed this was the case in antiquity. Writing in *The Hermeneutics of the Subject*, he explains it this way:

> Anyway, a certain particular form-of-life, which is distinct from all other forms of life in its particularity, will in fact be regarded as the real condition of the care of the self. So, in reality, the care of the self in ancient Greek or Roman Culture was never really seen, laid down, or affirmed as a universal law valid for every individual regardless of his mode of life. The care of the self always entails a choice of one's mode of life, that is to say a division between those who have chosen this mode of life and the rest.[58]

If there is no subject, I, or the self, what Foucault acknowledges in the impersonal "one" in the last sentence, the move to possess a form of life makes little sense. At the same time, the relation between care of the self and form of life remains unclear. Key to the difficulty is the role that choice plays when caring for the self. One can only care for the self to the extent that one has chosen a mode of life—to the degree that one has chosen possession. The problem, should we want to describe it that way, with care of the self lies precisely in the "always" that accompanies "entails." What Foucault cannot see (and see past) is the division between those who have chosen a form of life and those who have not. Admittedly, he couches his views on care of the self in a reading of Stoicism and not biopower and so it is difficult to separate his own views from those others he is discussing here. Still, Foucault's attempt is helpful to the degree that mythic violence and care for the self depend upon mutual origination as an appropriation of form of life. So much of Agamben's more affirmative response to biopower in *The Coming Community* hinges on weakening the relation between whatever singularity and the self. For Agamben, as for Foucault, however, whatever singularity and the impersonal depend upon a prior moment in which form is appropriated.[59]

Given how much of this reading of gratitude depends upon the perspective we adopt vis-à-vis form of life, allow me put some more of my cards on the table. The first comes from Ludwig Wittgenstein. Now it is true that Wittgenstein wrote very little about forms of life and that, when he did, he did so enigmatically. Any attempt to appropriate Wittgenstein's form of life for a reading of generosity risks pushing up against other readings that may either be more vitalistic or equally more in line with his notion of language games. Their brevity and infrequency notwithstanding, his observations do suggest ways forward in linking possession to forms of life. He notes for instance in "On Certainty" that "my life consists in my being content to accept many things." Later he will famously refer to the simple absence of doubt as "comfortable certainty."[60] Here is a relevant passage:

> Now I would like to regard this certainty, not as something akin to hastiness or superficiality, but as a form-of-life. (That is very badly expressed and probably badly thought as well.) But that just means that I want to conceive of it as something that lies beyond being justified or unjustified; as it were, as something animal.[61]

How are we to relate certainty to "form-of-life" if the former lies beyond "being justified or unjustified"? If certainty can be thought vitally, then so can degrees of uncertainty, which is precisely what the reference to comfort would appear to involve. We have degrees of more comfortable and less comfortable certainty, where that which is named is not actually certainty or uncertainty but rather how the thinker relates to both.

Wittgenstein's perspective suggests that form of life will be the form that skeptically holds its own level of discomfort around uncertainty.[62] About the nature of certainty itself, differences in forms of life will consist of the degree to which that form is comfortable with uncertainty. Another way of putting this is what matters most in a vitalist recuperation of Wittgenstein's form-of life won't be life per se but rather uncertainty.

Wittgenstein adds other pieces to his perspective on forms of life, the most helpful coming from his later *Philosophical Investigations*. In the first passage, he notes how "it is easy to imagine a language consisting only of orders and reports in battle . And to imagine a language means to imagine a form-of-life."[63] Later he asks: "Can only those hope who can talk? Only those who have mastered the use of a language. That is to say the phenomena of hope are modes of this complicated form-of-life." Hope may spring eternal, but for Wittgenstein, hope is to be thought of primarily in relation to the mastery of language and hence to the form of life that is human. Hoping indeed would be the activity linked to the mastery of language that sets the human form of life apart from other forms of life, including the animal. In terms of the directors soon to be examined, each in his own way offers visual languages in the dialect of attention.[64] That language becomes visible in the interaction among forms of life onscreen, which raises the question: What elements of visual language can be assembled so as to form a life onscreen? Unfortunately, Wittgenstein's emphasis on language as game suggests that speaking for him may be the only symbolic activity that matters. Rather than emphasizing speaking, the films move us closer to something like a practice of attention on forms of life as they arise. In my view, imagining a visual language is what Antonioni, Visconti, and Rossellini are after, but it isn't a language that is only spoken. Rather, it is a language of looking, attending, and not—at least initially—consuming. It is a form of life that attends to what is seen and unseen.

SYMBOLIC VITALISM AND TRANSITIONAL OBJECTS

My second card comes from Kenneth Burke and concerns the relation of form to the symbolic. In *Rhetoric of Motives*, Burke writes:

> The Symbolic should deal with unique individuals, each its own peculiarly constructed act, or form. These unique 'constitutions' being capable

of treatment in isolation, the Symbolic should consider them primarily in their capacity as singulars, each a separate universe of discourse (though there are also respects in which they are consubstantial with others of their kind, since they can be classed with other unique individuals as joint participants in common principles, possessors of the same or similar properties).[65]

Consider first the equating of form with act across "constellations" and "constitutions." Burke would have each individual translated out of its singular attribute and oriented toward form. One may well want to hear in such a passage a reference to potentiality but let's hold off doing so for the moment. Instead, let's reflect on what happens when we translate "constructed" act as a way of opening up form to reciprocity through symbolic action. To the degree we speak of forms of life as constructed, we do so because these singularities act in concert with others and their actions. In Burke's reframing of form through action, our perspective returns not just to Wittgenstein's speaking and to the language of singular individuals, but to the reciprocal nature of actions themselves as providing the horizon for "universes" of discourse to emerge. Singulars engage with other singulars through constructed actions that give rise to the symbolic. A first take-away: thinking form as constructed acts stretches form to the symbolic, moving the singular toward a shared "settling" among symbolic forms more generally. Admittedly, there remains the premise that these symbolic forms possess the "same or similar properties"—that they are participants in "common principles," which makes sense given the emphasis on the common throughout Burke's thought, on the shared proper that joins symbolic forms. In order to have properties in common that ultimately add up to the symbolic, these forms must be constituted by actions that give form to their singular universe. These actions do not take place in a vacuum, but are forms to the degree they are brought together with other actions collected under and by the symbolic.

Here we can register a further advantage in employing form of life as a term. As paradoxical as it might sound, forms of life enjoy more of a relation with the common than other terms precisely because of the constitutive features that the term enjoys with act.[66] This suggests an over-determination with regard to the cinematic apparatus and its relation to form(s) of life, an insight Visconti, among others, saw as decisive for his own filmmaking.

Cinema presents us with moving images of individuals and things whose form is constructed through singular acts, which then reach out to other forms on the screen and off. This is a fruitful way for marking another facet of cinema and its differences with other apparatuses. Is there a more powerful mode than the cinematic for treating these constitutions as singular(ities), the constituted nature of their form that accrues to them thanks to their acts? What would it mean to highlight the symbolic affinities between the viewer and the forms of life/act that appear onscreen?

Further discussion will have to wait for Chapter 2, but here I would only add that a commonality between forms of life onscreen and forms of life off screen concerns a different notion of exchange thought in terms of gratitude. Subject, self, and individual fail to capture the potential for opening up to exchanges that hesitate, evade, or suspend giving and receiving. And here another feature of form of life can be invoked, namely the relation of form of life to grasping. When employing form of life, we register in ways, which subject and individual often fail to, the being that is constitutively more given to identifying less with possession.

To see how form of life might name such an entity given to de-possession, let me circle back a bit to the earlier discussion of gratitude to introduce another of its features, namely play. On one hand, connecting play and gratitude ought to be an easy connection to make. We speak of graceful players, of playing gracefully, and grace notes. What is it about play that makes it so powerful when trying to think gratitude and form? In an earlier work, I employed a number of D. W. Winnicott's writings on play as a way of linking play and attention.[67] Here, as there, Winnicott's insight on how children (though not only) hold and let go of things is crucial to a discussion of what separates play from other forms of interaction with objects. Key is Winnicott's insight that when children play, the plaything is that which can be and is repeatedly turned back into a thing, and which contains the potential to become other objects. In other words, the plaything is not limited by the material make-up of the thing to only one function. In what will be a running argument throughout the remainder of this book, for forms of life to emerge, playful encounters with things are crucial as holding less tightly becomes an opportunity to identify less with the plaything's own form (indeed it may well go beyond the proper/improper distinction).

That we should again turn to Winnicott and transitional phenomena to describe such a moment isn't surprising. In his seminal essay "Transitional

Objects and Transitional Phenomena—A Study of the First Not-Me Posses-sion," he defines intermediate experience as the area "between primary un-awareness of indebtedness and the acknowledgment of indebtedness."[68] The reference to indebtedness moves us closer to the circuit of exchange first noted in Benveniste's etymology. The unawareness of being in debt, of being a being in debt, the fact that the infant has received a gift and then acknowledged that indebtedness is one we need to consider carefully. And let's remember as well that Winnicott also sees object and possession as comprising "a need for a specific object or a behavior pattern" and thus that transitional objects bear directly on reciprocal forms.[69] "If the adult can manage to enjoy the personal intermediate area," Winnicott writes, "with-out making certain claims, then we can acknowledge our own correspond-ing intermediate areas, and are pleased to find overlapping, that is to say common experience between members of a group in art or religion or philosophy."[70]

The question for a study of gratitude and forms of life hinges on the acknowledgment of these intermediate areas where claims are not made, what Winnicott will describe as the move in the infant from the possession of the transitional object to its non-possession. In a series of crucial insights, Winnicott shifts the focus of the argument away from the qualities of the object or the attributes of possession, emphasizing instead the relation-ship between object and infant. He observes, for instance, that the "infant assumes rights over the object," but that there is "some abrogation of omnipotence . . . from the start"; that the object "must survive instinctual loving, and also hating"; that, from the point of view of the baby, the object neither comes from without nor from within; and lastly that "it is not for-gotten and it is not mourned," but only that it "loses meaning" because it has become "diffused."[71] Interestingly, it is only when the transitional object has lost meaning that it "widens out into play and of artistic creation" as well as "fetishism, lying and stealing."[72] The phrase in this regard is telling: "He [the infant] comes within the wide definition of normal."[73]

Winnicott's analysis indicates that a space remains for a non-possession, which is to say there remains a way of receiving an object that does not make it a possession. The transitional object is a possession and so at least initially the gratitude one feels having given without consideration of re-ceiving anything in return seems difficult to locate. Yet consider another movement in the above passage, when the transitional object has "lost meaning." Then play and artistic creation as well as "fetishism, lying, and stealing" come to the fore. The transitional object, seemingly, has moved beyond good and evil.

At this juncture, it is helpful to recall that Winnicott, appropriating Melanie Klein, places the mother's breast at the center of the transitional object and that the loss of meaning of the object is accompanied by frustration "since incomplete adaptation to need makes objects real."[74] The breast is created over and over again "out of the infant's capacity of love or (one can say) out of need."[75] Thus, when thinking of gratitude, it's useful to remember that "the intermediate area to which I am referring is the area that is allowed the infant between primary creativity and objective perception based on reality testing. The transitional phenomena therefore represent the early stages of the use of illusion."[76] The infant believes she has created the breast, and hence her own capacity to create lies there. Transitional phenomena give the human being what is most important—"A neutral area of experience which will not be challenged"[77]—presumably because of the infant's belief that she possesses it. It is this illusion of mastery that results from the dialectic of reality testing—of having been given the breast, the illusion of having created the breast, of the breast as transitional object that has lost meaning—which in turn signals less identification with meaning.

It is tempting to move quickly over these steps in loss of meaning, perhaps because the steps aren't immediately clear. One access point may be to ask what happens when an object loses meaning as transitional object when we name such an object as a gift. Something similar may be in operation in a gift that loses its meaning as gift (keeping in mind that what some of these films are after is precisely the proximity of objects that lose their meaning with an intimacy with thing). In different words, if all transitional objects function as stand-ins for the good breast, then could we say that the domination of the object is premised on the belief that the infant has created the object herself? Such a view would account for the fear experienced by the child that something will be taken away and that the fear of losing possession can be linked to the fear in a loss of meaning. This seems like a good strategy to follow in that what underlies the reciprocity of the exchange of the gift is the expectation that the meaning of the gift—that it was once mine—won't go missing. It is this expectation of something in return that allays the fear of losing a possession. Possessions are exchanged, possession takes place in the future, but where then would the giving of gifts not named as such take place?

One name for the place of the non-giving of gifts is the "area of experience which will not be challenged," which is to say the neutral area of play. This is the neutral area of the giving that the "good enough" mother provides the infant so that the child is able to cathect to the transitional object. Winnicott tells us that this area between "primary creativity and objective perception" is the space of reality testing in which the infant engages. This neutral area of experience protected from challenge is one that he calls play.[78] We might choose to define gratitude, therefore, as the sense of relief that the infant or patient feels when a neutral area of experience opens. It is the gratitude of the therapeutic session for Winnicott—the testing of reality that arrives with no judgment. The subject of gratitude would be the one who plays in the neutral zone created by transitional objects, thanks to the capacity of transitional objects to escape the logic of exchange and calculation and circulation of giving and receiving. The problem with the calculation of giving and receiving is that it makes gratitude much more difficult to experience, given that calculation, or *nomos*,[79] names who has given and what has been received.

Oikos, economy, Aristotle's domestic sphere: These are realms in which a circuit of exchange holds sway—of giving and receiving, of ledgers and balances made, of debts calculated. Another circuit though becomes visible that presumes no possession either of the thing given or received. This is the milieu of no hope of receiving and no hope of giving. Such a realm would, I want to suggest, be that of play in which weak forms of giving do not add up to an improper gift. Herein reside the radical possibilities afforded us by gratitude. Necessary then to acknowledging these radical alternatives is avoiding the condition of agreeing to the exchange because to do so would move us again into the realm of *nomos*, circuits, calculation, and capitalism.[80]

SUSPECTED GIVING

We have come a long way from mythic violence, biopower, and biopolitics, which is another way of saying that many questions remain open. Too many perhaps. Some, I hope, will become clearer when I turn to the films of Visconti, Rossellini, and Antonioni, but in the meantime it may be helpful to consider again my earlier point about parataxis in a context of gratitude and play. Parataxis, we recall, is opposed to the construction of hierarchy, the placing of a cause or clause before the other. In the leveling of giving and receiving that gratitude names, no special status is awarded the giver or the receiver. It is a practice of placing side by side, much like what Dionysus does in Nietzsche's *The Birth of Tragedy*: equalizing by placing side by side; composing without posing or positioning according to status. "Dionysus," as Camille Paglia writes, "like Proteus, shifts through all forms of being, high to low. Human, animal, plant, mineral: none has special status. All are equalized and sacralized in the continuum of natural energy. Dionysus, leveling the great chain of being, respects no hierarchy."[81]

We are comforted in giving to receive, in doing the math, in receiving and then being obliged to give. Giving to receive, and receiving to give provide security by turning things into objects—turning the non-object into object. A first step then in avoiding the anxiety formation around giving—refuse to turn all giving into gift-giving. One result in adopting parataxis may turn out to be no ownership, either of the thing given or received. And no one more than Nietzsche recognized the possibilities of gratitude, or indeed an aesthetics of gratitude. He saw how "whole generations" were needed "in order merely to devise a courteous convention of gratefulness."

> Anyone who breaks new paths and who has led many others onto new paths, discovers with some amazement how clumsy and poor these people are in their capacity for expressing gratitude—and how rarely gratitude achieves expression at all. It almost seems that whenever gratitude wants to speak, she begins to gag, clears her throat, and falls silent before she has got a word out.

The transformation of the grateful into those unable to express their gratitude differs little in Nietzsche's judgment from the transformation of humans into animals, or the silence of objects—of people who lose their voice. Rather than judging, Nietzsche sees an opportunity for thinking gratitude: "The way [*die Art*] in which a thinker gets some notion [*spüren*] of the effects of his ideas, of their transforming [*umbildende*], revolutionary [*erschütternde*] power, is almost a comedy."[82]

Nietzsche's comment is striking for many reasons, not least for how easily in a passage dedicated to gratitude comedy emerges as a genre able to mark the "transforming power" of such a thought. What is it that links gratitude to comedy? Are there ways of following the effect of thought that make it more likely in resembling a comedy than others? Here the nature of the power at the thinker's command is key. When tracing the effects of his or her thoughts, what counts will be the "way" (*Art*) in which a thinker does so that makes it "almost a comedy." Presumably, tracing the power of a thinker's thoughts is possible precisely *because* of the difficulty that the thinker has in expressing her gratitude. It is only because of such a difficulty that the Nietzschean categories of spirit and genius will eventually merge together with gratitude.

The passage also tells us how difficult it is to say thanks. It also shows us the opportunity that arises for a thinker in measuring how much power the act of tracing effects has, over transformations occurring among those who "receive" thought. Is there a point, however, at which it is no longer simply possible to measure what is given without thought of return? If there is, then perhaps the Nietzschean genealogy so dear to Foucault may, in fact, be based on a lack of gratitude—that one can measure the traces of one's thought on bodies only in lieu of the expression of that gratitude. Seeing how one's thought convulses is a power trip and so it's not clear how giving without receiving might be possible. Indeed we may well be at the limit of Nietzsche's thought because he appears to be unable to let go of the thinker who traces the effects of her own thought. What if we could trace the power of generosity without the possessives—without his thought, my thought, and your thought—and instead imagine some *Art* that extends beyond or before possession? In different words, the product of so many thinkers prior to the one who thinks makes gratitude toward the person or the individual thinker less personal than it might otherwise need to be.

THE GENEROSITY OF COMEDY

An obvious question necessarily follows. What is it about the genre of comedy that offers itself as a space that can counter the power of exchange, of supply and demand, which is continually and almost always figured as a tragedy (the consumer as hero, as fated, the world that ends, destiny, the destiny of climate change, a negative entropic goal, or simply a new negative teleology)? Two perspectives about comedy and the comedic are worth pursing in this regard. First, let's recall that for Hegel comedy is not written in the language of fate or destiny, but often in a different language, that of "subjective caprice" and "subjective satisfaction." Implicit is the capacity of comedy to undercut the seriousness of tragedy and the epic. These capricious subjects—and here we will want to note the etymology of capricious and its affinities with a kind of becoming animal—are, according to Hegel in *Aesthetics*, "not seriously tied to the finite world [*nicht an die Endlichkeit . . . ernstlich gebunden sind*] with which they are engaged but are raised above it and remain firm in themselves and secure in the face of failure and loss."[83] The ability to remain firm for Hegel marks the borders of the comedic; further on he will remind us that the comedic is fundamentally about reconciliation and "subjective satisfaction" (*die Subjektivität der Befriedigung*) in which "what is comical   is a personality or subject who makes his own actions contradictory [*die ihr Handeln durch sich selber im Widerspruch bringt und auflöst*] and so brings them to nothing, while remaining tranquil [*ruhig*] and self-assured [*ihrer selbst gewiß*] in the process."

The key that opens Hegel's reading on generous comedy will be found in the phrase "not seriously tied," which I hasten to add does not mean that these subjects enjoy no relation to the finite world. They simply are not tied, he writes, as "seriously tied" very nearly defines tragedy and with it the fate of the hero. Here we might also note how more contemporary accounts of violence, myth, and law continue to privilege "tragic conflict," which is as true of circuits of exchange as it is of international strife. Every conflict is a tragic one.[84] The passage from Hegel earlier suggests a different perspective. If it were only a question of conflict, then tragic, mythic violence would continue to be the primary mode for naming it. When our gaze moves to reconciliation, however, to "the unity and harmony of the entire ethical order," then we move to comedy. What continues to linger in comedy is its relation to praxis such that the comical frequently appears as a mode of making ("to make his own actions contradictory," Hegel writes). The difficulty is how might a satisfied subject choose to make his or her actions contradictory, or how might contradictory actions bring about satisfaction?

The answer is precisely by giving without thought—giving without naming the action as giving. By bringing to nothing the circuit of exchange. By engaging in reciprocity that leads nowhere and in the process allows a mode of self-assuredness and tranquility to emerge. In the shadow of the infinite, the inhuman, et al., the comedic laughs. It says that the choice between finite and infinite worlds is a false one and that the world is both and neither and that what remains is only the question of the form of life best able to acknowledge that. On one hand, infinitude brings with it a form of life constellated around the militant. The finite—and this hasn't been remarked upon enough—might instead bring with it a multiplicity of forms of life, precisely because the condition for their proliferation is that their actions produce nothing—that is, that they escape the exchanges of giving and receiving.

This, to be clear, is not a question of nihilism à la Heidegger, but rather of locating a form of reciprocity not expressed in the liberal terms of exchange or neo-liberal terms of the *nomos*. Nor would one want to deny a role for violence here either—violence and comedy often go hand in hand—but far more important is the effect (and affect) that results from reconciling oneself to the fact that one's actions bring about nothing. All the same, it makes little sense to fear the no-thing. The no-thing belongs to that which has yet been named, but what we know brings tranquility. It is giving with an eye for receiving that creates disquiet; giving for receiving that sets in motion possession, what is mine or about to be mine and what is yours or about to be yours no longer.[85]

What is it about comedy and the thing that so fundamentally concerns giving? Here we ought to take seriously (though not too seriously) Hegel's descriptor of the subject of comedy as "capricious" and ask after the relation the non-capricious subject enjoys with the thing. In what sense does the comedic denote a mode of holding that entails a different relation to the thing as non-object, or the non-giving of the non-thing (because with no hands to grasp and the occasion for possessing no longer present)? Here, once again, Bataille precedes us with his emphasis on the animal. We recall Bataille's "obscure intimacy of the animal," with which he referred to a mode by which animals relate to things. Less noted, however, is the genre in which intimacy with things unfolds:

> It can doubtless be said, of the Protestant critique of saintly works that it gave the world over to profane works, that the demand for divine purity only managed to exile the divine, and to complete man's separation from it. It can be said, finally, that starting then things dominated man, insofar as he lived for enterprise and less and less in the present time. But domination is never total, and in a deep sense, it is only a comedy: It never deceives more than partly, while in the propitious darkness a new truth turns stormy.[86]

We could at this point turn over the threads of the sacred and profane that Giorgio Agamben uses to weave his narrative of *zoē* and more recently the monastic form of life.[87] We could also note the movement toward purity, which effectively exiles man from the divine. More decisive though is the relation that humanity enjoys with things. Bataille's insight here differs little from Lacan's reading of thermodynamics or Heidegger's discussion of mastery when employing technology,[88] though we note the emphasis on the danger of living "for enterprise," which allows less and less living "in the present time." We can also hear echoes of Benveniste's reading of the circuit of reciprocity too and the calculation that always goes into giving to receive. "Living for enterprise" fast forwards to the future in the same way that giving in order to receive does; both are premised on domination of the thing that occurs primarily in the past and future, with present time sacrificed. Yet, dialectically, such domination "is never total." This instance lies at the heart of the comedy of living less and less in the present—the comedy of living for enterprise.

What are the features of the comedic "living for enterprise"? Not surprisingly, they concern the circulation and handling of things. Bataille will observe how capitalism unleashes an "unreserved surrender to things, heedless of consequences and seeing nothing beyond them."[89] In the surrender to the commodity, "things generally prevailed and dominated the movement of the multitude, all the aborted dreams remained available: life (the global movement of life) became detached from them no doubt, but they still serve as consolation for troubled beings." The comedy, what Bataille calls "chaos," began when "in the most contrary ways, everything became equally possible."[90]

Bataille posits a relation of capitalism to a form of seeing that resembles a grip. We sense it in the way capitalism gives us images and things to see that simultaneously blind us as we are transformed into commodities. We can see "nothing beyond them." In the moment when things surrender to the commodity, they become less alive in their reciprocal relation to the multitude. The result is not simply domination of the thing but now the domination of the multitude. We think we dominate, we think we master, but in fact we are the ones who are dominated. Although Bataille doesn't sketch the details of the detachment of life from dreams, implicit in the surrender of things to commodities is the multitude's surrender to possession, which sunders the intimate relation that it previously had to the non-commodified thing.

Why the distinction between two registers of thing as opposed to employing the term object, surely a distinction he knew well? One reason might be found in the possibility of holding open a future in which a re-turn to the thing is possible. It is as if the thing dresses itself differently de-pending upon the various lenses capitalism uses, but that once the lens is refused, one finally senses the impenetrability of the thing. At that moment, intimacy is possible as a moment of reattachment to the thing and dream not as commodification or consolation. Perhaps in maintaining the thing-ness of the thing even or especially in the commodity, Bataille is imagining a way back from the precipice, something akin to the pieces of bread or clothing that a hiker employs to mark the path she had followed to that point.

Impenetrable things cannot be mastered and hence cannot chiasmati-cally master the multitude or the self. The reason has to do with mastery requiring an outside in order to arise. Mastery for Bataille is premised on closing the distance between inside and outside, between where one is and where one arrives. Thus, if we only had greater intimacy with things, an in-timacy involving more touch and less grasp, other scenarios might arise that would not necessarily involve surrendering to capitalism. "The unreserved surrender to things" is premised on the ability to see only things. It is seeing as grasping that makes all the difference in the "unreserved surrender."

Perhaps this explains why there continues to be so much interest in touch, and what touch offers in lieu of grasping as seeing. If seeing is be-lieving, then touching is about becoming intimate with, both individually and in the context of community. Accordingly, a thing requires an outside that cannot be penetrated, which presumes a role for touch as the experience of impenetrability. But when the thing has surrendered to the commodity, the outside expands to such a degree that we are led to consider it as mark-ing and naming all that it contains. We continue to forget what it means to approach a thing and to fail to grasp it. Prosthesis as trope or as biopolitical practice won't work here either because the engagement with the commod-ified thing has made seeing itself a form of prosthesis. Prosthesis, as the physical extension of the senses, is unable to provide an intimacy with our-selves as the non-commodified thing.

MANCEPS AND MANCHOT AS FORMS OF LIFE

Mastery and holding. Mastery as a form of holding. Comedy, caprice, and the letting go of mastery. This is where the previous curves and straightaways lead us. And no one more than François Lyotard drew the necessary conclusions.[91] In *Phenomenology*, Lyotard emphasizes how individuals "give themselves and others a meaning in a slice of time called the present,"[92] that the difference between Husserl and Hegel resides in the fact that "Husserlian description inaugurates the grasping of the 'thing itself' before all predication."[93] Yet nowhere more than in the essay "The Grip (Mainmise)" does Lyotard examine the relation of holding, griping, grasping, and possession.[94] "The Grip" is one of the richest of Lyotard's *oeuvre* as he is able to avoid setting in motion the machine of proper and improper giving, which lies at so much of the heart of much of the critique of giving. A passage from the opening page sets the scene:

> *Manceps* is the person who takes hold, in the sense of possession or appropriation. And manicipium refers to this gesture of taking hold. But it also refers to that (it's a neuter word) which is taken hold of by the *manceps*. The slave, that is, designated in terms of the regime of belonging rather than service. The slave does not belong to itself. Hence it does not have the capacity to appropriate anything at all. It is in the hands of another.[95]

Leaving aside the ambiguous position of "person" here, especially after the recent deconstruction of the term by Roberto Esposito, note the relation of taking hold and possession, followed soon after by making one's own.[96] A question comes barreling down on us. What lexicon is available when referring to the person that does not take hold in the sense of non-possession and non-appropriation? This wouldn't simply be the reversal of the *manceps* (the e-*manceps* presumably) because such a reversal would still be part of a binary structure that the reciprocity associated with generosity precisely is meant to forestall. In this regard, *manceps* appears not only as the one who holds, but that which is taken hold of. Indeed, when we speak of holding and the freeing of that which is held, we often fail to hear the rhyme between the two, that is between the person who holds and that which is held. With the emancipation of the thing that belongs—the slave in this instance—the *manceps* is freed as owner and possessor. This emancipation of the *manceps* is precisely what strikes at the heart of mythic violence in its current form of biopower. It does so as it frees the thing from its consumption as commodity and its owner from possession.

Dropping things, dropping into oneself, dropping oneself. Dispossession and non-appropriation, the non-appropriation of life. These possibilities often go missing in recent takes on the post-human and post-humanities. An alternative reading of the post-human would want to see therein a potential movement toward forms of life that are characterized by the degree one possesses (or not) one's self, person, beliefs. Lyotard glimpsed such a possibility when describing the problems associated with mastery. In "The Grip (Mainmise)," Lyotard cites Descartes on the entrance into taking full possession of ourselves. In the *Discourse*, Descartes counsels a "practical philosophy by means of which . . . we can . . . render ourselves the masters and possessors of nature."[97] As is often the case, such a possibility of non-mastery and non-possession comes with a caveat. How we relate to others cannot be pried apart from how we appropriate our self and our body. Lyotard's emphasis on possession and its translation into appropriation suggests other paths for thought that focus on how we wish to relate to, and to be in reciprocal relation with the self, without turning on the machine of appropriating. If seizing is not the only way of relating to self, other, thing, then different possibilities become available for the various moments of holding across our lives. This is simply because with possession comes the greater probability of "felt" harm; we have lost something.

In focusing on the relation among holding, belonging, and appropriation, Lyotard points the way to a mode of being that will focus on the figure of the *manceps*, especially in relation to mythic violence today—that it is the *manceps* on which the violent modes of "interaction" depend. We hold but sure enough at that moment we are also held. There can be no violence without a form of holding, a *manceps* that can only be emancipated by changing the grip or by not holding at all. Implicit in Lyotard's reading is the move to a different position with regard to the things around us. Not merely seeing them, but feeling them beneath our hands and feet. So too with ourselves, and designing a way of attending to the thingness that inheres in our sense of self.

Where does gratitude reside then for Lyotard? It will be found in no longer gripping. Writing of the slave and emancipation under Roman law, he notes:

> Who can tell the price the slave must pay in order to free himself? Is there even a common standard of measurement for those who are held and those who are free . . . Can there be emancipation by ransom? Is not the relinquishing of his grip always an act of grace on the part of the *manceps*? Grace, in principle, has no price. Can it even be obtained?[98]

Lyotard's foray into Roman law does not end here, but returns more broadly to Western thought in the wake of Roman influence. "Emancipation," he observes,

> consists of establishing oneself in the full possession of knowledge, will, and feeling, in providing oneself with the rule of knowledge, the law of willing, and the control of the emotions. The emancipated ones are the persons or things that owe nothing to anyone but themselves: Freed from all debts to the other.[99]

To the degree that the emancipated ones "owe nothing to anyone but themselves," Lyotard's reading offers itself as an immanent reading of generosity. We can engage with life through a reciprocity that does not involve possessing knowledge, will, or feeling fully. On one hand, there is exchange, which is encapsulated in the question of price. On the other hand, there is the relinquishing of the grip and so, along with it, price. In lieu of gratitude and the impossibility of obtaining it, the emancipated *manceps* signals the onset of individualism. The individual is the emancipated one "who owes nothing to anyone but themselves." This emancipation, however, is truly only skin deep. The question is precisely whether a further emancipation from the debt to oneself, to having a hand, might allow a space in which generosity can come to the fore?

Lyotard offers preciously few details on the relation between emancipation from debt of the material sort and freeing of oneself from the *manceps* of managing, administering, and hence owing something to the self. But he does add the following: "Anyone in the grip of a *manceps* is *mancus*, *manchot*, missing a hand."

> The one who lacks a hand. Emancipating oneself in these terms means escaping from this state of lack. In freeing himself from the other's tutelage, the *manchot* takes things in hand once more. He believes that his castration has been healed. This dream that we may put an end to lack is what gives rise to the emancipation of today. The dream of having done with my lack, with what I lack, with what made me lack, what made me have lack. I would make the claim, without defending it here, that the preeminent mode in which lack appears is time, and that time is also, inversely, what requires emancipation in order to put an end to the lack that is time.[100]

The object of the grip is not as we might expect someone incapable of movement, but rather someone who cannot use a hand to pry open another hand. This is because the *mancus*, the one who is in a grip, is missing a hand. Lacking a hand, however, there can be no emancipation—no freeing of the hand from outside, but rather only "escape" from such a lack.

Lyotard describes a dream in which emancipation exists and lack can be overcome. If we to translate this into this into the context of contemporary ontology, perhaps it is the belief that we still have hands, which makes us subjects—or better, the choice to imagine no hands might allow for the possibility of transforming our relation to self as one beyond appropriation and possession. I wonder—and the later chapters are an attempt to elaborate some of these beautiful reflections from Lyotard—whether emancipation actually takes many forms, which would mean acknowledging the degrees to which one cannot put an end to one's lack (and we note as well the reappearance of possession and what is proper and improper lack in the passage with "my lack"). What would giving away "my" lack entail? What forms of life might embody such a mode of relating to constitutive lack of a hand?

Another hypothesis follows from Lyotard's figure of the *manceps*. Different apparatuses enjoy different relations to the forms of life, including the cinematic apparatus. How might we understand the cinematic apparatus as making generous forms of life visible—that is, how does cinema show us the emancipated *manchot* and *manceps* and then how does it lead the spectator to identify and then not with this lack? On my read, cinema has the capacity to allow us to see generous forms of life becoming visible in ways that other apparatuses cannot. Decisive among the differences between the apparatuses will be parataxis, composition, and the implicit comedic potential of forms of life that are missing hands.

2

FREEING THE APPARATUS

The preceding chapter ended with the figure of the *mancus*, the one who is missing hands, which in a study of gratitude as a response to biopower and mythic violence seems paradoxical to say the least. What role does the *mancus* play in a study of the generous form of life as it emerges in a number of films from Italy in the postwar period? And to complicate matters further, how is cinema supposed to gesture to that generous form of life while at the same time suggesting that a potential future community can be imagined so long as we are able to conceive of a giving that does not require hands to master, let alone to hold on to.

As has been the practice to this point, I prefer not to meet the question directly, but instead want to take up an oblique position on the question by shifting our focus away from the *mancus* to the notion of apparatus, and in particular the cinematic apparatus. Let's begin with what may seem a ridiculous question. Can any apparatus be emancipatory? Can it be generous? This question lies at the heart of the following pages for here I want to consider the possibility that not all apparatuses are the same and that the cinematic apparatus can be read, at times, as enacting onscreen forms of reciprocity and gratitude. Some of the terms from Chapter 1 take a bow here, namely comedy and "subjective caprice," which makes sense given the search for the comic and generous potential of the cinematic apparatus itself. The question also looks forward to the next three chapters in which I sketch how films from Visconti, Rossellini, and Antonioni use the cinematic apparatus to make visible how non-grasping is possible, how they push the spectator to an identification with a lack that is not her own. We will, of course, need to be on the lookout for missing hands.

Apparatus. The word conjures up a skein of elements, uncertainties, and fascinations.[1] After the translations of the works of Michel Foucault, Gilles Deleuze, and Giorgio Agamben, the impression when considering apparatus is of an instrument, a piece of machinery, a device, or even a gear, and certainly those meanings are in play in the French *dispositif*, which apparatus often translates.[2] Yet unforeseen difficulties arise when we choose to leave untranslated *dispositif*, particularly when our attention turns to the visual ramifications of apparatus as opposed to *dispositif*. In a recent essay, Peter Goodrich notes how much of our reading of *dispositif* is indebted to the visual that apparatus connotes, along with ritual and liturgy. Working across the relation of law to personhood, he has this to say apropos of the value added of apparatus as the translation of *dispositif*.

> Turning from *dispositif* to *appareil*, from disposition to apparatus, can help explain this theatrical and properly liturgical modality of personality. The root of the word lies in *apparare* and means to be ready, to be prepared, *ut videtur*, so as to be seen. The apparatus is the mechanism by means of which the person comes into view. The French *dispositif* has this as one meaning, referring as it does to a mechanism and by extension to the arrangement of mechanisms and the techniques and orderings of appearances which machines make possible and facilitate. And thus by a relatively direct etymological link we move to the theatre of appearance. The apparatus is the mechanism or device by which the theatrical appears in the person of the player.[3]

Goodrich fastens on to the equivalency between liturgy and theater and so we might expect to see in his account the superimposition of the political and the theological.[4] But then he adds this:

> In an older language, the apparatus is the scaffold; the public staging of the spectacle of judgment, of execution, whose visibility, now as then, is the most charged of the dimensions of law's application. But the scaffold is simply the extreme, and modernity learned, as Foucault so well elaborated in terms of the disciplinary, that internal images and self-governance, the apparatus of the person *tout court* were likely to be far more effective—functional—mechanisms of governance than more direct expressions of repressive power. Manifest glory is preferable to explicit terror.[5]

Building on Goodrich's perspective, we might say that the cinematic apparatus prepares the "person" to be seen, that cinema systematizes things within the field of the visible, while making available some thing to the eye, allowing that thing to come into view which was not seen before.[6] In such a reading, apparatus would be one of the conditions for the formation of the "theatre of appearance," and thus will allow Goodrich to bring law back on stage. The scaffold and theater, the spectacle and appearance, all appear together when the law is applied, a point suggested as much in Benjamin's reading of mythic violence. With an apparatus, persons become visible who were not there before and thus are made subject to the law.

In Goodrich's analysis, apparatuses also work in terms of governance as it makes visible "internal images." Countless examples attest to the power of cinema in making subjects visible to the law. The gangster genre from the 1932 *Scarface* to *The Sopranos* heaped visual frame upon visual frame of the Italian-American as gangster; and indeed most genres might be said to function hand in hand with the cinematic apparatus with disciplinary effects as one result. When we speak of apparatuses, we link them to the capture of a body or life, or life through the edge of the body.[7] The limiting of life occurs so as to make that life a subject, which is true regardless of whether the apparatus in question be language, personhood, or a patent. Goodrich's larger point is simply that apparatuses make life appear in different contexts and under different guises, subjecting them to the law. Subject will name those entities, creatures, beings, and ontological spaces that are captured by and subjected to the apparatus in question.[8]

THE APPARATUS AND PRAEPARATUS

As much as Goodrich's insights lay bare how deeply apparatus depends upon theater and the spectacle, I wonder if a more nuanced reading of apparatus isn't available and here I have in mind the work of Vilém Flusser. Writing not of the cinematic but of the photographic, Flusser lines up apparatus ontologically with reciprocity by emphasizing the twin verbs *apparare* and *praeparare*. Here is Flusser:

> To illustrate in English the difference between the prefixes "ad" and "prae," one could perhaps translate *apparare* with "pro-pare," using

"pro" in the sense of "for." Accordingly, an "apparatus" would be a thing that lies in wait or in readiness for something, and a "preparatus" would be a thing that waits patiently for something. The photographic apparatus lies in wait for photography; it sharpens its teeth in readiness. This readiness to spring into action on the part of apparatuses, their similarity to wild animals, is something to grasp hold of in the attempt to define the term etymologically.[9]

The distinction between apparatus and the subject of apparatus returns us to the earlier moment of mythic violence noted in Chapter 1 as well as to Lyotard's reading of *mancus* and *manchot*—to what is grasped and what grasps. Consider the importance of the notion of thing for both apparatus and *praeparatus*. The apparatus is the thing that lies in wait to "grasp," according to Flusser; for its part *praeparatus* names the thing that waits "patiently" to be grasped. When reading of apparatuses, attention has often focused on the apparatus as capture, as what "lies in wait," but few have followed Flusser's insight to wonder about the nature of the thing that waits patiently. I'd like to do so next.

To begin, what happens when we substitute the cinematic for photographic? What results if we refer to cinema not only as an apparatus but as consisting of a *praeparatus* as well, or indeed as containing both elements (because the impression often is that apparatus and the *praeparatus* collapse on themselves when speaking of cinema)? Rather than choosing to make cinema both, what changes if we understood the spectator herself as a more likely candidate for the *praeparatus*? Cinema means little without a spectator, of course, and in this case we may want to consider, as many have, that the spectator waits for something. Cinema would name an apparatus to the degree it springs itself on the spectator, while the spectator in turn is prepared to wait patiently to grasp or be grasped, which amounts to the same thing.

From the origins of cinema, spectators have found themselves betwixt by the magic of cinema. Some of the magic was explained in the writings of André Bazin and Edgar Morin, and later the writings of Christian Metz, Laura Mulvey, Stephen Heath, and Jean-Louis Baudry. The latter four argued in works that continue to radiate their brilliance decades later how similar the imaginary constitution of the self is to the workings of the cinematic apparatus.[10] Working off a series of insights from Jacques Lacan,[11] they follow him in naming two conditions for such a constitution of the self: "immature powers of mobility and a precocious maturation of the visual process."[12] No one more than Jean-Louis Baudry drew the necessary conclusions from Lacan:

> If one considers that these two conditions are repeated during cinematographic projection-suspension of mobility and predominance of the visual function, perhaps one could suppose that this is more than a simple analogy. And possibly this very point explains the "impression of reality so often invoked in connection with the cinema for which the various explanations proposed seem only to skirt the real problem.[13]

In short, the state of waiting patiently to be captured by the wild animal of cinema depends upon the apparatus's capacity to constitute the viewing self by flashing all the teeth that the cinematic "wild animal" has: suture, *mise-en-scène*, montage, and point of view among them.

Is this the last word on the cinematic apparatus or is there another way of understanding Flusser's *praeparatus* as less an object than a thing, a living edge that is available for capture by the apparatus? Stephen Heath gets close to this possibility, which takes us back to the question of generosity, property, and what is mine.

> Cinema is the machine of a certain presence, the institution of certain conditions of the body. Hence the political question, the question of any radical political practice of film: how and to what extent is it possible to transform those conditions, that presence? The question can only be answered from an initial and fundamental recognition of the problems of the property of the image. The image is never the property of me or of this or of that person in the image; it is always an image for—for the film, its cinema. No referent can guarantee a discourse: the represented a discourse produces is grasped, realized, exists . . . A film is always a document—a documentary—of film.[14]

Heath's conclusion moves us toward a less paranoid view of the cinematic apparatus. Cinema is improper in its display of the movement of images that the spectator looks at. Implicit is the idea that the longer we look at something, the more we come to desire it. Similarly, the less we see a presence, the more we desire its absence. And here it is cinema that produces presence in its very absence: "It must not be forgotten that a body in cinema, in a film, is present in its absence, in the traces of an image (very different to the body in theatre). The position of a spectator of a film is often described as voyeuristic but voyeurs watch people not films."[15]

Cinema operates differently from other apparatuses to the degree that the properties associated with absent actors who provide presence do not offer a locus for belonging via a body or an image that has properties that belong to it. Perhaps Heath's question about a radical political practice and how to transform the conditions of the body resonates less today than another question: How can the cinematic *praeparatus* create a failure to identify with the properties of the image that appear on the screen? How can the spectator come to identify with an absence at the heart of cinematic presence so that the imaginary self projected back to her returns with a difference, namely with no properties or attributes?

> What is involved in cinema . . . is a certain imagination of the ego . . . the spectator "emancipated," unhindered by the existence of bodies, mobile in his or her images, the free play of an egocentric appropriation and fantasy relation . . . Cinema never shows the body you want but the body you want from cinema.[16]

Heath suggests that the "emancipated spectator" comes into being because images do not have properties. With no properties, the spectator can playfully appropriate those images.[17] Heath invites us to imagine the possibility that the cinematic apparatus is no one-way street of capture nor lines of flight á la Gilles Deleuze or Rosi Braidotti, but rather a practice in learning how to grasp less tightly—one that demands that we grasp, but one that also provides the tools with which to lessen the hold that the apparatus has.[18]

This possibility has often been overlooked in discussions of the cinematic apparatus.[19] Manipulations of the cinematic apparatus work dialectically, that is the possibility of reversal is contained therein.[20] The way to such a reversal begins in the practice of viewing the absence at the heart of cinematic presence as emancipation-producing. Literally. This emancipated spectator—the *mancus* from Chapter 1 and not Rancière's more famous one—is the one who, in ways deeply similar to the cinematic ego, has let go of identifying with one image. Here, too, there is the question of the proper and the improper, what belongs to cinema and in my view with the practice of a playful holding. Implicit in Heath's argument—and it is one we ought to keep in mind as we move toward the films I will be discussing shortly—is the equation of mobility and play, a mobility among images and how one holds them and lets them go.

The relation of the mobility of images to their missing properties is at the heart of a more affirmative perspective on *praeparatus*. Baudry, whom I quoted earlier, gets to the heart of the practice:

> Film history shows that as a result of the combined inertia of painting, theater, and photography, it took a certain time to notice the inherent mobility of the cinematic mechanism. The ability to reconstitute movement is after all only a partial, elementary aspect of a more general capability. To seize movement is to become movement, to follow a trajectory is to become trajectory, to choose a direction is to have the possibility of choosing one, to determine a meaning is to give oneself meaning.[21]

What modes are available to the apparatus to highlight the choice for determining a meaning that characterizes the spectator's interaction with the apparatus, that is to choose different meanings and to play with proper and improper meanings? What modes of unmasking are available to the absent presence of the actor, to draw out the apparatus? The task is to think of the apparatus as modeling a form of reciprocity not based on ownership or giving to receive, but rather something else.

THE SPECTATOR WITH NO HANDS

Consider again Benveniste's entry on grace and gratitude.

> Yet the reciprocal process of supply and demand can be interrupted voluntarily: here intervene services without return, offerings "by grace and favor," pure acts of "grace," which are the starting points of a new kind of reciprocity. Above the normal circuit of exchange—where one gives in order to obtain—there is a second circuit, that of benefice and gratefulness, what is given without thought of return, what is offered in thankfulness.[22]

The spectator can be (and not is) freed of his hands when he is invited not to identify with what appears on the screen. Cinema provides us with the image that we want from cinema, as Heath tells us, but the implicit possibility is of a cinema that continually fails to give us that image, and instead gives us one that highlights the path away from mere identification, away from all too easy mastery of the image. What happens if the apparatus were to provide an image that was not meant to be returned in the form of identification? This might lead to a new kind of reciprocity, keyed by interventions that interrupt the supply of images to be identified with and in so doing altering what the spectator demands. When something, in this case an image, is given without hope of receiving an identification with it in return, an interval opens in the reception of moving images[23]; even the nature of the subject who is subjected and sutured as a cinematic spectator. Here I have in mind David Dayan's classic reading of suture in film.

> When the viewer discovers the frame—the first step in reading the film—the triumph of his former possession of the image fades out. The viewer discovers that the camera is hiding things, and therefore distrusts it and the frame itself which he now understands to be arbitrary. He wonders why the frame is what it is. This radically transforms his mode of participation—the unreal space between characters and/or objects is no longer perceived as pleasurable. It is now the space which separates the camera from the characters. The latter have lost their quality of presence. The spectator discovers that his possession of space was only partial, illusory. He feels dispossessed of what he is prevented from seeing. He discovers that he is only authorized to see what happens to be in the axis of the gaze of another spectator, who is ghostly or absent.[24]

Most important is the notion of cinematic space created by the apparatus that is "unreal" and no longer "perceived as pleasurable." This space of partial possession and, for Lyotard, of dispossession depends upon its negative inflection for the spell of identification to be broken. But it is precisely in the spell having been broken that the cinematic apparatus differs from other modes of capture. It sets out ways for the spectator not to see but to encounter the frame.

MEANS TO A NON-END

The cinematic apparatus creates new circuits of reciprocity through its own principal mechanisms: cut and montage. Montage, as we know, is responsible for constructing the hypnotized gaze of the spectator, which has come to be called the "reality effect": I know I am watching a film or I don't. If we read montage in terms of reciprocity and gratitude, any break in the spectator's gaze may also interrupt her identification and possession of the image.[25] Continuity editing is part, on one hand, of the apparatus meant to push the spectator, in the absence of the noticeable cut, to continue to believe that what she is seeing is real. Continuity editing serves to make appear, but not to make disappear: With the cut occluded, the spectator believes she knows what is taking place at that moment onscreen. Continuity editing takes hold of the image and creates identification with it.[26] Today there are other ways to create identification with the image (see on this score *Avatar* whose resolution was seen as being too real).[27] This is not to say that directors no longer use montage, but rather that the level of sheer information contained in the moving images worked to make appropriation of the image—it is real and it is mine—easier. It awakens, to paraphrase Merleau-Ponty, "a delirium which is vision itself, for to see is *to have at a distance*."[28]

Ultimately, this is where the power of montage resides. It elaborates a lack of reciprocity, occluding the break into the dream, while pushing the individual viewer into the position of the spectator who receives something that has not been given. In other words, the spectator actually cannot identify with the image. Directors who highlight the image's constitutive impropriety, practice a generosity when they emphasize non-possession and non-mastery of images that lead nowhere, that block possession or that do not feature seeing/having at a distance. Admittedly, Heath describes an "egocentric appropriation" of the images, modifying it with "playfully," but we ought to acknowledge that if indeed it is a form of play, then it is premised on the possibility of weakening notions of what is mine and what is yours.

TO MEAN IS TO OWN

"The image is never the property of me or of this or of that person in the image; it is always an image *for* -for the film, its cinema." Heath's insight recalls, surprisingly perhaps, what Paul de Man in another context describes as the problem of the verb *meinen* in German. It may be helpful for understanding how the cinematic apparatus actually works against possession to see how de Man understands meaning and ownership. His gloss of Hegel complete, de Man continues:

It is, therefore, not only legitimate but necessary to hear, in the German word *meinen* (as in the sentence: Ich kann nicht sagen was ich nur meine) a connotation of *meinen* as "to make mine," a verbalization of the possessive pronoun mein. But that makes the innocuous pronouncement about the philosopher who, in humble self-effacement, has to progress beyond his private opinion, into a very odd sentence indeed: "Ich kann nicht sagen was ich (nur) meine" then means "I cannot say what I make mine" or, since to think is to make mine, "I cannot say what I think," and, since to think is fully contained in and defined by the I, since Hegel's ego cogito defines itself as mere ego, what the sentence actually says is "I cannot say."[29]

The cinematic apparatus cannot say "I" because the image does not belong to the spectator, to the director, or the actor. This accounts for the ubiquity and power of the image as it belongs to no one, as well as the emphasis that play receives in describing the movement between images. To return to Winnicott's insights once more in this context, the transitional object, as the "first not-me possession," eventually "loses meaning, and this is because the transitional phenomena have become diffused over the whole intermediate territory between 'inner psychic reality' and the 'external world as perceived by two persons in common,' that is to say, over the whole cultural field."[30] Winnicott, we recall, introduces both play and artistic creativity on the one side and fetishism and lying on the other as his subjects. In the context of de Man's reading of Hegel and possession, Winnicott provides a different perspective on how one possesses and how meaning takes place. Essentially, de Man is describing what Winnicott will call the "first not-me possession," which is language—language as what the ego cannot own, or as de Man puts it, "cannot say." Translated into a grammar of cinema, film is thought to belong to the spectator: What the film means depends upon the meaning I, the ego, give it. Film draws out the duration of the transitional object as neither internal object in a Kleinian sense nor as an external object. It is what Heath calls a "documentary" precisely because of the way in which the images belong to cinema, but are imagined by the ego as belonging to the spectator. A closer translation of transitional object is harder to find.

In the context of cinema, documentary names the property-lessness of the cinematic image as well as the experience of watching as witness (and less as voyeur). Naming the product of the cinematic apparatus as documentary acknowledges that what we desire from the apparatus occurs precisely because of its transitional status. It also suggests that the spectator, like the infant, can let go of the transitional object or not, what Winnicott will relate to illusion: "The transitional phenomena represent the early stages of the use of illusion, without which there is no meaning for the human being in the idea of a relationship with an object that is perceived by others as external to that being."[31] Or later: "If we shift the accent now from the object on to the word illusion we get near to the infant's transitional object; the importance lies in the concept of illusion, a universal in the field of experience."[32] Indeed, we might say that the apparatus generally constructs its product as transitional object that is meant to have duration.

The consequences of reading apparatus in a context of transitional phenomena are now clearer. Recall how Goodrich finds the apparatus's ability to capture so abhorrent as to find its origins in the guillotine that spectacularizes judgment. The motivation is to highlight the law and the way "persons" appear: With no apparatus, there would be no visibility, but no theater either. And here we see as well how deeply enmeshed apparatuses are in the production of the political, in the classic Schmittian definition of friends and enemies and a certain kind of playing of roles. What the cinematic apparatus can do, however, is to keep visibility open as a possibility, of that which is not (yet) completely mine. The cinematic apparatus differs in this from other "theatrical" apparatuses to the degree that we see making mine becoming visible. Cinema can be non-personal or, better, non-possessive in a way that the theatrical cannot; it can create through the apparatus intervals of non-possession in ways that other apparatuses have more difficulty doing. With cinema it is possible to register the possibility of non-possession and non-receiving therein at work.[33]

The move from the guillotine and its visibility of judgment to the theatrical and the visibility of the mask isn't simply the move to glory over terror, but is rather to greater mythic violence and the intensification of the political. This is key for appropriating persons as forms of knowledge, turning them into friend or enemy. Yet the cinematic apparatus is not simply a means for intensifying the political. Yes, cinema can make visible socially living beings, but given that it also depends on a relation to the invisible, a larger phenomenological horizon of the invisible out of which the visible is thinkable. The question then is this: What elements of the cinematic apparatus might be employed to counteract the possession and mastery of the image? How might cinema allow us to see what cannot be seen, to imagine what is not shown, and so doing push the spectator closer to something like an ethical viewing?[34] How might cinema assist the spectator in pointing to different acts of interpretation and non-possession, thereby creating a sense of responsibility for what we choose to make of a film? One way of thinking about this would be to see cinema not primarily as an apparatus or *dispositif* but rather as techne that allows for a practice of generous attention, what Bert Cardullo, writing of Antonioni, calls "creative spectatorship."[35]

TOWARD A PHENOMENOLOGY OF CINEMATIC FORMS OF LIFE

Shifting the frame from apparatus to techne, we begin to see how the spectator becomes more tolerant of objects, things, commodities, and persons seen onscreen so as to open up a space for thought around the question of how forms of life may be distinguished according to their grip. To elaborate this perspective, I want to turn, briefly at first, to Georg Simmel. For Simmel, writing at the turn of the last century, forms of life denote "patterns or any sort of contents in which psychic energy currently realises itself." The realization of life is key:

> Life cannot enter into form at all—beyond every attained structure it must at once seek out another one, in which the play—necessary structure, and necessary dissatisfaction with the structure as such—is repeated. As life it needs form; as life, it needs more than a given form. Life is caught up in the contradiction that it can only be lodged in forms and yet cannot be lodged in forms, that it passes beyond and destroys every one it has created . . . Life as immediately experienced is precisely the unity of "being formed" and "reaching out or flowing beyond form," which manifests itself at any single moment as destruction of the given current form. Life is indeed always more life than that accommodated in the form currently allotted to and grown from it.[36]

On a first read, Simmel's reading does not offer much for a reading of cinematic techne as his centerpiece is conflict among forms of life in which life cannot reside for long because to do so would mean the end of life. So, too, the constant striving of life to seek out another form and then another marks an idealized notion of life as conflict, struggle, and vitality. Indeed, many recent critiques of vitalism in Italian contemporary thought may be employed here against Simmel.[37] Yet the movement Simmel locates between satisfaction and dissatisfaction merits further consideration, with "structure as such" as well as the notion of forms of life in which "psychic energy realises itself." If we were to describe a cinema populated by forms of life, presumably it would be the one where psychic energy "realises itself," given the nature of the interaction between spectator and screen. It would be a cinema able to register the contradiction between the "lodging" of forms and the impossibility of that lodging remaining. If there were to be a cinema that features forms of life, it would be one capable of registering the movement between the "unity of being formed" and "reaching out or flowing beyond form." Here we might consider a piece that feels like a key to such a potential cinema—"life as immediately experienced." A phenomenology in which forms of life are experienced (and not captured for instance) suggests a cinema that highlights the unity of 'being formed" and "flowing out beyond form." Such a phenomenology would be one of play as well: the play between structure and dissatisfaction with structure. A cinema of forms of life would, in fact, be the one that shows life playing among forms and structures, adopting one form and then another. Such a potential cinema of forms of life certainly asks a lot both of cinema and spectator. It also asks a lot from any one national cinema.

The question is how a cinematic techne might move us toward such a space in which forms of life are experienced immediately and then followed attentively as life moves in and across them. Indeed, the reader may well wonder how such a potential phenomenology might work in terms of the directors and films soon to appear in the succeeding chapters. For now, one tentative answer will be found in how some films allow their protagonists to take leave of form and how such a leaving of form is made the object of attention in the spectator—a viewer who attends to how life moves across the forms on the screen and who is attentive to his or her own satisfaction and dissatisfaction. If there were such a thing as a cinematic techne, it would be one that creates conditions that make it possible for the spectator to look more closely at what appears on the screen—to focus on where and how life is manifested in and through form. Interestingly, the manifestation of life emerges in relation to things onscreen. It can be found in the interaction between those things in the *mise-en-scène*. The spectator and critic's task would be to move to where "patterns of psychic energy" can be attended to onscreen, and then to trace them attentively as they shift (or not).

One might well ask about the value added of doing so. That to do so ignores plot and, *pace* Heath, a host of formal tools for understanding cinema, that understanding cinema in terms of something so reductive or nebulous as attending to how life moves across forms misses the boat, especially if the point is to historicize the apparatus and cinematic history more broadly. Surely other objections come to mind: the implicit idealism of such a strategy of reading, the sneaking in of mere formalism into a discussion that by its very nature ought to contextualize and historicize such a move. My answer is that today in a moment of heightened violence and myth, as well as the proliferation of apparatuses in what often is experienced as pressure on forms of techne, paying attention to attention might help us to see and hold differently forms that are immanent to life and to cinema.

Rather than backing away from Simmel's "psychic energy" or the dialectic of life across forms, it's important to update Simmel's insights, translating them less in terms of ego and self, and more in relation to the key terms I have been using to this point: reciprocity, grip, touch, and thing. In such a reading of forms of life and cinema, capitalism will, on one hand, mark a form of life based on taking and holding; on the other, there will be the form that lessens or gives up its grip. A grasping of things, objects, persons and its object, the hand to be pried open. Cinema read as techne would allow the spectator to note how forms of holding, identification, and grasping come to characterize the increasingly limited forms of life that take place in our collective surrender to capitalism. Cinema as techne visually suggests that other forms of life are possible besides those that grasp—a plethora of forms that hold objects, their own form, or the frame, in ways quite different from the one-dimensional forms of life that capitalism features. All the while we remember that giving today often occurs without generosity. The primary techne associated with cinema able to create conditions in which these forms emerge or can be observed will feature primarily the long take, landscape, and *mise-en-scène*, especially with a view to the actor. Giving attention will name the techne associated with certain kinds of cinema that invite the spectator to identify less with what she sees or imagines she sees onscreen: to forego greater identification in lieu of the benefits of attending. It is here that Simmel's "life" may exceed the visible forms of life offered by the cinematic apparatus.

A cinematic techne allows us to pinpoint in ways that an emphasis on the cinematic apparatus cannot—where the visible and invisible meet, where the fold of the visible appears within the invisible. In such a fold, forms of life that may not be socially visible emerge: forms not linked to the person, to the mere functioning of the apparatus, but instead to what we might choose to call a non-idolatrous reading of cinema and with it the self.[38] By non-idolatrous, I intend an emphasis on those elements of cinematic techne not linked to fortifying or defending the self, or the ego.[39] The three directors under consideration shortly—Visconti, Rossellini, and Antonioni—work against precisely the idolatrous nature of the cinematic apparatus by forcing the spectator to pay attention and not to move immediately to what is visible—to seek out a distance between what we might call the Apollonian cinematic form and the Dionysian techne, what Camille Paglia years ago spoke of as "Dionysian liquidity," which is the "invisible sea of organic life, flooding our cells and uniting us to plants and animals."[40] Such a constitutive openness suggests, too, a relation with parataxis—Dionysus as the god of parataxis, with no penchant for constructing hierarchies among forms.

Each of these directors challenges the idolatry of the apparatus through a variety of means. The composition of the frame in particular stands out. In Visconti and then even more in Rossellini and Antonioni, what we see onscreen is often no longer a who but an object that changes form over time, which in turn becomes an invitation to identify less with the image/object.[41] To do so, each director will highlight the relationality the figures onscreen enjoy with other objects, landscapes, and spaces that open the same figures to different interactions and in so doing offering different (human and not so human) forms of life. Along the way, the films show how to hold open the visible to its other. Furthermore, they show how not to close off the visible by merely identifying and then identifying with it. Rather than a grasping, one learns how to receive the visible in a space that will suspend naming what appears there.

The questions these films answer is finally what form of life it is in which the visible actually is never known and mastered once and for all as visible. Such a perspective suggests that the attention evoked in the spectator presents itself as a way of becoming more intimate with the finite world of the non-commodity—to become less passionate about commodities and ourselves as commodities. On one hand, the term "apparatus" would name that which creates subjects and objects, making life available for capture. In terms of the cinematic apparatus, things are arranged, ordered, and captured as objects of the apparatus, and in that arrangement it becomes easier for the spectator to identify with these objects, which is to say, to provide them with meaning.

On the other hand, the ordering of objects and figures in the frame isn't the only story. What goes missing is another possibility that concerns a potential intimacy with the thing based on the thing's impenetrability. So much of what the apparatus does is meant to provide us with the illusion of mastery. A cinema that believes in the power of intimacy with things is a cinema that evades the viewer's supposed mastery by acknowledging that proper intimacy with the thing is based on the latter's attribute as solid and impenetrable.[42] Such non-mastery would involve holding things as things, seeing it as one would touch it so as not to grasp it.

Here, Luce Irigaray's reading of the caress is helpful:

> Of course there is a relation of the visible and the tangible. Is the doubling redoubled and crisscrossed? This is less certain. The look cannot take up the tangible. Thus I never see that in which I touch or am touched. What is at play in the caress does not see itself. The in-between, the middle, the medium of the caress does not see itself. In the same way and differently, I do not see that which allows me to see, that which touches me with light and air so that I see some "thing." This is perhaps, as far as I am concerned, what Merleau-Ponty calls the site of flesh in which things bathe. They begin to appear in a fog or a mist of invisibility. And it is still possible that my look—the most developed of all the senses?—disturbs the intelligence of my hand, of my touching . . . The visible and the tactile do not obey the same laws or rhythms of the flesh.[43]

The position of woman as the tangible invisible in a perspective on gratitude and responses to mythic violence absolutely needs to be acknowledged, especially given the prominent role that women play in the films discussed later in this book. The practices that make the "tangible invisible" to their object are also ones that are relevant for discussions of cinematic techne as well and with it gratitude. Here Irigaray suggests that just because we do not see form does not mean that it isn't tangible (as the tangible does not require a formal structure to be visible). Touching as seeing requires a greater intimacy with things, one that does not translate into mastery. In fact, Irigaray insists across all of her work that sight as mastery is precisely what we need less of. A techne of cinema would be one that creates conditions in which seeing is crossed with touch—a seeing that sees but masters less.

Why, we might ask, choose greater intimacy with things? One answer might be to sense the aliveness that becomes available precisely in the tangible contact with what remains invisible. Whereas with apparatuses generally, both subject and object fail to give way; a cinema of techne would feature the living quality of things that emerge in the moment of joined attentiveness when events, things, animals take form precisely because they no longer grip as they did before. In paying attention to the thing, a shared sense of flesh emerges linked to aliveness.[44] Or better: attention as a practice activates reciprocal aliveness.

For this reason, we can see why the animal figures so prominently in perspectives that promote notions of flesh. One would, for instance, not speak of an animal as having mastered a craft (though perhaps we might say that an animal or dog has learned a new trick).[45] Indeed, the animal is rarely if ever considered a master in any sense, perhaps because the animal's relation to nature dominates. Recall once again how Bataille linked "the obscure intimacy of the animal" with the "immense flux of the world." Irigaray and Merleau-Ponty's thought bring into focus the nature of that obscure intimacy, one based on non-mastery and non-possession—a non-possession of an object that the human has lost. *Pace* Deleuze, there can be no return to the animal and there is nothing, as I hope to show, in these films to suggest that such a transformation is needed. I would go still further and say that when we pivot to techne, we let go of the animal as the privileged road on the way to freedom from possession or non-mastery. Animals clearly do matter to the degree they gesture to a giving way to things in an "obscure intimacy." They still matter because for the time being we continue to live as social and political animals. Yet if we take form of life seriously as a rubric, then the role of the animal will be felt less strongly. This is not to say that the animal plays no role, but only that too often we fail to imagine forms of life as something other than animals. Or better, by focusing on animals, we miss an occasion for vitalizing relations between humans and living things, whose first step would precisely be the activation of attention.[46]

The move from gratitude to techne to forms of life—these are the key terms I want to carry forward in the next three chapters. Another is the comedic. What roles do the comedic and comedy play in pivoting from apparatus to techne? What place will "subjective caprice" have and how might we want to think about the relation between comedy and parataxis, as well as the leveling of hierarchy that is a part of comedy's *modus operandi*? Certainly, parataxis works well in terms of the comedic if we consider how much of the notion is about bringing the arrogant, the well-off, and the learned down to earth. But surely, there is more to the comical than that. As this brief reading of apparatus comes to a close, the principal question comes back to capture. Just how complete is the capture enacted by apparatuses? How fated to capture is the human? Where techne is highlighted instead of apparatus, capture may well give way to something else, namely a practice in which the invisible pushes up and past the visible; form once given and taken now holds off taking form. A spectatorship inhabited by techne would show how the apparatus is undercut precisely in the play between visible and invisible; between giving, taking, and observing.

One way of sketching a cinematic techne in these films is to adopt comedy as frame. Indeed the category of the comedic allows the critic to set out relationships among spectator, film, and forms of life in the frame and out, in ways that mere attention to apparatus cannot. For Kenneth Burke, such a frame asks us to be on the lookout "for those subtler ways in which the private appropriation of the public domain continues."[47] When thinking about gratitude and generosity via comedy, we begin to see how easily generosity can be transformed into a gift and how easily it can be made the object of a calculation. Capitalism, as we have come to know only too well, translates generosity into its human or social equivalents in exchange and philanthropy for what before would have been called generosity. By emphasizing the generic traits of the comedic, we can begin to trace a dialectic in the motivation of the "generous" act as part of an overall strategy that has at its core Burke's "private appropriation of the public domain." In the next three chapters, I read a number of films as displaying how hypertrophied non-generous forms of life have become, while also pointing the way to how more generous, more common forms of individual and collective life might begin to gain traction.

The last chapter ended on the figure of the *mancus*, the form of life whose lack of hands characterize a certain kind of giving. After considering the cinematic apparatus, we now are in a position to examine three directors who employ that apparatus in such a way as to highlight the generous features of a cinematic techne. In films such as *The Earth Trembles, Germany Year Zero*, and *Eclipse*, the cinematic apparatus isn't simply used to capture the human, but also includes within it a cinematic techne, which allows for a practice of spectatorship to arise not based on mastering what is on or off screen. Indeed, these are films deeply attuned just as much to what is off screen as to what is on. It is that interest in the interval between frame and what lies beyond that allows the spectator to hold on less to what he or she sees. In the possibility for not identifying and not mastering, something approaching the generous form of life becomes possible.

3

"DEAD WEIGHT": VISCONTI AND FORMS OF LIFE

The perils of giving and taking in a milieu of mythic violence: This is just one of the perspectives I want to follow up on next in my examination of Luchino Visconti's *The Earth Trembles*, the first of five films from postwar Italy to which the next three chapters are dedicated. Admittedly, the choice of this film may seem, well, odd. Just consider the tizzy some critics would work themselves into if they actually began to speak of neo-realist comedies—save for de Sica's *Miracolo a Milano* and Rossellini's *La macchina ammazzacattivi* of course—in terms of non-taking, non-giving, the comedy of a non-exchange, to the "event itself" as Andre Bazin calls it.[1] Yet that is just what *The Earth Trembles* offers: a compelling perspective on a cinematic and comedic techne worth pursuing.[2] In particular, the film provides us with a first take on the generous form of life, a cinematic *mancus* inhabited by the character Mara.

To introduce the relationship among gratitude, comedy, and forms of life in the film, let's begin with a contribution well known to scholars that Visconti made to a fascist-era journal, *Cinema*. These writings have, over the years, been read as a kind of theoretical diary preceding the filming of *The Earth Trembles*.[3] Furthermore, let's also remember that in the period between the films *Ossessione* and *The Earth Trembles*, Visconti wasn't by any means idle—he was busy making films about the Resistance as well as sketching his later films, all of which were accompanied by his philosophical musings in the pages of *Cinema*.[4] Of particular interest for this study is Visconti's call for a vital cinema and the role that the human plays in bringing a palpable sense of aliveness to the frame. Of the many essays and articles Visconti wrote, one in particular merits further thought, as it constitutes what we might call a manifesto for a cinema of living forms lacking hands.

For Visconti, the aliveness of cinematic bodies onscreen results not from their interaction with other bodies alone, but from their interaction with things in the frame over time.[5] Here is a first passage from that essay, "Anthropomorphic Cinema":

> My experience has taught me that the heft [*peso*] of a human being, his presence, is the only thing which really fills the frame; that he creates the atmosphere with his living presence. He acquires truth and character thanks to the emotion he undergoes, while his temporary absence from the screen [*rettangolo luminoso*] will cause things to return to the state of non-animated nature.[6]

Visconti uncovers three anthropological moments in the act of filmmaking, which he links to the "heft" of the human. First, he notes the role that creation plays in the frame. The act of creating will be found both in the human actor who appears in the frame as well as in the director who has composed it. The word "environment" also deserves scrutiny as that which the human being creates. The actor and director will presumably share creativity as both award the human his or her own proper weight—the actor because of the embodied power projected to things and the director for the mode with which the human body (or human "thing") can be positioned to provide optimal "weight" (a piece that we will return to in terms of gravity and the weight of the fall in *Germany Year Zero*).

The second moment concerns the importance of the human when placed inside the frame. For Visconti, the weight of human beings is joined to and measured in presence, and here we note the relation of "peso" (weight) with gravity as a property of bodies generally.[7] Not only is presence sensed, but no environment can be said to exist without it because every "thing" reverts to "non-animated" nature. "Environment," for Visconti, requires just such a presence. The pressure on the human "thing" in the frame necessarily will be great—in its absence, the frame continually risks reverting to a non-animated state. What counts here is not the appropriation of the forms onscreen by other "human forms," but apprehending these non-animated forms and in so doing allowing the forces of the human to be "expropriated" into them.[8] When noting the weight of the human, Visconti's choice of term lingers: The human being is the only "thing" able both to fill up the frame and to push what is contained therein higher ("colmare" has both the meaning of to culminate as well as to fill up).[9] Visconti would appear to be building toward a humanistically inflected reading of the cinematic apparatus.

From Visconti's perspective, the passions will function as a medium for presence because it is through them that the "human thing" is manifested.[10] Passion sets apart the human thing from the non-animate things in the frame, animating the frame away from its otherwise clear-cut destiny of non-animation. A cinema enlivened by the passions would be one that draws attention to the interaction among things onscreen, human or not. Whether the frame is alive or not will depend, therefore, on the role of the human as descriptor of "thing" (*cosa*). Yet how the human thing fills up the frame is obscure. Weight and presence are metonymically joined to "thing" when the descriptor of the human is added, but not before Visconti adds an element that shifts the line running from weight to presence to thing, and that is the relation of the human being back to the "environment" that he or she has created. Visconti in the passage does not say work or labor, but rather creation. The reason is clear: He is attempting to name more precisely the difference between man's "living presence" as opposed to the frame's dead presence. To do so, the creation that takes place in the frame has to be imagined impersonally—from him or her to living presence, to passions that "agitate"—and we suddenly realize that the environment acquires truth and meaning through the medium of passions.[11] When the human being occupies the frame, the environment comes alive thanks to the living thingness that is not only the attribute of the human being, but which can be awarded to the non-human things in the frame. There is something communicative about the nature of the relation between the "luminous rectangle," and the presence of the living thing as vitality is transmitted to the frame itself and thus to the cinematic apparatus that has produced it.

FLOWS, LIVES, COMEDY

The interaction between the human and non-human thing in the frame distinguishes Visconti's cinema from this period. It also moves our discussion to the question of the possibilities that inhere in a cinematic techne, including weight, passion, and the comedic. Why the comedic? The answer resides in gratitude, for in no other genre more than comedy does one find relief from the administration of violence or the weight that limits vitality.[12] To the degree that an analysis of cinematic techne allows us to register how deadness is made alive and how a non-animated nature is made vital, the fate of the apparatus to non-animation is lessened. To put my cards once again on the table, this is one of the principle ways Visconti's perspective on framing can help us. A translation of techne into comedic terms in *The Earth Trembles* may show us just how much the visible becomes hypertrophied when the apparatus is emphasized to the exclusion of techne and may show us how much the invisible becomes unavailable to the viewer as a potential *mancus*, who has some thing in common with the human thing onscreen.

A number of authors writing about cinema have noted a relation between life and apparatus. Siegfried Kraucauer, for instance, implicitly recognizes it in his notion of the "flow of life."[13] It is also a part of those memorable pages from Bazin on precisely the role that landscape plays in film and of course can be found in Deleuze's analysis of the time-image.[14] They may not call it the comedic, and certainly in the case of Deleuze anything that smells like the Hegelian dialectic is a problem.[15] On my read, however, the conceptual struggle between tragedy and comedy is played out in *The Earth Trembles* between apparatus and techne thanks largely to tragedy's relation to the apparatus and techne's to comedy: to one of fear and to another that responds differently.

As I observed earlier, no more eloquent proponent of the comedic as antidote to the violence of fear can be found than in the thought of American critic and poet Kenneth Burke. For Burke, comedy, or as he calls it across a variety of texts, the "comic frame" or "comic corrective," helps us be on the lookout "for those subtler ways in which the private appropriation of the public domain continues." He adds that the comic frame "admonishes us that social exigencies and 'goodwill' are as real a vein to be tapped as any oil deposit in Teapot Dome."[16] When thinking about gratitude and generosity in a comedic context, Burke's "comic corrective" gives us leave to recognize how easily generosity is calculated and made into a gift. Indeed, capitalism will find generosity's equivalent in social and human terms of exchange, which is to say in philanthropy, or what before went by the name generosity. Burke is not out to debunk philanthropy—or perhaps just a little—but rather to trace the dialectic motivating the "generous" act as part of an overall strategy that would frame "development" as an individual's appropriation of the common. For Burke, the comic corrective draws attention to the ways individuals make the common by how they hold things, others, themselves. Clearly, the comedic will not offer revolution as a response, nor will it seek directly to right the injustice of such an appropriation.[17] On the contrary, its purpose is to disclose how much of what appears as power covers over acts of appropriating what before was held in common.

If we adopt the comic corrective for understanding the cinematic apparatus, something interesting happens: the uncovering of the appropriation of the common occurs not just across narrative, but also in the appropriation of the common enacted by the cinematic apparatus itself. Said differently, the cinematic appartus limits through the frame what the spectator sees and doesn't.[18] A comic corrective to that appropriation will seek to highlight how the apparatus separates, divides, and pushes to the outside what is not seen as "belonging" to the frame. At the same time, a comic corrective permits the spectator to see how the apparatus makes possible other perspectives—that by waiting for the outside of the frame to be acknowledged, the greater relationality of the apparatus to what lies outside may be perceived. In other words, the comic corrective opens up vistas on forms that do not appropriate and it does so by creating conditions for the spectator to attend to the moment when what is outside the frame may come into view. The premise is that the spectator will not necessarily appropriate what she sees; will not take, but will instead give attention. Visconti's manifesto for a vital cinema plays out in the paradigm of the comic corrective in two ways: in his continuing attempts to remind the viewer of a landscape that shields the inhabitants (and viewer) from what lies outside the frame, and second, by showing the attentive film-goer the possibilities for the emergence of forms that are less subject to the whims of exchange and calculation.

MYTHIC VIOLENCE, MYTHIC COMMUNITY

Turning now to *The Earth Trembles*, let's consider the famous opening frame with its long shot of the village, Acitrezza, the small fishing village

Figure 3-1. The Earth Trembles

where most of the film's action will take place, and the slow pan that follows (see Figure 3-1). Moving from church to houses, barely lit against an approaching sunrise, the camera registers shadows and more shadows, which a collection of voices then interrupts. The camera, continuing to move slowly, even painfully, finally rests on the Cyclopean Isles, the jarring rocks that separate the village from the sea. The longer the camera holds on the Isles, the more we realize how much they occupy the frame, acting as gatekeepers to the early sequence and to the events of the film.[19] As anyone can attest who has lived on an island, Visconti's emphasis on the immovability of these rocks is not an accident.

Still, the effect of this early sequence and the frame provided by the Isles is ambiguous. On one hand, Visconti implies that no sharp division may be said to exist between the Isles and the fishermen. Given the long take and recurrent shot of the Isles throughout the film, the spectator sees a place that offers a view and looks back as well as a place shrouded in darkness and movement, all aided by the pan over the village, the trajectory of which ends famously back on the Isles.[20] Certainly, the voices and their dialect intensify the impression of the exotic and ritualistic, as does the difficulty of making out the outlines of any one individual.[21] Visconti's decision to linger over the bay in order to capture the voices and shadows as the boats are launched heightens expectation. We wait for a cut from the shot of the Isles to the bay, and when it eventually comes, it fails to give us the expected view of the village, Acitrezza, itself.

On the other hand, an unmistakable impression of violence is lurking here. We can sense it in the long take that transforms the sequence into something more like a photograph: a photograph that imperceptibly moves. Perhaps we first miss the violence implicit here, but if we look more closely, there is something that absolutely demands to be seen. We register it in the difficulty of discerning the lights and the boats and how forcefully the Isles dominate the frame. Roland Barthes described the violence of the photograph's demand to be seen this way:

> The Photograph is violent: not because it shows violent things, but because on each occasion it fills the sight by force, and because in it nothing can be refused or transformed (that we can sometimes call it mild does not contradict its violence: many say that sugar is mild, but to me sugar is violent, and I call it so).[22]

Expanding on Barthes's extrapolation of violence from the photograph, we might say that the opening shot, by holding on the Isles in the dawn, imparts a sense of anti-reciprocity to the sequence in which nothing can be refused, least of all the events that we will soon be a witness to. This demand that what we see must be accepted sets the sequence apart. Barthes's phrase—"nothing can be refused or transformed"—becomes shorthand for the workings of the apparatus and its role in the destiny of capture.

Visconti's images in the opening sequence visually illustrate Benjamin's mythic violence, which is linked to the destiny of non-individuation. Indeed the film might be said to describe the torturous path of failing to avoid that destiny for the Valastri family and with it, the effect of their failure on life in the village. In *The Earth Trembles*, life is premised on the impossibility of any lasting transformation of the family or the village or, to adopt Benjamin's language from Chapter 1, any hoped-for irruption of divine violence. The reason won't be found in the narrative or the dialogue, but rather in the imposing presence of the Faraglioni, the Cyclopean Isles that stand guard over the film's entire action. As I hope to show, the narrative of 'Ntoni and the family's failed individuation corresponds across the film to a visual language of precisely that sort of failure. To put Barthes into conversation with Visconti then: Destiny in *The Earth Trembles* is what cannot be refused, which is repeatedly concretized in ineluctability with what 'Ntoni and the family see and fail to see. Visconti relentlessly tracks down the consequences of this initial perspective on life in Acitrezza. Rarely are we given any point-of-view shots from the perspective of either of the brothers, 'Ntoni and Cola. Instead, the camera takes up a safe distance at the side or above them, suggesting that their missing point of view is mirrored in the film's content—attempts at individuation narratively meet the formal failure to award the brothers a consistent point of view.[23] Not only is nature unchangeable, it cannot be refused, nor, seemingly, can the film's *mise-en-scène* and with it the lives of those who inhabit the frame. On this score, let's not underestimate the visual cues that the Cyclopean Isles provide the viewer, recalling an ancient past of Homer's *Odyssey* and the Cyclops sequence recounted at the end of Book Nine.[24]

Certainly, Visconti was intent on framing the events recounted in the film with the *Odyssey* in mind. Writing in another essay that appeared in *Cinema*, and after highlighting repeatedly his origins as a Northerner, Visconti sees in Sicily and in Acitrezza "a primitive and gigantic world of fishermen and shepherds," which had "always appeared lit by an imaginary and violent epic tone; to my Lombardian eyes . . . Verga's Sicily seemed to truly be the island of Ulysses, an island of adventure and burning passions, proudly situated—immobile—against the waves of the Ionian Sea."[25] It is difficult to find a better description of how we experience these early scenes in the film: violent, immobile, and imaginary. Immobile particularly stands out in a context of mythic violence, what Visconti would surely have called epic violence. This context is informed by a Northerner's perspective—the words "primitive," "gigantic," "adventure," and "passion" call to mind the *topoi* of the South fitted into the usual wineskins of geographical identity. If we linger over the passage, however, it is "immobile" that identifies this earth, this *terra*, and the immobility of the island against the sea. This is the space of enclosure and fatedness. An island, its fishermen and shepherds, is fated to stand against the crashing waves and by extension, to face the violence of precisely that immobility. Let's also be sure to note how much Visconti's perspective is marked by a dehumanizing move in which the

South's relation to antiquity allows for a *glissando* from fishermen to adventure to immobility—all are of the same mythic violence.

What name do we want to give to such a space? Sicily, or more generally the South, comes to mind given the film's location and the adaptation of Verga's *I Malavoglia* on which Visconti worked for so many years.[26] So, too, does the more affirmative space of potential collective action, though again, perhaps because as we saw earlier Visconti remained close to Verga, that appears less the case the further removed the spectator is from the context in which the film was made. Let me suggest another name for the space and time of an individuation destined to fail: milieu. For a variety of reasons, milieu marks the space of mythic violence that characterizes the film. Of course, the term "milieu" dominates so much of our contemporary understanding of biopolitics, under the weight that Michel Foucault gives it in *Security, Territory, Population.*[27] A much earlier genealogy of milieu in Leo Spitzer's stunning essay of 1942, however, can help us see just how linked milieu is to fate.[28] Adopting Pascal's reading of milieu, Spitzer argues that where before milieu denoted a relationship to the outside that the individual desired, with Pascal, the locus for milieu is now fixed by the two poles of the absolute, to which finite man is "doomed." For Spitzer, milieu names a place in which man lives. The following passage from Pascal anchors Spitzer's reflections:

> This is our true state; this is what makes us incapable of certain knowledge and of absolute ignorance. We sail within a vast sphere [*sur un milieu vaste*], ever drifting in uncertainty, driven from end to end. When we think to attach ourselves to any point and to fasten to it, it wavers and leaves us; and if we follow it, it eludes our grasp, slips past us, and vanishes for ever. Nothing stays for us.[29]

Rarely do we consider milieu as a sphere on which we sail or drift, but in the Pascalian sense milieu names just these states of uncertainty that weaken our footing, of things held and things let go of, of things that cannot be grasped. There are other pivots and turns in Spitzer's tracing of milieu—the relation to medium is one that returns long after—but for the purposes of reading mythic violence and gratitude in *The Earth Trembles*, it is this incapability of "certain knowledge" as well as "absolute ignorance" that stands out. 'Ntoni and Cola fail to recognize the perils of individuation and remain unaware of the power of the forces arrayed against them. Visconti's camera records this in the choral insistence on the Cyclops.[30]

Yet the collective and individual lives captured cinematically do not tell the whole story. To see why, let's begin by re-evaluating the significance of non-actors in this film and more broadly in Italian neo-realism. I can recall the shifts in opinion, and perhaps the reader can, too, with regard to the question posed frequently over the last two decades and more. For a time, the use of non-actors in neo-realism was perceived as ideologically guaranteeing the reality of the film's representation of reality (dialect, dress, and so on). Later, other considerations began to dominate over questions of ideology. For Visconti, the motivation for using non-actors is clear enough. What counts in the use of non-actors is the weight their presence provides in the frame, namely in highlighting the anthropomorphic features of the apparatus that Visconti was intent on making visible: emphasizing the techne of cinema, and so pushing against the tragic features of the apparatus. The anthropological presence of the non-actor meets the challenge of the apparatus itself. In different words, their presence gives weight to the comedic possibilities of the apparatus itself.

Where and how does the viewer experience this weight, this gravity, on the part of the non-actor? It is felt in the mode of interaction that actors have with the camera, the way they remain oblivious to their own capture, the mode by which they fail to make a problem out of the workings of cinematic capture. The search for the non-actor who does not problematize the apparatus or who is not simply indifferent to it, responds to the growing power of the cinematic apparatus by employing "human material" in order to enliven the deadening effects of the apparatus itself. This is the sense in which Visconti speaks of "anthropomorphic cinema"—a cinema able to morph, not just the *anthropos* but cinema, too. The non-actors key such a reading of cinema as they provide the audience and the director with the possibility of witnessing in the frame what is able to counteract the workings of the apparatus itself.

Call it cinematic techne or "anthropomorphic cinema." Both put on the same footing those who are enclosed in the frame with those who are enclosed within the darkened room. Both non-actor and spectator are the subject and object of the capture of the apparatus. Rather than arguing simply about cinematic escape that the apparatus provides the filmgoer, however, Visconti points to a complex interaction between actor and spectator in which identification is both blocked and then opened. It is as simple as Visconti seeing in cinema the possibility of a commonality between the anthropomorphic potential of the non-actor and of the spectator herself. What is the nature of this commonality shared by the spectator and the non-actor? What does the projection of cinematic bodies onscreen in *The Earth Trembles* ultimately have to do with the viewer? The answer, according to Visconti, will be found in the repeated linking of living being with what that being has created. If the individual or body—sometimes it isn't clear where one begins and one ends both onscreen and off—fails to construct his or her own environment by creating, then doubts will arise precisely as to the degree of vitality that that those onscreen actually enjoy. It is through the labor of his or her hands and the interaction with the results of that labor—captured repeatedly in the *mise-en-scène*—that counteract the dead milieu and dead weight of mere registration. For Visconti, the power of the cinematic apparatus lies in the feedback loop running between the human being and the things that populate the frame as his or her creations.

On such a reading of apparatus, the imperative of creativity in Visconti's perspective on cinema intensifies. Writing again in "Anthropomorphic Cinema," Visconti recognizes how decisive the category creativity is for his own choice in becoming a filmmaker:

> What has led me to a creative activity in film? (Creative activity: labor [*opera*] of a living man among living men. With this term—it must be clear—I do not intend to refer to something pertaining exclusively to the realm of art. Every worker, living, creates something: as long, that is, as he is able to live) . . . I think that only through a genuinely felt experience, nourished daily by an objective and sympathetic scrutiny of human existence, can one arrive at artistic specialization . . . I have been attracted to film-making above all by the commitment to tell stories of living men: of men alive in things, not of things in and of themselves. The cinema I am interested in is anthropomorphic cinema.[31]

Creative activity for Visconti occurs in the setting of the other, with creation a condition for proving that one is alive in the midst of humanity. Visconti assumes that "in mezzo agli uomini," those less alive are numerous: one can, as a worker, not live and thus not create, which is precisely the point—creation is impossible for the alienated. What does it mean to live in such a way as to create? The switch is breathtaking—"his days are free and open," says Visconti. Days free and open are what the artist, worker, and artisan share. Note that Visconti does not discount the negative of his insight, namely that not all workers do create because not all are equally alive. The notion of work will necessarily change—an inverted form of work in which the worker does not create and thus does not live. Here again Visconti's Marxism comes into view (a Romantic one to be sure), and with it the critique of alienation that undermines the kind of creativity that every worker ought to enjoy in the fruits of her labor.

Another detail is easy to miss: Visconti's definition of a creative activity as "opera," not simply of an individual, but of one who lives among others, along the same lines with which Sartre defined generosity "as a passion properly speaking and as the only means of being."[32] How will we define the nature of what the human thing gives non-human things in the frame? What kind of reciprocity is at work? Let's recall the earlier passage about the movement from presence to weight to thing of the human being in the frame. One tack might be to bring together the environment created by the actor in the frame and the things that, when seen by the spectator, become not only real but also present.[33] Something similar is at work here, a resemblance between the frame and its objects when the human being is not present with the work that is done but lacking the presence of others. Cinema offers lessons in creativity by giving life to things thanks to the environment that contains the human captured on film.

To be clear, it isn't the act itself or the "opera" that renders an activity creative, but rather the act's relation to the presence of other individuals in the frame. If Visconti is right about vitality being contagious, then cinema itself would be based upon a relation not simply of life and death as Roland Barthes saw at work in the photograph, but also in the relation of the "created" environment to life. Where no relation between the things in the frame to human can be said to hold, something other than a vital environment emerges. The apparatus comes to the fore as it arranges bodies and things within the frame—giving life, making things come alive, but also withdrawing life, emptying the frame. The impression of life and death alternates in the rhythm of shots and it does so thanks to a cinematic techne that organizes what is seen around the creative potential of the human in the frame and in the audience.[34] The human, in such instances, is the mode by which things in the frame come alive, become visible, and then move back to the realm of the not seen and not alive. Visconti's perspective on creation provides another way of thinking flesh through creativity as we are looking at a flesh animated among things onscreen and off—a flesh alive thanks to the present thingness of the human being.[35]

ICONS OF CREATIVITY

At the same time, the aliveness radiated to things in the frame by the human thing moves us in another direction, a surprising one: the icon. How can we relate the icon to flesh and why attempt to do so in *The Earth Trembles*? We know that icon names a type of sign in which there exists a "physical resemblance" between the signifier and the signified (differently from what happens in the linguistic sign, where such resemblance isn't usually there. For linguists and semiologists, the icon isn't a proper sign because it lacks the arbitrariness in the association between signifier and signified).[36] For this reason, the icon falls outside the sign and with it arbitrariness, suggesting that tracing a commonality among things may be easier if the object in question is an icon. What distinguishes the icon from our earlier discussions of the idol and fetish? Recalling the decisive importance of mastery for both terms, we might now suggest the following question: In its resemblance to the sign, does the icon evade mastery in a way that the idol and fetish fail to? That is, might the arbitrariness of the sign in relation to the signifier as in language operate as one of the conditions for mastery? The questions are beyond the means of this chapter, but it's clear, I think, that by inviting the viewer to master, fetish and idol don't do themselves any favors with a genuine reciprocity that acknowledges uncertainty in relations.[37] And uncertainty is key to understanding both a cinematic techne as well as the *mancus* as generous form of life.

Visconti understood that the commonality between things and human beings becomes a possibility in the duration of the take and that in the shared thingness of the frame between things and human being as presence as weight, a resemblance with the viewer is created. A commonality with the thing and thingness of the captured human being presents us with the possibility of imagining a viewing practice that not only assumes that the apparatus will capture the human, but in so doing creates the possibility for marking the shared nature with the thing; a post-humanist perspective to the degree that aliveness becomes a possibility only in the presence of the human being, where "human" as an adjective is capable of moving from being to thing and back.

Other words come to mind for such a practice—such as "observation" and "attention." In order for the commonality between "my" thingness and the thing created around me to become visible, a stance must be adopted outside myself, which is to say an *ex-stare*: a standing outside that allows a framing of the body and consciousness. It would be one that allows an attending to movement, which opens a window on how environment comes alive thanks to the degree of a shared thingness. In such a perspective, the camera would operate as a kind of second-order observation, making possible a standing outside as opposed to a merely living inside. Creativity becomes possible to the degree that the folds of the thingness shared with other non-living things in the environment become observable.

ANTHROPOLOGICAL NON-MASTERY

We have come a long way from the respective milieu of divine and of mythic violence. How might we characterize, then, the milieu of Acitrezza after the foray into icon and the non-mastery of what we see onscreen? Many have noted the various anthropological features of *The Earth Trembles*—the distance and time of Acitrezza from Rome or New York or very nearly any Western capital. If there is another feature that deserves our investigation, it is precisely the village's missing relation to attention. It is just such a scarcity of attention that calls into question any possibility of transformation on the part of the villagers. In the film, Visconti asks the spectator to consider how decisive failed attention is on the part of the inhabitants of Acitrezza, not only for collective action, but also for the individuation of forms of life. Equally, Visconti invites us to consider how we as spectators engage with the frame and how we attend not simply to what takes place, but to what occupies the space in which the events take place. The film seems, on one hand, to associate the villagers with a natural guilt, a *blosses Leben*, in Benjamin's phrase, which has been made subject to mythic violence. Indeed mythic violence in the film often combines with nature itself to produce the tragic destiny of the brothers. The famous scene in which a fascist dictum appears on the wall (and soon after when the name of Mussolini appears behind one of the wholesalers near film's end) is but an indication of the first of the two poles of mythic violence (see Figure 3-2). The repeated shots of the bay and the Cyclopean Isles indicate an inevitable outcome to the events that we will witness.[38] To be sure that the spectator has understood the relation of violence to myth to the events recounted, Visconti offers near the film's closing a slow pan of the "Ciclope," the name of the wholesalers' transportation and selling operation (see Figure 3-3). It is here that the final moments of the film take place, framed again by the shot of the Cyclopean Islands (see Figure 3-4) in an alternation with the "Ciclope" shop. In what is one of the most moving long takes in all of Italian neorealism, we see 'Ntoni approach with the other brothers accompanying him. The storefront with the name "Ciclope" appears literally at the end of the road for the Valastri. The superimposition of Cyclops beyond Acitrezza and the Cyclops impersonated by the wholesalers asks the viewer to register visually the superimposition of mythic violence on daily violence. In the distance that 'Ntoni walks, framed between the Isles, to "Ciclope," all of the mythic violence can be measured as a fatedness to what has gone before.

At the same time, the film, while uncovering the doomed state of the villagers, gives something to its spectators in the form of a task: Allow attention to rest on what moves in the frame; attend, in ways that the villagers cannot, to what the villagers cannot see. Now any apparatus that places a living being in

Figure 3-2. The Earth Trembles

Figure 3-3. The Earth Trembles

Figure 3-4. The Earth Trembles

its crosshairs makes it an object of a certain kind of interpretation and a certain kind of writing. Moreover, it is also true that all living organisms interpret what happens around them according to their history, conditioning, and modes of experiencing. Yet consider how deeply the inhabitants fail to attend to what ails them. Or better, note how a collective form of life makes impossible the future individuation of other forms of life. If we were to describe the form that Visconti provides for the villagers, it is one that waits without knowing that it waits. It is also a form of life that cannot see how profoundly its individuation is blocked. There is no mass here waiting for revolution, but seemingly undifferentiated forms of life unaware of individuation alongside the small number who, aware, try and seemingly fail at individuation.

The spectator also waits. Her waiting, however, differs. Before answering how, it may prove helpful to ask a different question: What does the film ask of its Italian-speaking spectator? From the opening, Visconti emphasizes the skills the spectator must use in order to make sense of what occurs on-screen and off.[39] How many viewers have been unable to distinguish the fishermen moving in the morning darkness from the buildings of the village that stand above them? In the opening composition of the shots of the bay and the village, Visconti composes distance in such a way that the spectator cannot but confound persons and things, confound the living and the non-living. Closely related is the experience of separateness. The day begins with shafts of light and darkness that alternate, enclosed by the bay and the dawn sky. Images fold into each other, conveying the collapse of lines demarcating where a body or thing ends and another begins. The anthropological features of the film—the huts, the bare-footedness of the villagers, forms of life at the mercy of the elements, on boats or in their uncovered homes—create the distance necessary for the spectator to experience the obscure and fearful features of un-individuated forms of life.[40] As separateness and proximity are key to Visconti's political project in the film, we need to dig deeper into the elements of that distance.

THE PROPER DISTANCE OF ICONOGRAPHY

Here we return nearly by default to the issue of iconography in the film. Implicit in the attention demanded of the spectator when facing (and faced) with an icon is the construction of a relationship between the spectator and the frame based on unity in separateness. In an incisive reading from 1949,

Renzo Renzi describes the film as "a kind of Marxist mystery," arguing that ultimately Visconti's project breaks down as if it came down to a question "of an attitude, much like a long-planned study of the poetry of myth."[41] Renzi believes the search for poetry in myth to be unhealthy: "Furthermore, it's obvious that some of Visconti's discoveries, made thanks to Marxism—when they become dogma—begin to look like Destiny in *The Earth Trembles*: the Destiny of the proletariat is already spelled out in the three stages of revolt, redemption, and victory."[42] What does the spectator do, he asks, when faced with uppercase Destiny? "There is nothing left to do except contemplate. *The Earth Trembles* ultimately becomes a long, static contemplation of preordained events, in which the author does not participate, even if he really wanted to."[43] Renzi concludes: "The proletariat has been defeated because it remains victim to the sins of capitalism, with revelation nowhere to be found in anticipation of the event."[44]

In Renzi's view, the basis for contemplation lies in Visconti's composition of images: "Contemplation is manifested through an anesthetized care of how the images are composed: contemplation is made concrete in a true and authentic iconography."[45] Renzi's reading helps push us to some further remarks on gratitude and forms of life in the film. What are the features of the iconic relation between spectator and frame? How might we describe the form of life that contemplates what happens onscreen with the other form of life captured by the cinematic apparatus? Contemplation results from a composition of images whose ultimate point of arrival is to set off the spectator from what she sees onscreen and especially from the forms of life projected there. It is to increase the duration of the spectator's attending to forms onscreen. To do that, however, separation must include both the anthropological and the linguistic. What does it mean to put into symbolic action a movement between figures on the screen, villagers unaware of the possibility of event, and increasingly individuated forms of life, the brothers, who act? In other words, it is the villagers who wait, but it is the spectator who acts symbolically, putting images together, separating the living from the non-living. Micciché's insistence on the imaginary as the motor for creativity is apropos: "In Visconti—the most literary director of Italian cinema after silent movies—literature is given back its function as the primary creator of the imaginary: but his film-making, with some exceptions, doesn't pretend to be the visible establishment of a possible literary imaginary, but . . . the project for a different creative itinerary."[46]

Renzi senses much the same dialectical relation between the villagers captured onscreen and the spectator:

> Actually, it is precisely the necessity of postponing "revelation," which Visconti, logically—according to Visconti a political organism could have suggested "immediately" to the consciousness of the protagonist—induces the author to exit the situation of the present while remaining faithful to his preordained mythological schema, this despite the demands for realism from the spectator.[47]

Renzi understands a chief paradox of the film, which is to say that the film is mythological in how it constructs a choral landscape, and as such cannot be primarily considered as a documentary. But another paradox concerns these "realistic demands" made on the spectator, demands that have less to do with realism than with creating attention; in assisting the spectator in understanding, that is in seeing more than the "real life" features of the forms of life on the screen. To do so requires using the iconic features of the cinematic apparatus to instruct the spectator, not only on how to wait, but to make sense of the images composed before her onscreen. In the iconic features of *The Earth Trembles*—the mystical contemplation that so troubles Renzi—another possibility appears: a kind of giving we witness in the interaction between the form of life that attends and the one captured on film.

The affirmative potential of the iconic renders a cinematic techne different from apparatuses that capture humanity. To take up the question from a slightly different angle, let's reflect once again on the differences between icon and idol. In a discussion of love of the self, Luce Irigaray observes how on one hand, "in the icon, the passage from outside to inside occurs through the insistence of the invisible within visibility; the icon irradiates the invisible, and its gaze seems to gaze on the visible from out of the invisible, gaze of the gaze beyond our usual (?) perceptions."[48] The idol, on the other hand, "attracts the gaze but blinds it with brilliance that bars access to the invisible; it dazzles, it does not lead to another threshold, another texture of the gaze, of world, of meaning."[49] Charles Peirce is not so far away on this score:

> Each Icon partakes of some more or less overt character of its Object. They, one and all, partake of the most overt character of all lies and deceptions—their Overtness. Yet they have more to do with the living character of truth than have either Symbols and Indices. The Icon does

not stand unequivocally for this or that existing thing, as the Index does. Its Object may be a pure fiction, as to its existence.[50]

Taking up these perspectives on the icon, we might say that the frame of the Cyclopean Isles functions iconically to the degree that the Isles themselves stand outside in order to contain what takes place inside. The Isles occupy nearly every shot of Acitrezza that includes the villagers; they are especially prominent in the initial conflagration when the fishermen toss the wholesalers' scales into the sea. They enclose the actions captured on film and act as a mirror for the other side of the camera that looks back on us. Thus, when Renzi writes of a spectator waiting for revelation, that revelation cannot be thought of apart from the Isles and the sea that motivate the act (or lack of an act). Our waiting for revelation depends in this instance upon the icon of the Cyclops to give up its secrets, not to be what we see, namely the container whose power is precisely to get us to continue to look.

The Cyclops bear witness to and cast their shadow over the acts portrayed, working as a force that explains the ultimate motivation of both the brothers' actions as well as the reason for their failure. The scenic property of the bay permits certain acts, though none of them are sufficiently individuated for their momentum to last. These are a mass of men who cannot be said ultimately to act, but who only move. This may well explain the film's subtitle: "An Episode of the Sea." Episode (*epeisodion*), as Aristotle tells us, refers to the interval separating two choric songs—that is, the moment when the actor enters from the side on to the stage.[51] In terms of the film's politics, we might want to consider that the episode told here—the first of three originally planned—isn't just to be linked to the larger struggle of the proletariat, as Visconti himself noted, but one that is to be thought together with a very specific sea, the Mediterranean.[52] This relation to the sea finally troubles any reading of the film that would see it only in relation to its failure to meet a Marxian dogma. The sea names destiny to the degree it contains the act and the shots of the bay, while the Cyclopean Isles mythically remind the spectators of that destiny. And what is the destiny of the sea? The long takes of the bay and the spectator's wait for the Cyclops and sea to give up their meaning provide the spectator with leave to intuit what is happening in the film well before the narrative begins. The message? The iconography of the bay and Visconti's transformation of the long shot of the bay into an icon neutralize the narrative of the class struggle.

Visconti uses the cinematic apparatus to empower the spectator to participate in seeing, which takes us to the heart of the question on mythic
violence, the law, and the affirmative potential of the cinematic apparatus.
Unlike other apparatuses, the cinematic apparatus doesn't simply capture, but when employed in the way that Visconti does here, permits the
spectator to see what wasn't seen before. In that sense we can see, thanks to
the cinematic apparatus, things, objects, the past, all those elements of a
milieu that limit individuation. The cinematic apparatus seemingly has the
potential for charity and for uncovering for the viewer the complex elements of a milieu. In Visconti's films, the potential for charity is actualized
in the long take and the attention it demands of the spectator.

Consider the sequence of revolt and the slow pan that Visconti uses to
get us to see and touch the "event" of the film (see Figure 3-5). In this
moment, we encounter the individual faces of the collective village and

Figure 3-5. The Earth Trembles

the camera moves at a reasonable pace. The sequence is framed once again by the bay and the Cyclops, against which we see the coming and going of waves and the coming and going of the fishermen. Note, however, that the fishermen do not give their attention, do not see the bay and the Cyclops. They are unable to see where they are, which is to say that they do not possess enough distance to see themselves either individually or collectively as forms of life. Indeed, there is no distance between them, their collective actions, and what encloses those actions; that is precisely what operates mythically in the frame. There is simply not enough distance between them as observers and the object. What is missing in the film, but in particular in this sequence, is attention. The fishermen do not have sufficient distance to see what holds them in position, limiting the power of their actions.[53]

That, of course, is not the case for the spectator. She sees how mythic violence appears onscreen in the movement between those framed with the Cyclopean Isles and those without: all the film's action, including the domestic sequences with Mara and her sisters, is visually enclosed, delineating a milieu in which an immutable Destiny commands.[54] Yet cinematic techne provides the spectator with sufficient distance from the events through the rhythm of the shots. We observe the frame, pay attention to it, and see in the interplay among the frames and the absence and presence of the Isles, the interval over which Fate commands. We also experience the fear of which Benjamin writes. For the Valastri brothers, it is true that for a time change does arrive in the form of an elasticity to the demands of the situation; it is this elasticity that separates the Valastri from the others.[55]

A HOMELAND OF GESTURES

Focusing only on actions that make up the film—the fishermen's revolt, the battle between wholesalers and fishermen—in turn creates difficulties. We miss, for example, weighing properly the role of the young women in the household and the power they express. Although not given the same kinds of possibility as their brothers, they occupy a space of gratitude, perhaps even more so than their brothers. Of particular note are the gestures, the gazes, the touches, and the movement of the young women across the two dwellings of the film. The shots, especially the opening and closing ones of Mara, the closing shot of her and the photograph, linger long after, precisely because of the force of her gestures. In some of his most beautiful pages,

Giorgio Agamben tells of how he understands gesture and cinema, a reading that seems appropriate to introduce in marking the power of Mara's final scenes in *The Earth Trembles*: "Cinema," Agamben writes, "leads images back to the homeland of gesture."[56] In the film, events lead back to the homeland of Mara's mode of holding.[57]

It is to the homeland of gesture that 'Ntoni returns and, because I have introduced Agamben's reading of gesture, let's consider the importance of gesture in the context of gratitude. Agamben writes:

> What characterizes gesture is that in it nothing is being produced or acted, but rather something is being endured and supported. The gesture, in other words, opens the sphere of *ethos* as the more proper sphere of that which is human. But in what way does a *res* become a *res gesta*, that is, in what way does a simple fact become an event?[58]

Leaving aside the question of event as well as the problematic calling into account of what is more and less proper, the debut of *ethos* is suggestive for reading generosity in its catalogue of grips. In a milieu of the Cyclops that characterizes the life of Acitrezza, a series of things carried but also of grips loosened emerges.

Certainly in the gestures of 'Ntoni when he returns to the "Cicople" with his younger brothers, accompanied by laughter of the fishmongers, little would seem to diminish the tragic here. The laughter serves to mock 'Ntoni's attempts at individuation even more than before. The gestures of the brothers bear witness to this failure; they stoop under the weight of a Fate that has ruined them. Then another sequence follows, this one featuring Mara. After sending 'Ntoni off to the boats, the women once again gather in their new home. Mara is arranging objects inside, and it is then that we see her place the photo of the family on which she had focused her attention earlier in the film (see Figure 3-6). She places the photograph on the mantle alongside an icon, the Sacred Heart, an icon that was not seen in the earlier sequence. Her interaction with the photograph also differs now. No longer does she look at it as she did before. Instead she caresses it while arranging it alongside the other icon. This is no seizing, or if we prefer, it is "seizing upon nothing" and as such solicits "what slips away," or what has already slipped away.[59]

If tragedy is about the thing carried tightly and the gesture that bears burdens, then the comic is about holding less tightly, touching what we do not possess.[60] If tragedy is about grasping without acknowledging degrees

Figure 3-6. The Earth Trembles

of holding, then the way one holds oneself onscreen and off begins more or less tragically: We hold on to our identities for dear life; we hold them as if there were no tomorrow, as if the question were a matter of life and death. Here the comic offers Mara a different possibility, one in which holding less tightly takes the place of seizing. How do we to relate to tragedy, that is the question that Visconti is posing in the sequences. How do we relate to a situation when there is nothing that we can do to alter it—no amount of waiting for things to change so as to avoid the mythic violence that drives our defeats. Fear accompanies tragedy. Fear gives birth to tragedy.

In *The Birth of Tragedy*, Nietzsche reminds us that the wizard behind the mask of all tragic figures is Dionysos:

> The fact that there is a deity behind all theses masks is one of the essential reasons for the "ideal" quality of those famous figures which has prompted so much astonishment. Someone or other (I do not know who) once remarked that all individuals, as individuals, are comic, and therefore un-tragic; from which one could conclude that the Greeks were quite incapable of tolerating any individuals on the tragic stage. And in-

deed this does appear to have been their feeling, just as the reason for the Platonic distinction between, and deprecation of, the "idea" as opposed to the "idol," or copied image, lay deep within the Hellenic character. Using Plato's terminology, one would have to say something like this about the tragic figures of the Hellenic stage: the one, truly real Dionysos manifests himself in a multiplicity of figures, in the mask of a fighting hero and, as it were, entangled in the net of the individual will. In the way that he now speaks and acts, the god who appears resembles an erring, striving, suffering individual; and the fact that he appears at all with such epic definiteness and clarity, is the effect of Apollo, the interpreter of dreams, who interprets to the chorus its Dionysiac condition by means of this symbolic appearance.[61]

In her interaction, her holding and touching of the photograph of the family—a family that has been torn apart—Mara does not engage in any exchange, nor does she hold the photograph as a *res gesta*. In this movement that is not just a gesture, Mara exists outside the exchange that is featured in mythic violence. She is, in Nietzsche's words, the "un-tragic individual," the comic individual behind which the one "real" Dionysos will not be found. This is the piece we ought to take with us as we move to the next chapter and forms of reciprocity in *Germany Year Zero*. Touching, holding, and composing the photograph on the mantle, Mara engages with fate in a way that differs from everyone else in the film; she is the one who comes closest to the reciprocity that Visconti had spoken of earlier with regard to the spectator. This is not giving and taking, nor is it holding on as tightly as one can, but holding so as to touch, or touching so as to hold. She puts the photo on the mantle piece, and slides her hand across it. So doing she lessens the distance between herself and the photograph, which is precisely what 'Ntoni is unable to do when it comes to his own fate. In handling the photograph with openness to the present that isn't to be found in merely looking, a kind of comic physiognomy emerges.[62]

At the heart of her holding of the photograph is a question of seriousness and gravity. Henri Bergson helps us to cut to the chase.

All that is serious in life comes from our freedom. The feelings we have matured, the passions we have brooded over, the actions we have weighed, decided upon, and carried through, in short, all that comes from us and is our very own, these are the things that give life its oft times dramatic and generally grave aspect.[63]

The emphasis on owning and belonging are at the heart of 'Ntoni's fate. Consider, however, Bergson's follow-up: "What, then, is requisite to transform all this into a comedy? Merely to fancy that our seeming freedom conceals the strings of a dancing-Jack, and that we are, as the poet says, "humble marionettes / The wires of which are pulled by Fate?" He continues: "So there is not a real, a serious, or even a dramatic scene that fancy cannot render comic by simply calling forth this image. Nor is there a game for which a wider field lies open."[64] The film's response to the presence of the two Cyclops and mythic violence across all the relationships and actions of the film isn't to be found in some future event as such, but rather concerns how individuals relate to mythic violence. And here in Mara's handling of the photograph a wider field becomes visible, one of attentiveness.[65]

A perspective on attention and gratitude offers only this: 'Ntoni has not paid enough attention to a situation in which he and the Valastri family find themselves. In particular he has not paid attention to the weight that myth plays in their lives in the over-determination of Cyclopean Islands and the Cyclops Society of the wholesalers. 'Ntoni doesn't stand a chance—how could he? Visconti is asking us to adopt a perspective able to see in his tragedy a mode of holding, seizing, and identifying more open to a different kind of reciprocity in which what is given is not received and vice versa. The mode by which Mara responds stands out, especially in the way she attends to objects, holding them so that their qualities are seen and felt. 'Ntoni cannot see, or better, sees only what was true in the past in a reading that does not account for the situation itself. That inability is bitterly comical because by the end of the film, 'Ntoni's decisions have left the family destitute. As I argued in Chapter 1, aspects of holding, whether it is how one holds an object or one's body or how one holds one's self, are inextricably joined, and that is certainly true here as well. What separates Mara from 'Ntoni is how deeply Mara acknowledges that living in the present requires a composure that allows engaging with objects, one's self, myth, and the past in such a way that the present never retreats. This is not about receiving what life gives you, nor is it about taking what you need, but rather, it is about acknowledging the importance of how individuals hold themselves, how the un-tragic comic individual visually emerges onscreen.[66]

What is true for Mara is true for the spectator. The spectator of *The Earth Trembles* is invited to adopt an "elasticity," to employ again a word dear to Bergson, in order to engage with what is projected on the screen. And no one more so than Mara embodies that elasticity, particularly in the way that she engages with the photograph. Here is why the film and so many neo-realist films are more rightly considered comedies. Fortifying the *praeparatus* side of the cinematic apparatus, Visconti demands that the spectator pay attention, that she attend to what is onscreen in long takes and long shots. To what end? The answer finally will be found in the Bergsonian reversal I quoted earlier. Can the spectator see in Visconti's style the possibility of reversing tragedy into a comedy—to find ourselves laughing with the wholesalers as 'Ntoni enters because of Ntoni's inability to pay attention? Can the spectator identify in Mara's interactions a reciprocity that responds to mythic violence? These are the difficult questions that Visconti is posing. Kenneth Burke's dictum returns at this juncture: "Comprehensiveness can be discussed as superficiality, intensiveness as structure, tolerance as uncertainty . . . A way of seeing is also a way of not seeing—a focus upon object A involves a neglect of object B."[67] In short, the cinematic apparatus in *The Earth Trembles* forces the viewer to attend to what she cannot make out; she is asked to reconsider naming the situation differently from what the narrative of the film itself asks us to identify with.[68]

Where then does generosity in the film reside? It will be found in the form of holding that Mara embodies. To see how, let's begin by asking what is it that the brothers give and receive and here what they receive is a bout of destiny that they cannot avoid. In particular, they cannot avoid returning to their place with the other fishermen and villagers as part of community that is Acitrezza. We see this in the final shot of 'Ntoni, who is seen rowing out with his other fishermen, having returned to that group to which he had always belonged (see Figure 3-7). In this return, the film appears to say that no escape from the clutches of destiny is possible because destiny is demonstrated to be the impossibility of individuation for 'Ntoni. Indeed, no possibility exists for any of the fishermen to move beyond their station, which leads to the view that fate is figured as the impossibility for the oppressed elements of this society to escape on their own individually.

Figure 3-7. The Earth Trembles

The Earth Trembles visually elaborates the fatedness of community for some by showing the impossibility of the non-acceptance of one's lot as belonging to a certain strata of society. If we were to translate this into the lexicon of community, we might say that 'Ntoni's attempts to separate himself from the rest of the fishermen (who are visually identified with the community of Acitrezza itself), fails precisely because of the nature of the gift, that he and the Valastri cannot refuse. In other words, and here we will want to move slowly, there would appear to be in the gift that cannot be refused in the community of Acitrezza. This would be another element that involves violence, understood precisely as the violence that inheres in the fatedness of an obligation to the community that its gift must be received. This is how mythic violence relates to gift-giving in the film: There is no community that doesn't demand that its gift be received. The film posits at a minimum a foolhardiness that lies at the heart of any attempt at individuation. Visconti's perspective on the events besieging the family, to the degree he frames it as part of a mythic past, suggests that as much as the film relates the failed struggle, ultimately, 'Ntoni and the Valastri belong to Acitrezza. There is a kind of "told you so" to the proceedings, in what Renzi might call a mystic contemplation of destiny.

This leads to a troubling conclusion. The mythic violence of the film will be found in the community's success in asserting the nature of the gift over the brothers who, in their attempts at individuation, are also attempting a shortcut to individuation and with it freedom from gift-giving. The differences between failing to give gifts and individuation, however, aren't at all clear in the film. On one hand, there is one apparatus, one form of gift-giving of the community that we see at work in the film's narrative: in Visconti's choices in bringing to the screen the kind of tension between gift-giving and the refusal of gift-receiving. Still, not all apparatuses are the same. If we bring the notion of exchange and gift-giving to bear on what we mean by apparatus, we by no means ought to feel it necessary to make them of the same piece. The impossibility of refusing, which is at the heart of mythic violence is met by an apparatus, a mode of unmasking and making visible, between what is seen and felt onscreen and what is seen and felt in the darkened room of cinema. Unlike the Cyclops that guard and contain the events that take place in Acitrezza, another exchange, let's call it a cinematic techne, meets the prior apparatus that expropriates. This cinematic techne lays out a different circuit of reciprocity in which things, images, objects, are not given and not received, in which gifts are not given and received.

What does it mean in the context of the film to speak of the relation between apparatus and spectator as not involving gifts, but rather as concerning, fundamentally, things given without obligation of return? Here the word that comes to mind is affectability—the witnessing that cinema, this film, gives us in which we return continually to the choral nature of the isles and the bay. The return, the repetition of the scene, works differently for the spectator than it does for the brothers or the villagers. We are continually brought back to this scene, this angle, of Acitrezza; an image is given repeatedly, but the assumption is that we haven't received it fully, that we cannot master what it is that we see. What would we call something extended to us, but which we as spectators cannot receive and hence cannot master because we have no hands with which to grasp it? The static nature of the image suggests not an exchange—or at least not the exchange of consumption—but rather, an image that cannot be mastered precisely because its meaning cannot be pinned down outside of the frame of mythic violence. We look again at the Cyclopean Isles and see how they anchor nearly every frame. The previous reference to icon is crucial: In returning to the classic image of the Cyclops, we are asked to contemplate, though such contemplation never leads to anything approaching a mastering of the meaning of the image. We come back to the image to the icon of the bay and each time we contemplate it after further events have taken place in the Valastri tragedy. It is akin to seeing an icon repeatedly and so attending to something that was not present before.[69]

This is not something given and thus not something received as ultimate meaning, which is to say that there is no mastery understood as "a giving of meaning."[70] Nor is this a gift—it's unclear how an icon can, in fact, be a gift in the way that a fetish can be as there is no self that accompanies the icon image because no exchange will have taken place. Does this mean that repetition in cinematic form can have the effect of avoiding or evading a circuit of exchange that would bring with it the self that comes from exchange and gift-giving? Perhaps. Clearly though, given the way the spectator is asked to engage with the choral repetition of the image, it would be difficult to characterize it as gift-giving of the sort that we have come to know, nor is it similar to the kind of taking of capture that we know to be a part of the way apparatuses work.

The Earth Trembles offers the attentive viewer the possibility to engage differently with the images contained in the luminous rectangle as those beyond or beneath mastery. Yet a number of questions still remain unanswered. The principal question among them is how a number of films attempt to resolve the paradox of the mancus as both the form of life unable to give or receive but also able to pay attention. What means does a director have at his or her disposal to disable the giving and receiving of meaning among viewers and so doing elicit attention? I offer some provisional responses in the next two chapters.

4

PLAYFUL FALLS IN A MILIEU
OF CONTAGION

If one of the chief *dramatis personae* of these pages is the generous form of life, then what relation does that form owe to grace? Or better: To whom does grace befall? On whose head does the object of generosity land and thus who, ultimately, gets to practice greater relationality? In *The Earth Trembles*, fate appears in the interplay of shots of the village and the bay, which suggest that nearly all who live there are condemned to an un-individuated form of life. The lone exception is Mara, whose touch and caress intimate how the spectator might avoid such a fate. We might put it another way: To the spectator is reserved the possibility of those forms of life that avoid the fatedness of the Valastri brothers thanks to how Visconti employs the apparatus to highlight a vital techne of holding and letting go.

The questions around gratitude and fate posed in the previous chapter appear here as well but are transposed into a slightly different key. How does the spectator come to see for herself what the protagonists cannot? When does apparatus give way to techne? Can capture be turned back on itself so that the spectator begins to see those instances in which the film has seized its protagonists as well as the spectator herself? Can grace be understood as what results when one fails to take what has not been given or receives without grasping? Possible forms of reciprocity underpin an argument about how cinema can engage the spectator in her own practice of attending to individuation on screen and off.

We don't do justice to the potential of cinema to include in its workings a techne if we limit ourselves to tactics of unveiling destiny as the impossibility of non-individuation. It isn't a question simply of lining up individuation on the other side of the screen in the spectator who is able to pivot from merely seeing to seeing as a powerful form without grasping. What happens when the techne that anchors individuating of forms of life is made the subject and object of the film itself? These questions go to the heart of my reading of *Germany Year Zero* and more broadly Roberto Rossellini's film-making after World War II.

Before commencing, however, a *caveat emptor*. Given the subject matter of the film and the counter-intuitive reading that I am going to propose of comedy and generosity in the context of a parricide and suicide, some readers may find themselves feeling uneasy about where the chapter appears to be heading. Certainly, a possible equivalency between the suicidal act and the generous one is one that needs to be navigated prudently. For what it's worth, I also felt uneasy at times following where I believed Rossellini's portrayal of Edmund and Germany was leading. Some of the difficulty certainly has to do with the extreme case that is the subject of Rossellini's film: a country and city in which generosity becomes risky thanks to the results of a mythic violence that had reduced Germany to year zero. In such a context, it is difficult to imagine any spectator willing to adopt a generous form of life. Yet the limit case that *Germany Year Zero* represents is also the limit case for the *mancus*, showing us just how important the notion of reciprocity is for thinking, and more important, practicing generosity. The generous form of life requires other forms of life that are able to give and receive without calculation. In other words, *Germany Year Zero* pushes generosity to its extreme. If the reading I am making is to carry any weight—if the affirmative form of generosity is to become available to us as I hope it will in the next chapter when I turn to Antonioni—then that reading has to account for the limit case that *Germany Year Zero* presents. The point of arrival here, as before, is to shake up how we understand the comic and generosity in order that they do more work in a milieu of heightened biopower.

EDMUND AND THE EMANCIPATORY ACT

As the reader will recall, *Germany Year Zero* tells the story of a parricide in the aftermath of the war in Berlin. Young Edmund, motherless and looking ever the part of the "master race," fends for himself and his family in a kind of perverse *Oliver Twist* (see Figure 4-1).[1] The film relates the events that lead to Edmund's decision to poison his ill father and then to kill himself after having been abandoned by everyone in whom he had trusted. Criss-crossing the film are themes of German guilt as well as what some might call the reduction to bare life of the inhabitants of the city. Throughout the film, Rossellini paints a picture of a singular, massive breakdown in social relations.

Much criticism of the film has, of course, centered on what *Germany Year Zero* shares with other Italian neo-realist films from the period.[2] In a recent reading, Jacques Rancière takes issue with many and, in the process, both updates the film and complicates our understanding of it. Rancière's argument centers around the possibility that young Edmund's suicide can be seen as a liberating, emancipatory act.[3] For Rancière, Edmund's act represents a bid for freedom given the mode with which Edmund plays among the bombed-out ruins before his leap.[4] Edmund's act in such a reading will appear less a suicide than an attempt to free himself from the discord of the many voices that have wreaked havoc both on him and implicitly on

Figure 4-1. Germany Year Zero

Germany. The voices of year zero in Berlin make such a racket that Edmund has no other choice but to make a play for freedom. The jump into the void becomes, on Rancière's read, an attempt to act responsibly. Thus:

> Edmund is spurred to action by his vertiginous discovery of the pure ability to do so, or not do, what others say, the discovery that he alone is responsible for his act, the sole agent of its coming into being . . . But all that really weighs on Edmund is the crushing weight of the liberty of year zero.[5]

Because we are still removed from freedom and vertiginous discovery, Rancière adds:

> The fall that closes the child's improvisations—must know its profound kinship with absolute generosity or violence of the creator who freely reclaims what He has freely given. The call of the void to which the parricide child surrenders must reveal its proximity to the call presented by St. Francis of Assisi, God's juggler, who teaches his brothers that the way to decide where they must go is to spin round and round, as kids do, until vertigo throws them on the ground and points them in the direction of the call.[6]

For Rancière, no cause grounds Edmund's jump or fall, just as one cannot say that the brothers of St. Francis knew where they were going, except in the direction of "the void of unlimited possibility."

Much, maybe too much, can be made of Rancière's reading.[7] First, note the emphasis on choice and responsibility in the passage as well as the reference to "pure ability" and the none-too-obvious choice of phrase, "spurred." Edmund is "spurred to action." The thrust of Rancière's reflection comes to depend upon an equivalency between weight and gravity, moral weight and liberating gravity, gravity and choice, and ultimately agency and ability.[8] Edmund is "spurred to action" by freedom, ability, and the void itself. We also note the reference, strange at first glance, to generosity. Edmund playing among the ruins of a bombed out city is akin to the creator who practices either absolute generosity or more menacingly, violence.[9] At the heart of the question is a gift that is returned, or reclaimed as Rancière puts it, and then freely taken back. Grace in the context of generosity, play, improvisation, and violence comes to name not a gift but the reclamation of what was freely given and now freely taken back.

For Rancière, grace is linked to the pure ability "to do so"—that is, to be "spurred to action," to kill oneself because one has felt on all sides the weight of liberty.[10] It is an incongruous mode of reading that would find choice in Sartrean fashion, leading to the ultimate choice to take one's life (and so in some sense to take issue with the circuit of exchange that characterizes year zero in Germany). Relatedly, and this will shortly become the hinge for my reflections here, Rancière clusters a number of terms together that are meant to name the child's improvisations. These include play (parenthetically, it would be helpful to track the moments when Edmund is a child in Rancière's argument, and when he takes on the essential features of an adolescent or even adult). We also note how Rancière figures the unalterable series of events that constitute the call of the void. There is no subjectivity here, but rather an impersonally felt command given in a context of searing freedom and the improvised, which leads to self-annihilation.[11]

THE IMPERATIVE OF GRATITUDE

Impersonality brings us to a voice that can be heard in the spaces of Rancière's argument as well as in Rossellini's own filmmaking. That voice belongs, of course, to Simone Weil.[12] Rancière will invoke Weil in justifying Edmund's turn/fall to vertiginous freedom in terms of grace and gravity, but the connection to Weil's thought runs deeper than that. This becomes apparent when considering the work the term "gravity" does for Weil generally. Gravity for the French mystic refers to obedience, sin, and the corruption that arises thanks to the "function of language," which is to say what expresses "the relationship between things."[13] Additionally, gravity for Weil also appeals to a form of categorical imperative in which "whoever suffers tries to communicate his suffering . . . in order to reduce it."[14] For those able to express their suffering, the law of gravity functions fully in what Weil calls a kind of human mechanics in which states of suffering can actually be reduced. For those who do not have the power to mistreat anyone (or who cannot transmit their suffering), the effect is poisonous. On just this point, Weil observes that the "tendency" is to spread evil beyond oneself; when the possibility for communicating one's suffering is blocked, the "poison" turns back on those without power. The power to mistreat others marks the most significant feature of Weil's gloss of gravity, not just for those with power, but those who fail to communicate suffering. She calls this failure a negative power because she sees in it the undoing of our valuation of beings and things as "sacred enough."[15] This rhymes with her defense of the impersonal in another essay, "Human Personality," in which what is considered sacred is what cannot be thought of as "personal."[16]

Here we can begin to understand why Weil's writings hover as much as they do over the film and Rancière's reading of it. Year zero marks the moment of spreading contagion. The gravity that Edmund experiences not just during his fall, but more intensely prior to it—the capacity of everyone else to treat others miserably regardless of age is simply shocking—is to be thought alongside his powerlessness in stopping the spread of contagion, or better his suffering beyond himself. Paradoxically, if Edmund had been able to communicate, the fall into the void would have been unnecessary as he would have been able to express through language the "relationship between things." Rossellini relentlessly shows Edmund's inability and need to communicate suffering and at the same time the impossibility for him to do so.

Consider Edmund's father's loquacity, especially in the moment when Edmund administers the poison (*Gift* in German) to him.[17] His father continues to speak of his wish to die to Edmund, begging for pity. Compare that moment to the many others in which Edmund fails or refuses to seek pity. It's here that Rancière hits on something else just as important: that when poisoning his father, Edmund actually fails to reduce his own suffering. Grace appears as the possibility of moving into the void—a favorite term of Weil's as well—in which play, purity, improvisation, creation, grace, and violence all merge into a moment of bliss and death as the moment of escape from the contagion of year zero. Joyful death, graceful violence, and the host of fused nouns that are meant to mark the truth of the fall follow.

Yet something doesn't quite work. To see what, let's suspend our judgment of Edmund's final moments and its possible motivations. Is there a way to move beyond the good and evil of his deed, be it an overwhelming sense of grief and guilt after having committed parricide or his choice of radical freedom in annihilation?[18] One way that both dovetails with and eventually distances us from Rancière's argument about Edmund's crime concerns the relation of gratitude to reciprocity. Consider now another thinker on gratitude, who, surprisingly has often been marginalized in readings of the film. Melanie Klein's reading of gratitude and envy, particularly the question of enjoyment and its relation to gratitude, needs to be considered.

> The fact that envy spoils the capacity for enjoyment explains to some extent why envy is so persistent. For it is enjoyment and the gratitude to which it gives rise that mitigate destructive impulses, envy, and greed . . . greed, envy, and persecutory anxiety, which are bound up with each other, inevitably increase each other.[19]

Doubts about the "possession of the good object," which in Kleinian fashion originate with the good breast, correspond to "uncertainty about one's own good feelings." Such doubts contribute to "greedy and indiscriminate identifications," with the result that one no longer trusts one's own judgment. Gratitude for Klein involves constructing a relation to a good object, which "underlies also the appreciation of goodness in others and in oneself." For Klein, full gratification at the breast means that the "infant feels he has received from his loved object a unique gift which he wants to keep. This is the basis of gratitude. Gratitude is closely linked with the trust in good figures."[20]

I haven't done justice to the depth and beauty of Klein's argument, but the passage does provide us with terms for understanding the relation of generosity and violence in *Germany Year Zero*. For all kinds of reasons—a missing mother, an invalid father, a weak brother, and a former untrustworthy teacher—Edmund moves from identifying with and trusting in his father to trusting Herr Enning, the pedophile and former teacher, to trusting no one. Yet this is not enough to provide a motivation and meaning for Edmund's fall. What does is the milieu that Rossellini goes to such great lengths to construct so as to match the terrible events recounted in the film. Along with the relentless complaining from the inhabitants of *Germany Year Zero* is the impossibility of enjoyment. There are no good and bad objects with which to identify or not—no "good figures"—but rather for Edmund an indiscriminate identification with all of the figures populating this ruined world. In a milieu of envy, it is impossible to feel as if the ego "possesses goodness."[21] The result is a landscape of objects and individuals that work against trust.[22]

Let's also recall another feature of Klein's gloss of gratitude. For her, gratitude moves dialectically to possession as it emerges initially out of a desire to hold onto the loved object: that is, the desire to be fully gratified at the breast. It is the possession of the good object, Klein tells us, that is the first step toward assimilating the object. It is also the condition for sharing of gifts with others. *Germany Year Zero* shows a boy who is unable to assimilate the object; who continually shifts his identifications across the film; who trusts, but whose trust is continually revealed as misplaced. More damaging is the fact that the lone moment in which he actually does give a gift it is the gift of death given to his ill father, when he confuses one gift for another. This is what makes the film's perspective on reciprocity in *Germany Year Zero* so interesting and so troubling. It is as if gratitude has been turned inside out; in lieu of good and bad objects and the gratitude that arises from enjoying them, the expected enjoyment leads to the law and to guilt. In Edmund's only attempt to share, he succeeds and fails.

The film shows us a year zero for generosity. Yet rather than the fall somehow driving a politics of absolute freedom and violence, or a staging of some sort of dissensus that is of a part with certain of Rancière's notions of the political, the fall marks the separation between gratitude of the Kleinian sort and its coming to fruition (or dialectical completion) in grace as a form of non-possession and non-holding. It is only by forcing a reading of grace in terms of fall and void, moving grace outside the orbit of gratitude, that Rancière's political reading becomes possible. What if, rather, Edmund's fall, jump, suicide, or however we choose to name it, casts a light onto a milieu of failed reciprocity, a zero point of gratitude or a negative perspective that becomes visible as Edmund's parricide stands out increasingly against the very incongruity of the gift of death that Edmund "gives" his father.[23] According to Rossellini, this is precisely what characterizes Germany after the Thousand Year Reich; one of the only forms of gift-giving available is the gift of death and Edmund's jump into the void becomes the sole moment of reciprocity. What is shared (and not freely given) is death administered by son to both father and son.

A corollary. In the absence of good objects and bad, in year zero a devastated Berlin mirrors the ruins of the internalized and idealized object that is Nazism. The film presents us with a milieu of contagion in which the former idealized object has not only come crashing down but has left as its legacy a persecutory anxiety.[24] At the same time, when faced with the knowledge that the formerly idealized object is truly horrific—in this case Nazism embodied in Herr Enning, the schoolteacher—the only answer, seemingly, is to embrace the void. *Germany Year Zero* recounts a young boy's search for something with which to identify, but such a search ends ultimately with the one interest that had before been the sole identification, Nazism. This explains the import of the early scene in which Edmund attempts to sell recordings of Hitler's speeches. Any interpretation that focuses on the fall into grace therefore risks missing the cost of a boy's struggle to find an object with which to identify in a milieu characterized by a generalized incapacity among its people to possess a good object. This, in turn, points to the possibility that the figure of Edmund (and by extension a generation, as Rossellini suggests in the opening titles) represents a waning of feeling in the self as "possessing goodness" of its own. The fall into the void registers the moment when such knowledge is acknowledged. If we were to follow this line of inquiry out further, we might review how the film, obliquely at first, and then more explicitly by the end of the film, shows Germany under Nazism covering over when not hiding outright the good object, attempting to appropriate the good breast for its own ends. What is missing and what the film is asking us to reflect upon, is what happens when gratitude is no longer possible. Rossellini movingly peers into the collective unconscious of Germany after the war by focusing intensely on the contamination of greed and envy at all levels of Germany society (and here the American occupiers are implicitly a part of the problem). What appears to be blocked is the ability to accept the loved "primal object . . . without greed." It is impossible to find, let alone invest, any object with libido that the self is able to protect, including obviously Edmund's own self. The result is the impossibility of sharing gifts with others and hence, at the risk of a gross understatement, the creation of a less "friendly world," as Klein puts it.

In ways that rehearse Adorno's juxtaposition of fear and gratitude that I introduced in Chapter 1, Rossellini in *Germany Year Zero* visualizes what happens to a society of adults and children when giving is blocked—when gratitude, understood as the assimilation of the good object, has come to an end. Edmund represents that failure in vivid and distressing ways. Clearly, the lack of a mother (as opposed to a father, which is surprising given the war and the enrollment of nearly every adult male in conscription) captures the denial of the good object. It is a year zero of relationality, of non-giving (but also non-accepting) that results from the lack of trust in good figures. This lack—in teachers, neighbors, the military, other children, and implicitly the Führer and Nazism itself—is reciprocally inscribed in the envy and greed that characterizes the Berliners of the film.

A MILIEU OF ENVY

The image lingers. It is that of a sprightly, blond-haired young boy who walks with eyes downcast. Despite, or on account of, the awkwardness of his body, he steps lightly and with purpose. Edmund's later fall works to such devastating effect precisely because of the innocence with which the spectator desires to see him as innocent, as a child who simply is walking despite where he walks.

The film's narrative recounts the story of a boy who helps his family survive. Indeed, Edmund initially appears as the locus of what is affirming in the film, what Klein calls the life-instinct. He moves, he jumps; when he moves, we see him move. Whenever he enters at night, light follows, while during the day often he gives no shadow. All that changes, however, when he kills his father and when Renzo Rossellini's terrifying score takes hold.[25] Before that, the film suggests a child with a large capacity to love and to experience gratitude. Yet as the film progresses, the figure of Edmund becomes more complex. He appears to exist liminally; he lives among older children and the younger children, those who ultimately refuse to play with him at the end of the film. He moves along the margins of the adult world as well until the crime, though clearly the influence of the adult world is felt wherever Edmund strolls. Indeed there is no moment in which the film doesn't register adulthood as threat.[26] Edmund's awkwardness when he plays at the end of the film becomes increasingly obvious; his legs are too long and he seems simply too old to be playing (see Figure 4-2). The impression of a boy not yet an adolescent stuck between two seasons of life goes missing when we choose to emphasize the fall or Edmund's playing at the end of the film. He plays alone because he inhabits the zone between childhood and adolescence.

In Rancière's reading, what matters in the fall is the recognition of responsibility, but also freedom of choice. Another way to consider the gesture—if indeed that is what we choose to call it—is as a kind of boycott of Germany. Karl Abraham's description of the *dementia praecox* comes to mind: "He thus carries his self-isolation so far that in a certain measure he boycotts the external world. He no longer gives it anything, or accepts

Figure 4-2. Germany Year Zero

anything from it. He grants himself a monopoly for the supply of sense impressions."[27] This is the ultimate meaning of the title *Germany Year Zero* in which nothing is given nor anything received. Should we choose to accent the fall as graceful, we ought at least to be aware of the dangers of nothing given and nothing received when a milieu such as this one is in place.

It is tempting, of course, to read Edmund's suicide as an attempt to hold himself differently than before, but here, too, I think we need to be wary of such an argument. Nothing in the choice of the fall into emancipation suggests a break in the monopoly of sense impressions. How could there be if this is precisely where *Germany Year Zero* leads all of its former children, both adults and the nominally young? This explains why the film continues to distress so many and why so many students (though not only) seek a way out for Edmund by pointing a collective finger at Herr Enning;[28] anything to lessen Edmund's responsibility for his actions. Yet suspending our judgment about personal responsibility—which in point of fact is the shared horizon between Rancière and the film's earlier critics—it is clear that in

Germany Year Zero, no one escapes their guilt. This is what year zero looks like and no amount of play provides an escape. When Edmund, after trying and failing to play, looks out on the landscape of his home and after the funeral hearse arrives to pick up the body of his father—all of it framed through the blown-out perspective provided by *Germany Year Zero*—only then does the monopoly of sense impressions end. After ascending the building, and finally after having finished playing, Edmund gains a perspective on the previous events. Rossellini places the camera in a point-of-view shot in line with Edmund so that the camera's attention to detail is matched by Edmund's own. It is when Edmund's vision is superimposed over the camera's—when he sees as the camera sees—that Edmund masters enough attention to understand the full extent of what he has done (see Figures 4-3 and 4-4). It is at this point that the external world refuses to be boycotted. No turning away from objects or deeds is possible, which in Edmund's case, amounts to the same thing.

Figure 4-3. Germany Year Zero

Figure 4-4. Germany Year Zero

As for the Edmund as *mancus*, one possible perspective is to see his itinerary across the film as moving away precisely from non-giving, from his status as *mancus*. Indeed, for the greater part of the film, he doesn't receive gifts nor give any. He listens attentively, but again he is on the move so much that the occasions for giving and receiving are few. At the point, however, when his father tells him how much better it would be if he were dead, Edmund, by killing his father, gives a gift. What matters less here is a reading that marks the pharmakon of gift as *Gift,* and more that the act of giving occurs as part of a circuit of exchange of poisoned gifts being exchanged all across Germany in year zero. Again, my sense is that prior to killing his father, Edmund doesn't give much at all, as no one can receive them as proper gifts. Who is there to receive his gifts? The search for work and a few marks has meant a living in the present and less chance to hold onto what he has. That changes dramatically after Enning espouses his views on the weak and old and ill, as Edmund holds these words differently than others directed toward him (and let's note that the same holds true for how Edmund hears and holds the words his father uses to describe his own pain and his wish to die). What is interesting is that in each instance Edmund identifies deeply with their views, leading him to believe that what they say is exactly what they mean. Doing so, he gives them a gift that in other circumstances would not necessarily lead to Gift-giving. In a world of envy without any good figures, the result is a limit case of gift-giving in which the only proper gift is a *Gift*.

Gift becomes a poison in a context in which other gifts are no longer possible to give or receive. Or better, the difference between gift and *Gift* is one that is felt less strongly in lieu of forms of life such as Edmund's that have gone missing in year zero. Had Edmund been able to receive less tightly what was given to him by Enning (but also by his father), he would not have confused gift and *Gift*. For that is what is at the heart of the film's *ethos*: a confusion of gifts brought on by Edmund's inability to hold what has been told to him. We might say that in this, Edmund stands in for other Germans who, during Nazism, held on too tightly; who believed they had figures whose words could be trusted; who believed that these figures were worthy of giving gifts because they knew how to receive them. The form of life of the *mancus* is the one who hears but is not the one who can give the *Gift* of death. In that sense, what Germany needed were more *mancus*, unable to identify too tightly with gifts received and those given.

COMMUNITY AND ENVY

What becomes of community in *Germany Year Zero*? A comparison with *Open City* may prove helpful because both films show that community falters when gratitude has gone missing. Let's recall just how prominent the roles of Don Pietro and Manfredi are in *Open City*. Trust in them both by other adults—even the Nazis—as well as children is one of the elements that underpins the collective sharing of gifts, speech, and food that sets the Roman community apart. Despite the German occupation of the city, enjoyment of life and one another remains possible in Rome.[29] This capacity for enjoyment in *Open City* and its absence in *Germany Year Zero* makes each film the negative of the other. Gratitude and ingratitude, envy and sympathy, good figures and none—this is the broad horizon they share.

Yet here too things are not quite so simple. Pina is gunned down in *Open City* and so another child has lost a mother. The repeated absence of a mother, and with it the good breast, suggests that here, too, what separates the films unites them. Indeed, the form of relationality in both films is premised on just such an absence/presence. With no Pina, there is no primal loved object (and we note, as so many others have, that she is pregnant, which serves to heighten her narrative qualities of mothering). Following up on the earlier approach to gratitude through the role of the good object leading to "feeling a unity with another person," relationality in *Open City* is anchored to trust, generosity, the sharing of gifts, and the introjection of a friendlier world. Naming it a friendlier world doesn't mean failing somehow to see the Nazis as occupiers or failing to fight them.

Perhaps the difference in the films can be summed up in the way that the characters (and actors, the difference is often blurred) hold themselves as good objects, which is registered in the distinction between "receive" and "accept." Consider the following entry on "take" and the connections running to accept in Crabb's *English Synonymes*:

> To receive is frequently a passive act; whatever is offered or done to another is received; but to accept is an act of choice; many things, therefore, may be received which cannot be accepted; as a person receives a blow or an insult . . . What is given as a present may be both received and accepted, but the inferior receives and the superior accepts . . . what is accepted is a matter of favor either on the part of the giver or receiver . . . Animals and things, as well as persons, may take; things may receive; but persons only accept. An animal may take what is offered to it; things take whatever attaches to them, but they receive that which by an express effort is given to them.[30]

What forms of reciprocity are displayed in *Germany Year Zero*? First, nothing suggests that the inhabitants do anything other than receive; what we do not see is acceptance of their lot as an act of choice and that is presumably because Germany lost the war. What are they given? Not gifts, certainly. Let's note, too, the reference to "person" in Crabb's definition. Perhaps the difference among communities of persons will depend upon the degrees to which its members receive and accept. A whole host of life forms (and non-life forms) take or receive, but only "persons accept." With such a reading in hand, *Germany Year Zero* exposes a society of receivers unable to accept their lot, their history, their present—in a word, unable to accept their responsibility in their own destruction. *Rome Open City* shows us instead what acceptance looks like: Don Pietro's martyrdom as well as Manfredi's torture and death at the hands of the Nazis. Both have chosen. So, too, has Pina. So, too, the boy army on which the film closes. In *Germany Year Zero*, we see the same but now in the negative. The only moments of acceptance are those concerning Edmund. His acceptance lies in having killed his father, which is exactly what separates the form of life associated with him from nearly everyone else in the film.

Rossellini is asking the filmgoer to hold Edmund as both good and evil in a way that again reflects the influence of Simone Weil. For Weil, "evil is the shadow of good. All real good, possessing solidity and thickness, projects evil. Only imaginary good does not project it."[31] Continuing, she writes:

> As all good is attached to evil, if we desire the good and do not wish to spread the corresponding evil around us, we are obliged, since we cannot avoid this evil, to concentrate it on ourselves. Thus the desire for utterly pure good involves the acceptance of the last degree of affliction for ourselves.[32]

Acceptance rings across the passage. Superimposed over *Germany Year Zero*, Edmund is not simply evil, but nor is he good. Instead, his goodness cannot be distinguished from his "evil" actions. When seeking to do good deeds, he kills both his father and himself. In that sense Rossellini can say that the ending was positive because, by killing himself, Edmund took the evil with him.[33] Perhaps *Germany Year Zero* resembles nothing so much as *The Exorcist*, hitting the same marks: evil, possession, and the acceptance of "affliction."

THE GOOD AND THE BAD

What are the roots of Edmund's goodness? Here, too, the answer will lie in the reverse image of gratitude, which, according to Klein, is envy:

> A particular cause of envy is the relative absence of it in others. The envied person is felt to possess what is at bottom most prized and desired— and this is a good object, which also implies a good character and sanity . . . Such an attitude, which includes gratitude for the pleasures of

the past and the enjoyment of what the present can give, expresses itself in serenity . . . Those who feel that they have had a share in the experience and pleasures of life are much more able to believe in the continuity of life.[34]

Germany Year Zero is about gratitude and envy writ large. Edmund, however, envies no one. He goes to work, he sells things, and he rarely if ever appears to take more than what he needs. This lack of envy of others sets him apart from the world of children and the world of adults. Paradoxically then, Edmund is sane. To borrow Klein's term, this is true even when he chooses to give the "Gift" to his father; the parricide isn't premised on envy but rather on the result of Edmund having listened attentively in a milieu in which gratitude and envy are dialectically intertwined. But here, as Lyotard indicates in his analysis of the grip, gratitude must not be confused with holding onto oneself, one's possessions, or one's father too tightly. We are led to the conclusion that there is a gesture, which under certain conditions is unavoidable for generous forms of life. Edmund's form of life in a negated community leads to his fall.[35] In *Germany Year Zero*, envy seems to precede gratitude everywhere, much like hate precedes love in Freud's famous formulation.[36] Rossellini asks us to consider the possibility of an indeterminacy surrounding generosity; that envy trumps gratitude in year zero and that year zeros are constituted by the dominance of envy.

Thus, the routines of lament that characterize so much of the interaction among the inhabitants of Berlin begin to take on a different hue. Much of the way the film communicates the features of the envious community is through talk; everyone drones on and on in the film, save for Edmund. Paradoxically (as it leads him to kill his father), Edmund knows how to listen. Indeed no one listens as intently and attentively as Edmund does. He listens to his father and he most certainly listens to Herr Enning. His radius of attention is wide indeed, which we see repeatedly in the way the camera follows him across a ruined city. Edmund at times comes to stand in for the camera itself, heading to heights and depths in the same way that the camera does.[37] Focusing on Edmund's lack of envy, we can well understand Rossellini's decision to follow Edmund around Berlin because Edmund's objective stance highlights the perilous increase in envious speech; a bombed-out city mirroring a bombed-out speech. This kind of speech is precisely what makes difficult the kind of relationality that is required for a generous form of life. It is a ruined speech whose effects are toxic and contaminating. It is a speech that assumes that no one takes the meaning of words seriously or that the effects of speech do not matter. Edmund is different. He takes people at their word.

My central point is this. Rampant envy devastates Germany in year zero in a community fractured by hollowed-out words and brutalized language. It is space in which care for self and others is impossible, with the case of Edmund offered as proof. We see Edmund's attempts to care for his father and family, noting where such a generosity leads and does not: For Edmund, generosity fails to provide the necessary conditions for further generosity and with it a care for the self. This is another limit point of Rossellini's perspective on generosity and so for now it is ours too. For Rossellini, gratitude cannot be imagined in year zero that doesn't ultimately end in suicide. For us, generosity as a response to mythic violence requires a communal milieu to support more generous forms of life, especially more generous when it comes to oneself.

PLAYING ONE MORE TIME

In much of what I have written to this point, I have avoided the role of play because I don't believe that Edmund merely plays in the film. Or better, he plays at something, but what that might be remains unclear. Edmund is a kind of *flâneur*.[38] He walks and strolls across a ruined landscape with purpose. We see him continually walking, and it is the classic medium shots of Edmund that remain with us. He walks with head held high, inclined at times, so as to see what lies up ahead. That is the beauty of the film's first half, which intensifies the tragic nature of the film. Edmund may not be up to the specific challenges of the city's other "Artful Dodgers," but he attends to others in Berlin in ways that no one else in the film does.

His attention to the city (as well as Rossellini's camera) changes over the course of the film, moving from the tactile to the optical.[39] The key moment occurs after his last conversation with Herr Enning, and is registered in the series of shots preceding Edmund's fall. If we look closely at the sequence, it isn't just that play precedes the fall. There is as well Rossellini's superimposition of Edmund's point of view with that of the camera. Both the camera and Edmund look on as the hearse pulls up to his home. Up to this point, the camera has stayed ahead or to the side of Edmund, rarely matching his point of view, save for the moment when Edmund and the spectator truly see the bottle of poison. Here, too, Edmund and the camera's perspectives match just as they do when his father's body is being taken away. Without these point-of-view shots, Rossellini's camera is content to show Edmund looking, but rarely to show what he sees so intensely.

Something else may move us forward and that is, in the absence of these shots, the spectator finds it easier to award Edmund's vision elements of the tactile rather than the optical; the film recounts Edmund's *Bildung* as a haptic form of life.[40] Haptic, we recall, refers to the sensorial mode of appropriating proximity. Derrida provides a helpful gloss:

> Because of the proximity value, because this vector of close presence finally determines the concept and term "haptic," because the haptical virtually covers all the senses wherever they appropriate a proximity, Deleuze and Guattari prefer the word "haptic" to the word "tactile." "Haptic" is a better word than "tactile" since it does not establish an opposition between two sense organs but rather invites the assumption that the eye itself may fulfill this nonoptical function.[41]

The introduction of the haptic helps us make sense of the film and Edmund in ways we weren't able to before. If we consider the haptic as involving a number of senses and a mode of making proper what is not one's own or what is in fact improper (appropriating a proximity in Derrida's terminology), we can detect a movement from the tactilely haptic to the more optically haptic. Why the need for such a precise distinction of the continuum between them? The haptic is too blunt an instrument to read the subtle movements of the film. If we simply use the haptic to cover how proximities are appropriated, we risk losing an important piece of where the film and with it Rossellini's entire *oeuvre* are pushing.

The move from the tactile to the optical is really about modes of holding, grasping, and allowing to weaken that have been, up until now, at the heart of this study: forms of life characterized by their degrees of holding. The more such an appropriation of an object or an identity is seen as tactile, the more the form of life can be said to possess. The more it moves to sight, the more such a life enacts a non-having. Walter Benjamin captured the distinction well: "Possession and having are allied with the tactile, and stand in a certain opposition to the optical. Collectors are beings with tactile instincts . . . The *flâneur* optical, the collector tactile."[42] In *Germany*

Year Zero, Edmund is a *flâneur* for most of the film. When he sees and then administers the poison, he becomes a collector.

It is in this context that the sequence leading up to the fall emerges as decisive. Edmund for the first time ascends a building that has remained intact. Note what he gains by moving vertically. With the ascent comes the possibility that the tactile moves to the foreground in ways it hadn't before. In a series of subjective shots that follow, we see Edmund looking, taking in the events, and touching the places of his childhood from a different, elevated venue. In this moment of seeing the apartment building, Rossellini frames his looking around the blown-out holes of the apartment building from where he stands. The effect is to heighten the intensity of the looking as if he were touching them. At this point Edmund experiences what he has done, touching by sight what he has been given. The implication is that Edmund undergoes a *Bildung* of sorts concerning seeing.[43]

Taken together, the ascent and the subjective shots lead to the realization of a form of life that experiences dispossession in ways quite different from other forms of life. Given the frames through which Edmund sees—the historical context of the environment that surrounds him; the envious speech that fills up this environment; and the dominance of a negative reciprocity—the haptic form of life is inflected decisively toward the tactile. The questions multiply, of course, as soon as we translate the film's meaning in terms of the construction of less haptic forms of life. I turn to some of those in the next chapter, but before I do, we need to pick up one final thread.

UNCOMMON ENDS

André Bazin was the first to register the intimate relationship in Rossellini's filmmaking between aesthetics and politics, what we might call a pedagogical approach to filmmaking. Here is Bazin describing the workings in both de Sica and Rossellini in a passage that lays bare the stakes of *Germany Year Zero*:

> The rules of its aesthetics are plain to see. It fits a vision of the world directly adapted to a framework of *mise en scène*. Rossellini's is a way of seeing, while de Sica's is primarily a way of knowing. The *mise en scène* of the former lays siege to its object from the outside. I do not mean without understanding and feeling—but that this exterior approach offers us

an essential ethical and metaphysical aspect of our relations with the world. In order to understand this statement one need only compare the treatment of the child in *Allemania Anno Zero* and in *Sciuscià* and *Ladri di Biciclette*.[44]

In this remarkable passage, Bazin hits on the implicit relation between exterior and interior in Rossellini's films, which is to say the weight afforded the landscape/cityscape and their relation to the so-called "interiority" of the characters. Insightful, too, is the notion that the outside "lays siege" to the inside in Rossellini's films in ways not dissimilar from how the apparatus impacts the spectator. Fundamentally, the question for Bazin is seeing how the *mise-en-scène* makes communication difficult, what he will call "a desperate awareness of man's inability to communicate."[45] On this score, Bazin writes:

> It follows that Rossellini's direction comes between his material and us, not as an artificial obstacle set up between the two, but as an unbridgeable, ontological distance, a congenital weakness of the human being which expresses itself aesthetically in terms of space, in forms, in the structure of his *mise-en-scène*. Because we are aware of it as a lack, a refusal, an escape from things and hence finally as a kind of pain, it follows that it is easier for us to be aware of it, easier for us to reduce it to a formal method.[46]

Rossellini directs sparsely. He employs distance as a mode of communicating suffering, which is found in the non-correspondence between what we see and what we don't. Furthermore, his direction separates the viewer from the material, the story, the documentary, and the film itself. Space is part of the distance between spectator and material. If the human being is weak "congenitally," how then can one show that? Here we have the answer to the earlier question about the means through which a film can make clear that its characters are in the act of interiorizing what is outside. That answer will be found in the "structure" of the *mise-en-scène* in *Germany Year Zero*, a process that occurs by equating emotional poverty with spatial poverty.

Clearly, space is toxic in *Germany Year Zero* as it is structured not simply to block communication, but also to intensify certain forms of communication, the most perfidious of which is envy. It is a *mise-en-scène* that does little except to isolate the individual from others.[47] As such, it is no social space, but something closer to a space in which social relations among forms of life have been curtailed thanks to the difficulty for gratitude to emerge. To circle back to my earlier discussion of envy and gratitude, this is a space in which good objects fail to be acknowledged, including most importantly the self.

No one more than the psychologist Wilfred Bion noted how much the lack of a good object brings with it not only frustration but thought itself:

> The model I propose is that of an infant whose expectation of a breast is mated with a realization of no breast available for satisfaction. This mating is experienced as a no-breast, or "absent" breast inside. The next step depends on the infant's capacity for frustration: in particular it depends on whether the decision is to evade frustration or to modify it. If the capacity for toleration of frustration is sufficient, the "no-breast" inside becomes a thought, and an apparatus for "thinking" it develops.[48]

For Bion, this psyche "operates on the principle that evacuation of a bad breast is synonymous with obtaining sustenance from a good breast." The result? "All thoughts are treated as if they were indistinguishable from bad internal objects; the appropriate machinery is felt to be, not an apparatus for thinking the thoughts, but an apparatus for ridding the psyche of accumulations of bad internal objects." Bion's perspective draws us toward accumulation and time, but just as decisively, is the effect that the realization of no-breast inside the good breast will have. Thought arises. Following Bion's line of inquiry, tolerating frustration appears as the ground against which thought arises as well as the means by which frustration is managed. Thinking responds to frustration and is a means for tolerating it.[49]

What does this have to do with Edmund and *Germany Year Zero*? Only this. We now have another perspective on why all the inhabitants of year zero, including Edmund, are incapable of tolerating frustration. Indeed, no one is more incapable of tolerating frustration than Edmund by the film's end: The frustration that his father is suffering and the desperate straits of the family continue to avail Edmund. Perhaps we can speak of these inhabitants as having developed a trained incapacity after thirteen years of Nazism to tolerate frustration and thought.[50] The results of a successful training in incapacity deserve our attention. Here is Bion again:

If intolerance of frustration is not so great as to activate the mechanisms of evasion and yet is too great to bear dominance of the reality principle, the personality develops omnipotence as a substitute for the mating of the pre-conception, or conception, with the negative realization. This involves the assumption of omniscience as a substitute for learning from experience by aid of thoughts and thinking. There is therefore no psychic activity to discriminate between true and false. Omniscience substitutes for the discrimination between true and false a dictatorial affirmation that one thing is morally right and the other wrong.[51]

Rather than thinking so as to engage with and evade frustration—which is the least we can say about the other inhabitants of Berlin in year zero—Edmund comes face to face with the enormous gap between the reality principle and what he wants. For others who had lived under and with Nazism, Nazism allowed them to avoid facing the abyss between reality and desire. When Nazism is no longer available as a mechanism for evading frustration or a mode by which reality is kept at bay in lieu of thought, omniscience results and with it a waning of "learning from experience by aid of thoughts and thinking." Thinking, thought, and yes, the gratitude that arises toward frustration as it leads to thought as a coping mechanism are nowhere to be found.

Now consider the cinematic apparatus. How does film show the spectator the way to move toward frustration—that is, toward acknowledging frustration while developing a response in kind that would involve holding together good object/no object, good breast/no breast? Matters are complex given that one apparatus, the cinematic, meets Bion's apparatus for holding thought. Perhaps it's something as simple as the more we acknowledge the no-breast/good breast, the more we move toward experiencing reality as reality. And if we sense this in rising levels of frustration, we know that reality can't be far behind.

What if the cinematic apparatus frustrates the spectator and so provides the means by which such frustration can do work, and can be productive of a certain kind of thought that acknowledges the frustration inherent in the good object and the no breast? Is the issue with Edmund, Germany Year Zero more generally, and across Rossellini's films even more profoundly, how precisely the cinematic apparatus frustrates the spectator and thus calls forth thought? What would a breakdown in the apparatus for dealing with thoughts look like? What or where would the spectator note the break-down in the apparatus for dealing with the thought, or the switch between the cinematic apparatus working one way and then moving in another? In *Germany Year Zero*, the question for Edmund concerns the knowledge of parricide and the apparatus of thinking that is unable to deal with that thought.[52] Rossellini shows us what happens when an apparatus isn't working in a context of a collective psychological catastrophe. That, I think, is what the film portrays and the choice of Edmund as the locus for that playing out in all the senses of the term is a stunning and frightening one.

Differences between the form of life of the spectator and Edmund, a form of life in *Germany Year Zero* who practices a different form of reci-procity, come into focus. Edmund's form of life does not accumulate guilt over time, but acknowledges the obligations that accrue to individual forms in a world and year in which reciprocity as it had been traditionally prac-ticed is no longer possible. It is a form of life no longer able to evade frus-tration through thought. This is the omnipotent form of life that emerges in the interaction between living being and apparatus, the form of life that emerges out of a circuit of failed reciprocity, of receiving that which harms and giving what can only do harm. The point is that language is not the only apparatus humming along in the film, but that in the circuit of giving and not giving, receiving and not receiving, other forms of life emerge. Can there be any doubt that the principal form of life in the film is that of the ingrate, a form based on a zero degree of gift-giving? Trans-lated into terms of envy, the film provides us with a terrifying account of envy run rampant and the price that comes with an attentiveness that ultimately moves against the self. In a context in which gift-giving and gift-receiving have been sundered, the form of life that results is marked as negative: the form of life that not only does not give, but the form of life that does not know how to receive. We are witness to the birth of a society in which it doesn't pay to pay attention, nor to receive what the senses provide.

What do all these loose ends add up to finally in terms of gratitude in the film? We recall that making gratitude visible is all in the way one re-ceives and that a reception that is an acceptance is so regardless of the con-ditions in which a gift or a present is given. This is Derrida's "interruption" that qualifies a gift as proper. Given how few material objects there are to give in Berlin at the end of the war, an exchange value attaches itself to nearly everything. With the dearth of things to give and in their place the sheer number of things to be sold or traded or stolen, including children, words take on enormous importance. The importance that they are given is readily seen in how Edmund weighs the words spoken to him. He receives the words of others by listening attentively to them. How he walks through the city is how he listens. This attentiveness, however, comes with a price. This isn't to lend one's ear, though there is that part of it as well. All exchanges are elaborated in terms of wanting something, which suggests that *Gratitude Year Zero* might be a better title for the film.[53]

If we connect the dots in Bion's perspective on the apparatus of thinking—"inability to tolerate frustration can obstruct the development of thoughts and a capacity to think, though a capacity to think would diminish the sense of frustration intrinsic to appreciation of the gap between a wish and its fulfillment"—then we should be heedful of the moments before Edmund falls. Here, interestingly enough, we have Edmund literally adopting a higher perspective from the new building at the end of the film. It is the moment when Edmund's perspective is most closely aligned with the camera and the spectator's. In that moment of superimposition, Edmund's inability to tolerate frustration obstructs the development of thought, which would consist in the acknowledgment of the larger role that the milieu in which he finds himself plays in his choices. The word, obstruction, is clearly merited for in that moment Edmund has an unobstructed view of the meaning of his actions. It is then that the gap between reality and wish becomes too great. With an unobstructed view of reality, Edmund is forced to see what he has done, at which point the capacity for thought emerges. In *Germany Year Zero*, however, thought offers little in the way of easing frustration, especially for those like Edmund whose mechanisms for evading frustrating are rudimentary at best.

What Edmund, and more generally other forms of life in *Germany Year Zero*, are unable to do is hold together the idea of the good breast/bad breast, good object/bad object. Holding them together is frustrating, but it is precisely the need to hold them together out of which the capacity for thought emerges. In a feedback loop, the result is eventually a greater capacity for handling frustration. Another approach would be to think less—that there are insights and experiences that do not require the apparatus of thinking to emerge. With this, a certain form of making visible not only is possible but necessary. In the suspension of thought, a form of life might emerge able to see—without obstruction and without judgment—the features of life in 1945 Germany.

What name will we want to give to this form of life? Let me hedge my bets a bit because the form of life that appears does not do so fully formed in the film. Perhaps the term "spectator" suffices though I remain unconvinced that spectator names that more generous form of life or acknowledges the importance of attention that Rossellini and as we will soon see, Antonioni, are intent in pushing us toward. To be subjected to, to be the spectator of, suggests an inability to see the effects of the apparatus and *praeparatus*. What is required is a term that marks what the cinematic apparatus not only does but what it potentially allows us to touch.

For now, a helpful way of seeing this is to let forms of life resonate with both subject and spectator, to hold open what names we might choose to give to the subjects we see onscreen and the kind of spectatorship that the film produces.[54] The longer we defer naming, the more we move in a direction that feels less tragic (the tragic genres of subjects and spectators that we have come to know too well over the last forty years) in which the possibilities of future action and future words are held hostage to an absolutely certain and inexorable denouement that is often called "capture."

Saying so does not deny that what forms of life may provide in terms of a different relation to fate may also mean giving up some of the hefty theoretical ballast that subjectivity and spectatorship provide. That seeming lack in form of life does present advantages, however, that other categories often fail to provide. They consist in the possibility that the cinematic apparatus creates intervals for the spectator to move or not, to hold or not. One might respond that my reading of Rossellini's *Germany Year Zero* is at best far-fetched and at worst just wrong. And so I may be forgiven, if in continuing to make the case for the generous form of life, I turn to Michelangelo Antonioni's films, *L'avventura*, *La notte*, and *L'eclisse*, for help.

5

THE TENDER LIVES
OF VITTI/VITTORIA

Has there ever been a director more boxed in than Michelangelo Antonioni? Critics have been happily hemming in him for more than fifty years,
enabled admittedly by Antonioni's own often obscure pronouncements
("About Nothing—With Precision," the most notorious) as well as his, shall
we say, often enigmatic style. Thus we have Antonioni, the existentialist,
and Antonioni, the Marxist; Antonioni, the geographer, and Antonioni, the
ecologist.[1] No one will be surprised to find lurking in the margins of the
following chapter, Antonioni, the bio-politician. Truthfully, little scholarship has elaborated such a profile of forms of life or forms of reciprocity
across his films. Among other things, in the following chapter I attempt to
do so by bringing together holding, generosity, and violence in a reading
of three of Antonioni's most important films: *L'avventura*, *La notte*, and
L'eclisse. I do so by adopting a perspective on reciprocity that in turn evokes
play and attention and so is situated as the negative image of Edmund
and generosity presented previously. Here, surprisingly, the reading orbits
tightly around the actor, Monica Vitti, and the possibility that her command and evasion of the cinematic apparatus might actually help equip us
for living today in our own milieu of fear. In the process, we might also be
able to see where and why it makes sense to move away from mere aliveness
to something approaching playful existence.[2]

The key terms concern attention and reciprocity. What would an attentive form of life look like on film? What would we, as spectators, see the
characters doing (or not) that could enlist us in paying more attention?
Girding my discussions throughout is the idea that something like a pedagogical project lies at the heart of Antonioni's cinema. Although we might

begin our discussion with Antonioni's early films and shorts, for reasons soon clear, it makes sense to begin with attention as it unfolds in the first film of the trilogy, *L'avventura*. If there is a mode of connecting the three films, it will be in how attention very nearly becomes a kind of character across the trilogy.

FALLING OFF THE BOAT

L'avventura begins where *Germany Year Zero* ends—with a fall. *L'avventura* famously recounts the aftermath of the disappearance of a young woman, Anna, and then the failed attempts of her friends to find her. The film also tells of the consequences of that disappearance on all of them, but especially on her friend, Claudia, and on Anna's fiancé, Sandro.[3] The combination of the failed search and the increasing desire on the part of Sandro for Claudia, played by Monica Vitti, and vice-versa, touches on a relation between search and desire; the search leading to greater desire, with Thanatos driving not a little of the former.

The film also relates desire to the cinematic apparatus itself, specifically through Antonioni's insistence, even obsession, with touch. By "touch" I have in mind certainly not just the sense of touch, but also the images of touch framed as a holding, a grasping, or a release, which are framed as desire.[4] Yet there is more to these connected moments of touching than simply marking desire. In *L'avventura* Antonioni displays kinds of holding, touching, and grasping that bring into focus how to think about the relation between the holding that characterizes both the spectator and forms of life onscreen.[5] Another hypothesis: *L'avventura* visualizes how the cinematic apparatus captures the film's protagonists, where it holds them in its grip, and then how such a grip may be lessened.

Some preliminaries to get us started. What kinds of holding do we see on display in *L'avventura* and then why call it holding? Returning to Lyotard's translation of the term "grip" (*mainmisse*) on which I concluded Chapter 1, recall how Lyotard joins the grip to moments of possessing. The crucial term for him is *mancus*—that is, "the person who takes hold, in the sense of possession or appropriation."[6] Antonioni's films appear readymade for such an analysis, as they seem to reply *avant la lettre* to the question of whether there can be a holding that is not at the same time a taking.

L'avventura answers affirmatively and then sets out to show the spectator what degrees of holding look like—that there can be a holding that isn't a taking hold of, and so also a holding that does not qualify as possession.[7] Holding, in other words, has transitive and intransitive forms.

One solution might be to line up the apparatus with the transitive and *praeparatus* with the intransitive. And so the spectator waits. This characterization of spectatorship shares many features with the strategy of defamiliarization that comes down to us as one of Russian formalism's signature contributions. "Habitualization devours work, clothes, furniture, one's wife, and the fear of war," writes Victor Shklovsky. He adds:

> If the whole complex lives of many people go on unconsciously, then such lives are as if they had never been. And art exists that one may recover the sensation of life; it exists to make one feel things, to make the stone stony. The purpose of art is to impart the sensation of things as they are perceived and not as they are known. The technique of art is to make objects "unfamiliar," to make forms difficult, to increase the difficulty and length of perception because the process of perception is an aesthetic end in itself and must be prolonged.[8]

In a context of defamiliarization, the spectator loses her moorings and the result is the creation of worlds perceived more than known. Yet such a strategy doesn't have to end there. In Antonioni's films, the defamiliarizing possibilities of the cinematic apparatus are dramatically employed so as to invite the spectator to consider his or her own proper relation to things and to the often terrifying moment of identifying with what and who appear onscreen. Defamiliarizing depends upon the "making difficult of forms" by rendering them unfamiliar and so increasing the length of perception. Antonioni makes explicit Shklovsky's terms, in particular what conditions give rise to attention. For Antonioni and for us, the bridge connects how we hold and the forms of life that result (we could simply say forms of possession or what belongs to "I"). What bridges between the two in these films is precisely the grip and how to think together holding with life.[9]

How might we imagine Antonioni proceeding with his display of holding and taking in *L'avventura*? Primarily, he focuses our attention on the relation of appropriation to taking hold of, of how characters are placed in relation to objects, to each other, to other gazes, to the camera, and lastly to themselves. The audience is led to see that at issue for Antonioni is always the way in which his characters hold (and are held) by the objects around them or the thoughts within them.[10] If we were to adopt a reading that focuses relentlessly on holding in the film, what would we discover? What would it look like if we were to read the film in terms of holding and then how might we connect holding with mastery, that is with knowledge or indeed an existence that is unfamiliar to us?[11]

UNCANNY GRIPS

Sequence 1. A boat sways. A well-heeled passenger, Sandro, is looking for his fiancé, Anna, who has gone missing. He hears a voice on the island: "No trace." The voice belongs to Corrado, another passenger who is also searching for Anna. As the boat lurches forward, Sandro leaves the frame (see Figure 5-1). The camera, however, keeps hold of the island with the waves crashing into the rocks. The camera then lifts off the boat to show us just how high a fall might be (see Figure 5-2) and then returns to the boat and another two passengers (Raimondo and Patrizia), whose backs hold the center of the frame. The camera holds on Patrizia who grasps one of the center poles of the boat (see Figure 5-3). A sharp cut follows and we are smack in the middle of the island with Claudia, the actor Monica Vitti, foregrounded and looking forlorn (see Figure 5-4).

Something uncanny hovers over these frames and it is linked to the way the pole divides the human protagonists from the non-living rock.[12] Hands separate the frame by holding on, an echo of an earlier moment in which Claudia and Anna had both held on to the same pole (see Figure 5-5). Now her grip appears much lighter than the others and indeed from her own in the earlier scene, this because not only Claudia and Anna grip differently, but also because Antonioni continues to focus our attention on Claudia and the way she grips.

The earlier shot of Claudia and Anna lingers for other reasons. There is the strangeness of Claudia's one hand separate from Anna's two. Anna is clearly frightened by the voyage and seeing her hold on with both hands after the close-ups of love-making with Sandro implies as much. For her part, Claudia, as the boat makes it way to the island, moves across the boat freely without fear of falling, despite that fact that she could fall in, seemingly at any moment (see Figure 5-6). The choppy seas threaten; falling into

Figure 5-1. L'avventura

Figure 5-2. L'avventura

Figure 5-3. L'avventura

Figure 5-4. L'avventura

Figure 5-5. L'avventura

these waters would be easy. The sequence ends with Anna covered in shadow and Claudia bathed in light.

Sequence 2. Anna is now missing and the passengers have spread out and are canvassing the island. Claudia peers over a ledge to see if her friend has perhaps fallen there, which then leads to an arpeggio of shots of Vitti's hands as they grip, fail to grip, and then attempt to grip, again, the rocky terrain beneath her (see Figure 5-7).[13] Here Antonioni focuses again on Vitti's hands, how they hold, and how they allow her to stand up. The effect is to separate her hands from the rest of the body. Vitti's face comes into close shot as she pushes herself up from the ground. Again, we sense something out of the ordinary when not uncanny.

For two decades, if not longer, "uncanny" has been one of the most overused terms in the theoretical arsenal. That won't stop me from employing it here. Consider this reading of "uncanny" to see why: "The absence of what ought to be present is eerie," whereas "the presence of what ought to be absent is uncanny."[14] This formulation from Nicholas Royle helps us make

Figure 5-6. L'avventura

Figure 5-7. L'avventura

sense of the succession of images of Claudia and the proliferation of images of the hand that characterize the film in nearly every shot of Vitti on the island. In terms of eerie, Anna's disappearance surely qualifies, but Antonioni doesn't leave it there. Instead, the camera gravitates to the island's strange landscape, heightened in black and white: the empty villager's house, the island's moonscape, and lastly, the full-throttled estrangement of the couples on the island. Yet the presence of something that ought to be is absent? What is it?

One answer is the death drive, sitting astride the intersection of what is eerie and uncanny.[15] Nothing is more uncanny than the death drive for how it "ought to be absent" and yet inhabits the island like a bad dream; what ought to be present is made absent (Anna) and what is absent is made present, namely the death drive itself. The sheer number of frames in which a grip, a hold, or simply a hand are at the center of the frame, points to the strong presence of the drive in such a landscape. Everyone on the island and on the boat is quite literally holding on for dear life, sitting astride vistas that beckon a fall or a jump.[16]

If the film has an unconscious, then the death drive is it.[17] It will be seen in the way that bodies hold on or don't hold on to the boat, railings, rocks, essentially all the objects in the frame. We see it in the way that bodies hold themselves against the sides of what Visconti called the luminous rectangle. Indeed, the island interlude resembles a literalizing of the drive toward death; we begin to pay attention to the way each character holds on as they are knocked about, and as they knock themselves and each other about. Indeed, the island interlude ultimately seems to be about obliging the characters to hold on. One wonders whether in privileging the grip, Antonioni is actually associating holding on and holding oneself to the death drive, a situation that changes obviously once they leave the island, into Eros. The death drive for many lies at the heart of the cinematic apparatus's unconscious as well. In this sense, the forms of life we see onscreen are ones the death drive inflects, which is registered in each form's ability to hold on to what life gives.[18]

Given Antonioni's emphasis on the grip, an obvious question is how a reading primed to register a cinematic techne might actually work. A first approach would surely involve linking the film's forms of life as a response to the presence/absence of the death drive. Pursuing this line of inquiry, we will need to be on the lookout for modes of holding—that is, ontological forms linked to how the hand or hands take, receive, and give. As my seven-year-old son knows so well, throwing something is never akin to giving because there is no way for the recipient to receive it. One catches what is thrown, but we would hesitate to say that she receives it. And in *L'avventura*, there are as many forms of life as there are degrees of holding and as many deaths as there are falls or throws.

TO HAVE AND TO HOLD

In *L'avventura*, forms of reciprocity become visible in the difference between holding and having.[19] Consider the etymology not of holding (which we remember is linked etymologically to having), but of *tenere*. A Sanskrit dictionary shows the following entry under *tan*:

> 1. Tan stretch, trans. and intrans.; extended, reach; spread over; 2. continue, endure; 3. stretch (a weft or line); continue (the line of a family); 4. metaphorically, of sacrifice and supplication (which are compared with a weft), perform, make, stretch (Ger. *dehnen*, stretch).[20]

Now the second meaning: "resound, thunder," and the next, "*tanú -*" thin, *tenuis*, slender as subst. f. body; person, one's own person, self, used like *atman*, outward form or manifestation. [prop. 'stretched out, thin']." Possession is nowhere to be found. Instead, we find a stretching and reaching, which in English recalls attention, attending, and of course the lovely words "tenuous" and "tender."[21] Superimposing holding and "outward form" joins form to forms of holding and not teleologically to forms of having, with its connections to possession, identification, and the like. It is the legal distinction between *habendum* and *tenendum* that one employs in contracts. That's certainly fine, the reader may well respond, but why insist on holding and not having?[22] The reason has to do with the space available to us to consider a different relation to life within the notions of having or possessing—one that doesn't move through ownership, but rather through attention to form. Here lies the preference for some of us for forms of life. To employ forms of life evokes a holding whose emphasis on shaping and creating differs from having as well as from labor and mastery.[23]

How does the spectator experience the distinction between having and holding in *L'avventura*?[24] The contrast emerges in the nearly constant repositioning of the hands in the island sequence, especially the repeated holding and releasing of the grip. Here compare once again Claudia's grip and Anna's as they travel to the island. Claudia's grip features a lightness of touch, but also an inability to grab hold of the island itself, with its moon-like surface, its ragged cliffs, and the sky that hangs over the proceedings like cinema's largest curtain. We could say that Anna and Claudia's respective grips represent two intensities of holding, but that isn't specific enough. To the degree that Claudia properly establishes a grasp of an object, there is no way for her to feel whether she has done so unless she lets go and then repeats the process.[25] A metaphor: Claudia plays the spaces of the film's landscape with her hands.

True expressiveness in the film resides in and lingers across hands and touch.[26] Antonioni provides us with a phenomenology of different holds, grasps, clenches, fingerings, and touch, all anchored and performed by the hand. Objects and landscapes are held and released and, in so doing, spaces open. With the familiarity of the hand for holding, letting go and holding again, the hand(s) become familiar with gratitude, not closing finally around what they touch, but rather by repeatedly gripping and releasing. No mere synecdoche for gratitude, the film finds it in the opening and closing of the hand. Naturally, we cannot speak of a form of exchange based on gravity; on taking or having, which is to say that it is impossible to read Claudia, sprawled on the island, grasping and releasing, as engaged in any exchange of a hierarchical nature. Rather, hers is a body with hands that accomplish distance. In this nearly constant work with the hands, Antonioni effectively composes a map of the modalities of holding.[27]

Antonioni is asking the spectator to consider a different lexicon for viewing films, one that bridges from subjectivity to a kind of exposure to what lies outside. We will want to name the form of life that underpins modes of holding—a form of life in which form also includes that which has not yet been formed. In such a perspective, Claudia's role is crucial. Nearly all the touching, holding, and playing that take place in the film involve her. We see it in the relation between *L'avventura*'s entire *mise-en-scène* and her. Its objects—the purse in the opening scene of the film, the island, the rocks, the poles on the boat, and especially in the film's concluding scene—not only move across the frame but relate directly to her. Claudia understands that living with and among things means being in relation to them. The rest of the party are seemingly caught in mere words to the degree that they avoid or refuse relationships with each other.

The weight Antonioni affords the *mise-en-scène* bears some reflection. If forms of holding are to be thought in relation to forms of life, then the kind of objects that appear here will need to be sketched. A name I would like to propose is one that appeared in Chapter 1, namely "transitional objects." We recall the term appeared in Winnicott's description of the "intermediate area":

> From birth therefore the human being is concerned with the problem of the relationship between what is objectively perceived and what is subjectively conceived of, and in the solution of this problem there is no health for the human being who has not been started off well enough by the mother. The intermediate area to which I am referring is the area that is allowed to the infant between primary creativity and objective perception based on reality testing. The transitional phenomena represent the early stages of the use of illusion, without which there is no meaning for the human being in the idea of a relationship with an object that is perceived by others as external to that being.[28]

What actually changes when we read *L'avventura* as an exploration of the boundaries of Winnicott's "intermediate area" given to Claudia and which reside between "primary creativity and objective perception?" In Claudia's struggle, literally, to get a grip—she also searches for an object that lies between having and not having, where having lines up with objective perception and primary creativity with non-possession. Holding will name the space between creativity and reality testing—to the degree one holds less, one moves toward creativity. As one begins to test reality, possession comes more to the fore. If my reading has hit the mark, then we might view modes of holding in terms of a not-me possession whose task it is to relate inside to outside. The result would be a zone of experience of what is not yet mine. This is what sets apart the original not-me-possession.[29]

To return more forcefully to the film now, Antonioni reveals not so much what happens when transitional objects appear; nor does he delve in a sustained way into the relation between adults as children and their relation to objects. It is more complex and also more troubling than that. In Claudia's difficulty of possessing anything on the island, she experiences the lack of transitional objects and so is unable to navigate the terrain between having and not-possessing. The premise is that with fewer and fewer transitional objects, inside and outside necessarily remain blurred. The effect of the blurring is to create a situation in which the spectator begins to see the effects of Claudia's struggle. Admittedly, to assume this means that transitional objects are not-me possessions and hence the fewer of the not-me possessions that are available to us (to possess without involving the "I"), the smaller becomes the zone for experiencing reality.[30]

That is precisely what separates the island opening from the remainder of the film. In the film's second half, the number of objects increases exponentially, but these are not necessarily transitional objects or not-me possessions. One wonders if the island's barrenness doesn't actually mark a space in which transitional phenomena are precisely *not* available. Getting off the boat sets in motion an adventure characterized by the lack of playthings. Bareness, rocks, dusty artifacts, not a holding of objects, much less a consumption of objects, but rather an encounter with a lack of transitional objects that characterizes a particular zone of reality.[31]

What then are we finally left with when returning to forms of life? One answer is to take a step back from the individual frames and the pedagogy of holding to ask after the work the cinematic apparatus does in these scenes, especially with regard to partial objects. Here Christian Metz's classic argument on the fetish is decisive:

It [film] does *contain* many potential part-objects (the different shots, the sounds, and so forth), but each of them disappears quickly after a moment of presence, whereas a fetish has to be kept, mastered, held, like the photograph in the pocket. Film is, however, an extraordinary activator of fetishism.[32]

Thanks to the principle of a *moving cutting off*, thanks to the changes of framing between shots (or within a shot: tracking, panning, characters moving into or out of the frame, and so forth) cinema literally *plays* with the terror and the pleasure of fetishism, with its combination of desire and fear.[33]

More generally, the play of framings and the play with framings in all sorts of films, work like a striptease of the space itself (and a striptease proper in erotic sequences, when they are constructed with some subtlety). The moving camera caresses the space ... Most of all, a film cannot be *touched*, cannot be carried and handled: although the actual reels can, the projected film cannot.[34]

Certainly, Antonioni's *L'avventura* knows its fetishes well; the strong impression of hands lingers as potential part-objects. In order for the part-objects to come together as fetish, however, they must be mastered: They must be "held." The relationship between mastery and fetish is one that often goes unremarked in the film, though it does figure in earlier readings of the apparatus.[35] For Metz, the continuum will be found between, on one hand, the cinematic apparatus that offers part objects without providing the spectator with the means for mastery initially, and the other based on capture.

Metz finds a remedy in suture against the fetish: against holding on to an absence or against being seduced by an absence. Film activates fetishism but doesn't necessarily provide the means for the fetish to be mastered. *L'avventura*, in particular, blocks the constricted holding of partial objects, which is implicit in Metz's reading of the difference between film and photography. And yes, while it is true that Metz will go on to note how film plays with "the terror of the fetish," another more affirmative possibility is that film may actually weaken the hold the fetish has.

NO MASTERY, NO FETISH

If fetishes exist to be mastered, then what does a film have to do to keep the fetish at bay so as to break off mastery? What does the spectator hold on to and then master as part of what is seen or not? How we answer will depend upon how we understand the part-object and its disappearance.[36] Here Antonioni invites us in *L'avventura* to see how shots, frames, and duration can be mixed and matched so as to interrupt mastering the images that appear onscreen. The spectator begins to notice just how close the unexpected is to the island group but equally just how close the unexpected is to the spectator herself, who must navigate the frames that appear to go nowhere. The effect I would suggest is making certain that the spectator cannot master fully the part object.[37]

Recall once again an early scene on the boat. Claudia and Anna's hair are framed, a quick cut to the pearls of the necklace, then a hand that holds one of the boat's poles, but not too tightly. Another shot, this time of a hand centered in the frame that holds on. We suddenly realize that it is impossible to link the hands that hold on to the bodies; they are unidentifiable. The impression is of an anonymous, non-gendered, pose. How often do we find ourselves in front of another cut, another back of the head with a shot of hair, and then another realization that we have confused both Claudia and Anna with one another. With their backs turned and the hand that holds on, the impression is a scene out of a different genre, perhaps science fiction or horror. We see a creature that appears to be merely attached to a grip. If this is a form of life that emerges on the screen, it is broken up, fragmented, helped along by Antonioni's repeated failure to provide any recognizable medium shots or close-ups of the face. Rather, we merely see the back and neck, a creature from the Mediterranean lagoon. That, I think, is the point. The spectator pays attention more intensely when the face is initially unavailable.[38]

Or when a body goes missing. This is also how we ought to approach the empty shots of the island, the visual hints of where Anna may have fallen or jumped. Rather than a haunting, the effect is to liberate the apparatus and to show the spectator how distracted a tool the camera can be, how easily the apparatus invents its own story without recourse to a human point of view.[39] We might assume a link to Visconti and the Cyclopean islands that doom the 'Ntoni brothers to failure and we might be on to something. Unlike Visconti, however, Antonioni shows us what the experience of looking back and backwards feels like. The sea and the coast hold the gaze of everyone. It is only Anna, who before was holding on for dear life, who escapes the spectator and passengers' gaze.

If we were to imagine Anna's as a form of life, it would be the one that holds tightly and lets go recklessly. There is no holding of the other as all of film's couples refuse that possibility. Indeed, the lack of intimacy is revealed in Claudia's repeated attempts to claw her way back literally through the movement of holding and letting go. For his part, Antonioni shows us that holding an object, another person, a gaze, or indeed oneself, is part of a continuum and that on one side is Claudia who learns to hold and release (or who doesn't hold at all). On another, we have Sandro, who poses for Anna in the opening moments of the film and who will hold that pose again while refusing to lessen his grip on Claudia. The result is a catalogue of grips and holds in a wider context of life and death.

In *La notte*, Antonioni expands on the possibility of forms of life as linked to degrees of holding. Here, too, the form of life that is most able to recognize its hold or non-hold or degrees of holding is the film's female protagonist, Lidia. This reminds us how profoundly Antonioni conceives of forms of life that are able to practice generosity are nearly always gendered as feminine.[40] In this film, the form of life that practices holding and letting go as the principal movement is Lidia, but it is a Lidia repeatedly doubled for Monica Vitti's Valentina in the film's final half hour. That *La notte* also fundamentally concerns holding and form may seem to some like a stretch. Rather, the film would appear primarily to recount a matrimonial crisis. Giovanni, a writer, drinks in the shadows; he appears at the drop of a hat or the opening of a door. Impulsive and blissfully unaware of the effects of his actions, he rarely says anything to Lidia, his wife, though they are able to recall earlier moments even if they remain separated physically and emotionally from each other.

Lidia does not want to return to the past. As many analyses have made clear, the film describes a communication breakdown that is meant to extend to the larger world of the Italian bourgeoisie during the boom years.[41] The crisis appears to be related to the difficulty with which the various characters populating Milan in the early 1960s relate to themselves and to one another. It is this difficulty of relating to things held in common that forms the heart of the well-known Antonioni critique of capitalism, the West, and Antonioni's own unique form of existential filmmaking.[42]

Undoubtedly, such a critique plays an important role in Antonioni's cinema. The critique operates as well at molecular levels in the film. Thus, we notice how often people nearly run into each other in the film: A car door opens and a bicyclist nearly hits the car; an elevator door opens and closes and those exiting nearly knock the others over. A woman assumes that Lidia is meeting someone for a rendezvous in a squalid part of town; two young men fight silently while Lidia looks on along with other spectators, until her final "Basta!" ends the sequence. Typically, these moments of proximity are represented as conflictual, though they do not add up to full-fledged conflict. Instead, separation keys pivotal moments of the film: the separation between bodies in the car—Lidia and Giovanni's—which sit near (but not too near) and, of course, the greatest area of separation in the film, the abyss between thoughts and their expression. *La notte* lays bare a society in which the majority of its characters feel and act as if they do not belong together.[43]

All relations featured in the film are broken: the physical and mental crisis of the couple's friend, Tommaso; the conflict between Giovanni and Lidia, but also Giovanni and the reading public; the difficult interaction between Lidia and Valentina, but also the three of them; and even, or especially, the crisis of the cinematic apparatus that appears to go off on its own, leering, following, stalking its female leads. There doesn't appear to be any possibility of a return to some earlier moment of fullness or peace, let alone serenity. Giovanni says as much to Lidia after picking her up after her walk. You remember this place, she says, we were here before, years ago. Yet the moment ends just as quickly as it began. By film's end, the past remains inaccessible with only knowledge of the present possible.

That knowledge concerns fundamentally the objects and persons and the commodities and fetishes that move across the city. The Milan of *La notte* positively shines, both inside and out. Really, has there ever been a shinier, more hygienic hospital ever filmed? Not content to show us these surfaces, Antonioni demands in *La notte* that we contemplate what we see onscreen.[44] He doesn't offer a plot or a solution (which amounts to the same thing) to the riddle that is Milan buckling under the weight of modernity. He chooses instead to show—relentlessly—what modernity has wrought on those who live within the city's reflected exteriors and empty interiors. Antonioni transfixes the spectator by highlighting the distance between these dazzling worlds and the forms of life that move, often lethargically, within them. To see that in its duration and up close, the spectator has to wait.

In this the spectator differs from the majority of the characters in the film, none of whom seem capable of waiting. For those who can—Lidia and Valentina, in particular—it is their capacity for attending that urges us to adopt a different language for describing what they have in common, and that is precisely a form of life that is attentive.[45] Here again, Antonioni invites us to superimpose Lidia and Valentina as the generous form. Unlike Giovanni and nearly all the men in the film, these women are invited to wake from their sleepwalking.[46] The emphasis on sleepwalking as deadness, and the dead of the party, extends across the film because we usually don't speak of the dead or the living in quite this way.[47]

Traditional perspectives on Antonioni abound to highlight the devastating picture the film paints of Italian society after the economic boom: falsehood, empty spaces, isolation, and of course alienation. Still, the question that continues to vex is this: How are we to link the modernity of what an apparatus has captured on film—nearly magically in the film's opening and justifiably famous shot of the Pirelli building—to the empty spaces that characterize interactions in the city? If *La notte*'s women are meant to provide an alternative to those that sleepwalk, then why does the critique seem so muted? Why does that critique, represented by Lidia and Valentina, often consist of silence or, more precisely, silent movement; how might we refer to this mode of witnessing, or even observing intently?

What sets Lidia and Valentina apart is precisely how they hold what they see and thus how they attend. In a word, they come to stand in for the spectator who, too, is asked to hold what she sees in a certain way on film and what she does not. If we shift our frame from the critical and tragic frame of alienation to reciprocity, holding, and attentiveness to the figures of Lidia and Valentina, then Antonioni's project might be seen as affirming a form of life that sees without identifying utterly with what it sees. On this score, I'm reminded of Simone Weil and her framing of contemplation, philosophy, and image: "The proper method of philosophy consists in clearly conceiving the insoluble problems in all their insolubility and then in simply contemplating them, fixedly and tirelessly, year after year, without any hope, patiently waiting."[48] Antonioni, for his part, philosophizes to the degree that he forces the spectator and his female protagonists to wait "fixedly and tirelessly" in contemplation. This is what tires Valentina in her encounters with both Giovanni and Lidia, while Lidia seems to be nothing other than exhausted throughout the film—the shadow under her eyes continually lit in such a way as to emphasize it (see Figure 5-8). So, too, *La notte* exhausts the spectator by withholding narration in what legions of undergraduates and others have simply called "boring." It is also how Valentina ends her conversation with Giovanni and Lidia: The couple has exhausted her.

Lidia's is also a critique of thought. Indeed, a disbelief in the benefits of thinking in lieu of attending peeks through in her implicit critiques of Giovanni's writing. Antonioni has Lidia offering a then fashionable critique of the bourgeoisie as dead, but significantly that critique falters over the course of the party. The spectator, too, is drawn into Valentina's game like so many of her fellow partygoers. We begin to wonder as well what truths

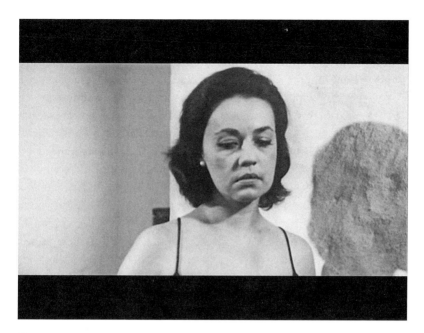

Figure 5-8. La notte

and falsehoods Roberto and Lidia are telling each other in the car. And then
we recall the drama of the final scene in which Giovanni offers a self-critique
of his position and his failure to recognize his own experience. Yet each moment ends in futility for the character onscreen as well as the spectator, the
point simply being how insistently the film demystifies not only the intellectual but also language itself and the recording of it. Here we might also
note that Valentina does not write by pen but employs a tape recorder.[49]

THE WALKING SLEEPWALKERS

This context helps us understand the weight Antonioni gives the thought
of Hermann Broch. Although passages are not cited directly in the film, we
can construct our own hit list from Broch's enormous output. Here he is in
two passages from "The Spirit in an Unspiritual Age":

> Over and over again, humanity loses its language, and over and over
> again the spirit, the absolute, slips from its grasp, time and again humanity

is thrown back to the muteness of its dim origins, still apparent today in the apathy of primitive peoples . . . This mute silence weighs heavily on a world that has lost language and spirit, for it has had to put its faith in power, and in murder without which there is no power. Muteness now rules both individuals and groups, and is the muteness of murder.

Amidst all this, the Church broadcasts its message, but mechanically, unceremoniously, drowned out, banalized and annihilated by the clamor of earthly life. It is the awful wordless clamor that goes with murder— rhetorical in itself, a muteness elevated to the noise and pathos of the rhetorical. It is a muteness that sounds like speech, but is not—a syntax of shouting, an element of language, admittedly, of just its word- less part, but in this wordlessness there is only fear, or desperation, or courage about to erupt. The rhetorical knows no dialogue, no argument or counterargument, it comes not from the sphere of the intellect, but from darkness. It does not convince, but enthralls and fascinates through the power of darkness, through the allure of darkness, through this dan- ger that no one can escape . . . Wherever this dark silence finds an outlet, exploding into life, it goes for the heart . . . Rhetoric, that anthem of both heroism and desperation, serves the religion of power.[50]

Muteness, noise, lies. The relation among them could be taken as the under- lying theme of the film. It would certainly account for the trouble in which the spectator finds herself when watching the party scene and when the noise of the party reaches deafening levels. Alongside the aural din, we also register the visual noise of indistinct bodies moving across the frame. So, too, outsides invade insides; the noise of an airplane throws Lidia off balance in the hotel room. And then words, Giovanni's in particular, do not carry truth, but seem to have been emptied of both affect and meaning. This is empty speech that empties subjects.

Rhetoric serves the religion of power, Broch tells us, which Antonioni sounds as one of the film's major chords. Giovanni, we learn, will be hired by an important industrialist and taken on as manager. The scenes at the book launch and later at the party are characterized by nothing so much as the emptiness of what each person says: the generalities of the content, what and who needs to be saved or not. The point of these scenes and many others like them is to inform the spectator how easily silence and speech serve power. So, too, the *mise-en-scène*, which marks the kinds of speech and the forms of life that speak them. The tractors, the seemingly empty lot hiding a squat in the early scenes, the walk across a bustling Milan into a nearly deserted and depraved suburb—all echo simultaneously the cacophonous and silent soundscape.

Broch writes that such a clamor accompanies murder and though we might want to diminish that perspective, make it less a killing than the end of a relationship, we need to hold on to the risks that silence entails for those who inhabit such areas. The paradox is that a mute silence is one in which a speaker isn't prompted to speak rhetorically. It is as if the film's characters do not know or remember how to speak; do not know how to speak to each other;[51] and most importantly do not know how to speak to themselves. Such a separation is made even more unbearable by the lack of a space that might bring them together. Each of the set pieces in the film, but especially those of the party, are meant to match the hardness of the landscape with a missing language.[52]

HOW TO HOLD A CITY

What does all this add up to in terms of holding and attention? For Antonioni, in a moment of postwar Italy and, more broadly, modernity, the risk is of empty speech and sleepwalking under the effects of a certain milieu spreading. Yet are there those who are more cognizant of their relation to the outside? How might a film show us a different relation to the outside, one that would presumably also concern a relation with what remains stationary inside? By the traditional mode of contrast, no one enjoys that relation to an intimacy with their surroundings more than Lidia and Valentina. Their intimacy features a kind of holding that is remarkably different from that of Giovanni and the other male characters. In marking these different degrees of intimacy with their environment, we can sketch a milieu that is the relation between forms of reciprocity and forms of life.

In a milieu of only human forms of life, Lidia stands out. In her often remarked upon walk across Milan, what endures is the way she travels across the city. She smiles, she touches objects, she crosses streets, she comforts a child, and so becomes one with the city's movement of objects and individuals. The question to ask is this: What makes her engagement with the city so obviously the opposite of sleepwalking? How does she receive what it is that she sees? Where others fail to notice just how unfamiliar their surroundings are, Lidia values a sense of remaining unfamiliar with the objects of sight. Hers is a not a mastery of the visible, one based on the belief that what we see has already been seen and therefore is remembered and mastered. Rather the impression here, helped along by the repeated superimposition of her perception with a camera empowered to go and to look both with her and at her, is that she is seeing for the first time. The parallels with Edmund of the previous chapter are by now obvious, but what sets Lidia apart is her capacity to hold uncertainty about the future, about her life, about Giovanni without identifying with it.

Lidia's chief interest in the sequence isn't based on a search for inward or outward security, but rather involves a break with the past so as to discover the new. Nor does there appear to be a pattern in where she walks or whether what she makes sense of what she is seeing. What she sees—perhaps for the first time—is the essential: the laughter of two friends, a piece of paint that peels. The word that comes to mind is "wonder." Antonioni transmits this sense of wonder through a series of medium shots through which we see not classic reaction shots to what she is experiencing, but something like a response to "what is."[53] Sometimes that wonder is captured in a smile, a glance, a tightening and then a lightening of the face. Wonder involves the entire body in movement and in particular Lidia's hands. Her body is engaged in her walking and seeing so much so that we ask if this is the first time that she has truly walked across the city.

Her stroll doesn't add up to a mastery of the city. Or better, the effect of the sequence is not to show Lidia acquiring a quality or becoming something else. Her stroll differs from others to the degree that she doesn't appear to be postponing or avoiding what is. Said negatively, Lidia doesn't create more time by accumulating and then later using what she sees, which is to say there does not appear to be a conclusion toward which she is working. Rather, the episode in the city involves an acknowledgment of the actual moment in which she walks.[54] It will be found in the way that touch and eyes work together and here no moment captures that better than the one in which Lidia reaches out to touch a piece of peeling paint (see Figure 5-9). There is no appropriation, no proper name given to what she sees. What she sees, she perceives, without any move to make it her own, even or especially in the case of the infant who has seemingly been abandoned. She

Figure 5-9. La notte

sees with a sense of openness to what is around her and refuses to avoid what she sees. That openness is on display in the later encounters with Giovanni and especially Valentina, where she doesn't resist what is by depending upon time to overcome Giovanni's infidelity and ultimately failure of memory.

If speaking of such openness is difficult to grasp, it's because we still do not have a language to describe what Lidia is up to because Lidia, actually, isn't up to anything. How does one speak of an activity that features attentiveness, which culminates in the joining of touching and seeing? This is a mode that can distinguish between what is seen but not held or grasped. Indeed, the moment of touch as sight, and touch as non-grasping, is what separates Lidia's mode of interaction from the others in the film. Lidia understands that what she sees cannot be made her own and that is as true of her stroll across Milan as it is in her relationship with Giovanni. Such a moment of diminished grasping comes to stand in for a mode of being that is attentive and receptive.

How are these moments caught on film and so communicated to the spectator? Antonioni frequently employs a visual strategy of parataxis that limits the construction of hierarchies across the film. He does this primarily in his staging of scenes. Describing a winter scene he witnessed in Rimini of two impoverished children playing and singing, Antonioni writes: "The words were absurd at such a time, in the mouths of those characters, but the tone was not. I must say it had a kind of mystery. And that's a limit when staging scenes: forcing words into events which reject them."[55] Here and elsewhere Antonioni uses montage and shifts in points of view to make identification with what a character sees difficult, but also what the camera itself is seeing or doing. Causal relations among shots and sequences become disjointed such that the spectator is continually thrown back on the experience that she is watching a film. The effect is akin to pulling the rug out from under the spectator in order to show a form that doesn't avoid what is onscreen, by choosing to blame Lidia or Giovanni or for that matter Antonioni. It's when the spectator's attention has been provoked that a shared commonality with Lidia emerges, one located in the shared attention of both to what does not resist the paratactic moves, the cuts, the long takes, and pans that more often than not go nowhere. Like Lidia, the spectator is learning how to see and to hold images paratactically and not in a hierarchy of meaning.[56]

Antonioni has given us with Lidia a form of life at ease in not mastering what is seen. Lidia walks as she talks as she holds, without any regard for ranking what she sees or touches. Indeed, the impression is of a hand that sees. This ability to move across a cityscape or a party seeing but not mastering, is juxtaposed to those who can only speak about what they see (and here we note how often mastery in the film is linked to speech, to what Giovanni and the others can say about a particular event, book, or context). If, for Adorno, parataxis is one of the principal ways that gratitude emerges, then gratitude will be found in the mode with which Lidia touches, holds, but not grasps. And no moment better captures the features of gratitude than when Lidia strolls across Milan.

As we know, parataxis responds to subordinate construction, the weighing of priorities, of what deserves attention, and so becomes a principal tonic for weakening mastery. This is because in order to master one first has to be able to create order based upon the looking and classifying of objects, be they objects of thought or of the hand; weighing them and then opting for one or another.[57] For its part, parataxis works against a hierarchy of meanings or things from which a hand chooses. Instead it functions as a rhetorical and ethical practice, which asks that we accept what we perceive and only that. Mapping parataxis in *La notte*, Lidia names the form of life that attends to what is seen and touched without identifying or judging it. There is no seizing of what she sees that comes when the symbol-using animal that is the human being believes what is seen can be translated into symbols. Here the difference between Giovanni and Lidia will consist of Giovanni's domination of the language of symbols, while Lidia appears instead as the form most at ease with non-symbolization.[58]

Peter Brunette comes closest to the relation I want to draw between the forms of life in Antonioni's films and the forms of life that make up spectatorship. Writing of *Blow Up* and the famous tennis match at film's end, a sequence that stills confounds many viewers, myself included, Brunette writes:

> We [the spectators] are part of the way there, in other words, if not the whole way; an act of will, like Hemmings's, can presumably complete the loop of communication. It is also suggested that membership in this group is only a logical extension of film spectatorship itself, through the film apparatus, which, after all, is already dependent on a group understanding of cinematic codes. The camera ostentatiously participates in this construction of meaning from the beginning of this scene, when it "follows" the arc of the invisible ball through the air, over the fence. The camera then comes to rest on a specific point in the grass, implying that even if we cannot see anything there, the camera does, or better, it puts it there, through its very act of attention.[59]

We don't often speak of a camera having the capacity for attention, but that is how Antonioni puts into play the action of the camera. Yet such acts of attention are not limited to filming a ball or a wall or a hand. Rather, in *La notte* and soon enough as we shall see in *L'eclisse*, the apparatus is employed to show the spectator what attention looks like and feels like, introducing her to the pleasures of unfamiliarity.[60] Acts of attention, however, aren't the end all for Antonioni. In fact, they precede what often appears to be the ultimate aim of Antonioni's films: preparing the ground for parataxis because that occurs thanks to a prior moment of attention on the part of the spectator.[61] The apparatus practices acts of attention; the spectator participates in them and thus constructs (or construes) those acts as part of a chain. We may not see anything hidden within Lidia's touch of the wall, but that frame becomes part of a chain whose sense is deeply linked to the spectator's ability to place them side-by-side without joining them together in hypostasis. We, like Lidia, are invited to touch without grasping, and to see how "matter plays along with man."[62]

One final piece remains before pressing on to Antonioni's extended account of attention in *L'eclisse*. Brunette's insight into a community of spectators able to extend attention from the apparatus to themselves suggests a further commonality between Lidia and the spectator as forms of life. Both are able to recognize in parataxis the possibility of attending to how apparatus "plays" (*mitspielt*) with the spectator.[63] Without wanting to overstate the case, we might say that Antonioni's use of the cinematic apparatus to create and prolong attention works to block mimetic repetition, which was integral to the spectator's response from the dawn of cinema today. Parataxis, for its part, makes it difficult to identify with any one element of what is seen. This is especially true in *La notte* for there the spectator struggles to identify with anyone onscreen, thanks to the mutual intensification and deintensification of some features of the apparatus's power.[64] With few point of view shots and Hollywood cuts to elide suture, the spectator struggles to identify with one form over another, save for Lidia, precisely because she too must let go. Rather, Antonioni is intent on creating a relation between a form of life onscreen and off with the apparatus's act of attention.

Furthermore, let's recall that for many, such as René Girard, it is precisely mimetic repetition that causes violence.[65] If that is the case, then in *La notte* we face a cinema that is trying to do something radically different. The issue is not the human being distinguished by mimetic repetition, but instead the human animal, which becomes more attentive. Such an animal doesn't imitate or act immediately because it now believes utterly in what it sees. Antonioni is proposing a critique of the acquisitive desire of certain forms of life that want what they see and the time they need to get it. Nearly everyone in *La notte* asserts their mastery by making what is outside theirs through acts of appropriation, none more so than Giovanni. Lidia differs as hers is not an imitative mode of being, but one based on the possibilities that inhere in touch for an anti-mimetic, anti-imitative form of life—this because touch is a less mimetic act than sight. With that said, Antonioni doesn't give us a purely anti-mimetic model to follow, but rather creates conditions such that the spectator might opt for a mode of viewership that might, upon reflection, resemble Lidia's. In the possibility of choosing to be attentive, Antonioni provides something like Adorno's momentum for the spectator, namely that in not continually being forced to identify and desire what we see onscreen, we are led to seek other possibilities.

L'ECLISSE

Much of what I've written to this point may be little more than a prologue to a film that continues to enchant viewers more than fifty years since it first appeared. L'eclisse speaks to many of the issues I have raised here and builds in profound ways on questions related to gratitude and forms of life. As before, I put Antonioni's perspective in the larger service of reading how forms of life onscreen touch, hold, and fail to grasp. This film, in particular, points to reciprocity and forms of life that encapsulate what has come before while looking to more generous forms of life to come.

L'eclisse differs from L'avventura and La notte to the degree in which the film wants to make equivalent forms of life and degrees of holding. As was the case in the previous films, L'eclisse pivots on reciprocity, only more intensely. In L'eclisse, we see forms come into being; we see how they experience duration in the mode of their grip. And yet the film is no easily sung hymn to letting go. Instead, Antonioni visually associates forms of holding with forms of life, with those forms associated with appropriation on one side, while on the other, a form of holding embodied in Monica Vitti's Vittoria, who offers non-appropriation, affect, and non-grasping as touchstones.

Three questions will guide my discussion of the film and the forms of life therein. First, if we were to speak of milieu as we did previously with Visconti's La terra trema, how might we describe it here? What arrangement of forces presents a problem to the film's protagonists as well as to the spectator? Second, what practices does the film encourage as a response to such a disposition of forces? And lastly, what role does gratitude play, both as a new form of exchange, and as an impetus for the transformation of future forms of life?

The arrangement of forces in the film's milieu is admittedly difficult to discern. In a number of opening shots, we witness what apparently are the final moments of a breakup between Riccardo and Vittoria (we note in passing that this very nearly is where *La notte* left off). In what some have called a mannered approach, Antonioni delivers a variety of perspectives on the physical and emotional distance separating the couple.[66] There is much more to these scenes, however, than merely filming a space to mirror the personal distance between Ricardo and Vittoria; I will want to refer to these moments again in terms of defamiliarization as I did in the earlier pages dedicated to *L'avventura*. Here, as there, the spectator is separated from what transpires in the scene by the freeing of the cinematic apparatus from its prior uses so as to elicit attention and waiting in the spectator. The lack of smooth suturing, the self-conscious montage, the holding of certain angles—filming from above Vitti's head on more than one occasion—all contribute to a feeling of defamiliarization (see Figure 5-10).[67] Why? For some, like Roland Barthes, it is a question of pertinence:

> For you, contents and forms are equally historical; dramas, you have said, are plastic as much as psychological. The social, the narrative, the neurotic are just levels—pertinences, as they say in linguistics—of the *world as a whole*, which is the object of every artist's work; there is a succession of interests, not a hierarchy.[68]

For others the scene and the film itself more generally showcase a simulacrum: We, the spectators, experience the alienation that the characters onscreen feel; in both cases perceived reality becomes unreasonable or off-putting.[69] We see this in one of the first scenes of the film in which Vittoria rearranges the objects that before had been framed (see Figure 5-11), all eerily accompanied by the sound of her footsteps and the noise of the fans.

No one reason comes to mind when we try to locate the cause for their break-up. It isn't as if Vittoria seems unreasonable, nor does Riccardo for that matter. Yet there is a creeping, abstract feel to the proceedings, one that gives the spectator the sense of a social order that isn't at all interested in allowing the film's protagonists to make sense of what is happening around them. The awkward shots, a stillness intensified by the rhythm of the fan, soon give way to the abstract movement of the Borsa. Everyone here appears to have had one espresso too many; the movement never ends. In ways different from Visconti's use of the photograph of the Cyclopean

Figure 5-10. L'eclisse

Figure 5-11. L'eclisse

Islands, Antonioni uses movement in the Borsa sequences not only to attribute to these forms of life a mobility that was missing with the fishermen of Acitrezza, but also to match the movement of the camera with the movement of objects and bodies onscreen. That the movement takes place in the confined space of the Borsa contributes obviously to the film's sense of speed, but also to claustrophobia that characterizes all of the sequences there.[70] So much of the film's action takes place here as well, and it is where we are introduced to Piero, a cross between a gopher and a trader in stocks in an era of telephones before computers. The Borsa and the particular form of reciprocity it stands for make up the principal situation to which L'eclisse responds. Over the years, these details of the film, however, have given way to what most people remember—a series of startling images at the end of the film, in what has become the film's signature moment: a seven-minute epilogue filmed across the major locations of the film, but now bereft of the presence of the protagonists.[71]

How does Antonioni respond in L'eclisse to the forms of life associated with holding and reciprocity associated with the Borsa and the form of life featured there? The response is in no way straightforward. First, Antonioni conflates Monica Vitti, the actor, who is subject to the apparatus, and Vittoria, who is placed in opposition to the forms of life associated with the home of financial capital. He does so by focusing continually, even obsessively on Vitti. Yet this is more than an obsession. Antonioni places Vitti in the center of the apparatus's attention—to pick up on Brunette's earlier analysis—in order to emphasize her vulnerability. Vitti's response will offer the spectator visual clues in how to practice a cinematic techne that is able to counter the power of the apparatus to capture her. In the apparatus's attempts to shape and mold Vitti's life, a conflict arises and with it an environment in which such conflict is managed. On one hand, we have the technological conditions of the apparatus, and on the other, the result of that environment, Vittoria/Vitti. What features characterize the environment of which she is the reaction, and then how might we think about her response in terms of reciprocity?

The environment of which Vitti is a part prominently features a mobile point of view, indeed a desperately mobile one, the effect of which is to set off the form of holding and life that characterize Vittoria.[72] The same is true of the apparatus. Moving seemingly of its own accord, the camera adopts points of view that go nowhere or are employed simply because they are available. The camera moves constantly, leering at its female protagonist just as it did in *La notte* or willfully taking up angles and positions that seemingly go nowhere. The impression is of an unstoppable need to look, see, and possess. That, too, is another feature of Antonioni's emphasis on the ability of the camera to position itself in order to capture movement. But just as Paul Virilio recognized three decades ago when writing about speed and control, Antonioni also recognizes the connection between speed and possession in *L'eclisse*.[73] The camera cannot stop looking and possessing, cannot stop trying to master what it sees and what we see. The camera thinks and possesses.[74]

This insistence on looking as possessing stands in for the kind of mastering associated with the film's perspective on financial capitalism. The milieu of the film—circulation of money, people, and emotions—is matched by the speed of the apparatus with its different angles, shots, and cuts. It becomes one of the principal ways by which the cinematic apparatus collaborates in the creation of the film's milieu. The apparatus shows objects and persons flitting across the screen, and as it does so, the spectator experiences the speed as well as the sheer mobility of the cinematic apparatus. Indeed, at times Antonioni appears to be celebrating the apparatus's ability to film whenever and from whatever perspective is available to it at that moment. Moreover, nearly every frame of the film acknowledges the power of the apparatus not simply to see, but to make what it sees its own by insisting on and promoting different perspectives. Antonioni clearly understands the possibilities provided by the cinematic apparatus, and employs it in the service of filming and appropriating what it sees. In *L'eclisse*, the apparatus moves and looks wherever and whenever it wants, which is true even or especially at the film's conclusion, when the apparatus returns to earlier places and spaces *sans* the film's protagonists.[75]

For all that, the cinematic apparatus differs from other apparatuses as it also provides a strategy for responding to a certain alignment of forces. In *L'eclisse*, the response to a milieu of grasping will be found in the exchanges between the apparatus and the character of Vittoria, or better the persona of Vittoria as played by Vitti. Vitti had been featured in Antonioni's two previous films, but nothing prepares the viewer for the kind of responsibility she has in the film.[76] For long stretches, she is the object of both the apparatus as well as the object of Piero and Ricccardo's gaze. The question Antonioni is posing by conflating Vitti and Vittoria concerns how an object of an apparatus might elude the attempt to hold in place the object of the grip, whether it is that of the apparatus or that of the possessive form of life known as the stockbroker.

On one hand, Vitti, the actor, exists as a foil to the cinematic apparatus itself. In a milieu of incessant movement, Vitti literally holds her own, by which I mean that she faces her capture by the apparatus head-on; she acknowledges the reality of the power of the apparatus to capture her and to be framed by it.[77] She responds not by evading the gaze but by accepting it, which by no means suggests that she acquiesces to it. Instead she deflects.[78] The impression noted in her gaze, which hovers just outside the camera lens or in her use of the window to evade Piero's desire in a later scene, is that Vitti and Vittoria are responding to a lightning-quick apparatus.[79] There is something undeniably forensic about Vitti's performance. She meets the apparatus directly with her gaze and then pivots, avoiding, or absenting herself from the frame, in her by now classic gaze that flits above the camera while a sly smile moves across her face (see Figure 5-12).

Thus the formal situation posed in *L'eclisse* lines up this way: Given the increasing power of the cinematic apparatus to reflect perspectives not linked to specific points of view, more, much more is required of the actor.

Figure 5-12. L'eclisse

When one is the object of an apparatus, what possible attitudes toward the apparatus can be adopted? In *L'eclisse*, Vitti is absolutely the object of the apparatus, and just as clearly Vitti surely recognizes the increasing power of the apparatus to make her the focus of its attention. In lieu of surrendering to the apparatus's capacity to make visible from different perspectives, however, she acknowledges its power and at the same time absents herself by accepting and then elaborating the conflation between herself; Vitti, the actor; and Vittoria, the protagonist of the film.[80] Where there is no conflict between the milieu of the film—the boom years in Italy—and the characters, and no conflict between the increasing power of the cinematic apparatus and the actors filmed, there can be no I or self that is a reaction to it. Both Vitti, the actor, and Vittoria, the character, become forms of life that not only pay attention, but also are forms at peace with the milieu in which they are located.[81] Each frame requires different responses and in the flurry of those responses, the commonalities among them add up to a form of life.[82]

The form of life that attends to and accepts the perspectives that Antonioni adopts is able to evade the apparatus. It is a form of life that by embracing defamiliarization is able to create an interval in which no conflict between milieu and form can be observed. We shouldn't be surprised, therefore, at Vitti's fortitude in managing responses or for that matter in Antonioni's increasing identification with the power of the apparatus.[83] A quick look at Antonioni's *Screentest* in *I tre volti* reveals a director searching for actors capable enough of withstanding the power of the apparatus. There can be no hope of possessing an identity when the apparatus is humming along so intensely. Instead, in *L'eclisse*, Vitti's strategy is to fight against moments of capture while seeking opportunities to forget (or dare we say forgive) the apparatus. The responses she adopts are those that work against identification, where we understand identification as a form of possession, be it of self, the other, or the performance. In other words, faced with domination by the apparatus, Vitti doesn't assert her own mastery; or better, her own mastery will be measured in the ability not to hold her own against the apparatus. Much will depend upon the expressiveness of her face.[84]

Admittedly, such moments are difficult to describe because we continue to be habituated to a language that involves strength, resistance, and power. Difficult, too, since so much of the spectator's response to Vitti's non-response (or constantly morphing response) begins with surface impressions and experience. With that said, when framed and filmed in a context of being possessed, Vitti's strategy is to hold on to what has been called the "alienating power" of the apparatus.[85] She offers the possibility of moving out from under, of discounting the apparatus's ability to make visible by making her image the center of focus. This is no mastery over the apparatus, a fight to the death. Her response, rather, is to see each shot, each frame, as a new situation requiring a response that accepts the power asymmetry and then to work out from within to become actual, that is to hold open an interval in which no conflict can lead to no self as a reaction to the apparatus.[86]

The reader will perhaps have heard in the preceding sentence an echo of those earlier sections in which attention, open spaces, and play were featured in Winnicott's investigation of transitional phenomena. To the growing power of the apparatus and the willingness of its human operators to allow it to capture ever more of the visible, Vitti responds by playing. If play can be conceptualized through the notion of attending, understood as a reaching out so as to compose the field of experience, here much will depend on the way that the Vitti/Vittoria attends to the apparatus as a potential plaything and thus as an occasion for repeatedly practicing attention.[87] Typically, she will play with the apparatus mostly by looking nearly directly at the camera, unobtrusively so, naturally so, using her eyes and her face to receive the attention of the camera, by accepting that the camera is intent on taking something from her (in Italian the camera is a machine that grabs, *macchina da presa*).

In the series of moments in which some thing, her image is being taken, Vitti communicates to the audience as well as to the camera and to the eye of Antonioni that this taking is not taking when one accepts that this is the nature of "what is"—when one accepts the ontological stakes of being the object of the apparatus. We register it in the series of frames before she wafts out of the frame before *L'eclisse*'s coda (see Figures 5-13 and 5-14). We see it when she adopts different masks when playing with her friends, and we see it in the way that she responds to another kind of *macchina da presa*, Piero, who is intent on making love to her. To see how she plays with the apparatus, we need only look closely at these moments with Piero: the feints behind and between the windows, the giving up of ground—seemingly—and then the moving out from under his grasp. This isn't so surprising given the frequency with which the apparatus, the *macchina da presa*, grasps at Vitti.

Figure 5-13. L'eclisse

Figure 5-14. L'eclisse

VITTI, VITA, VITE

This isn't the only element of ontological play that the film privileges. In a milieu of increasing circulation—of goods and bodies moving, of seemingly irresistible forces pushing bodies left and right, out of spaces of interior spaces and into others—another space centers around Vittoria's placement within and interaction with the other elements of the *mise-en-scène*. Vittoria resides at the heart of the film precisely because she seems immune to those forms of life associated with the financial capitalism: of savings lost and futures denied.[88] Antonioni does this by superimposing the apparatus of the *Borsa* on the cinematic apparatus, which is to say that he repeatedly has Alain Delon's Piero stand in for the apparatus. This is not just a question of the male gaze that joins Antonioni to Piero, but rather the attempt by two apparatuses to hold Vitti/Vittoria's image. The key to understanding Vitti's response as Vittoria is to frame this action precisely in terms of reciprocity, which is to say, how she responds to taking.

Across the film, Antonioni shows Vittoria in moments in which her relation to the objects of the *mise-en-scène* are highlighted.[89] We see her repeatedly handling and manipulating objects in the frame and depending upon that interaction, the ontological status and the form of life onscreen change. Said differently, the relationality she brings to the film depends in large measure on gesture. In this way, ontologies come into view that were unavailable when she failed to play. Vittoria attends to objects; she investigates through touch a different realm of experience that wasn't available to her in the opening interlude, though clearly there, too, in her handling of the frame, touch is foregrounded. The intimacy with objects is decisive as it creates a tension between the mode of taking that defines the *macchina da presa* and another mode that limits taking or the demand that a gift be made, which nearly amounts to the same thing.

Antonioni is inviting the spectator to think about the power of the *Borsa* and the cinematic apparatus, and their respective capacities to create hierarchies between those who take and those who are forced to give. Vitti/Vittoria responds to both by continuously searching for the limits of the frame in which she finds herself. The impression is of a subterranean film that parallels Vittoria's encounter with Piero, in which Vittoria must establish "what is."[90] We see her struggle in a variety of sequences across the film, none more important than her visits to the Borsa. Here Vittoria graphs through touch the contours of the milieu in which she finds herself. Why else does she continue to remind herself of what is by touching that which she sees are walls, columns, and people? Are they solid and if they aren't, what is the nature of the I or ego that touches them? It is this attempt

Figure 5-15. L'eclisse

Figure 5-16. L'eclisse

to fix and weight the solidity of objects that distinguishes Vittoria from all the others in the film (see Figures 5-15 and 5-16).

ON GESTURE

In what may seem counterintuitive, Vitti, the actor, responds to the apparatus by embracing what in an earlier moment of cinema studies was referred to as alienation. She does this through gesture as a response to the incessant demand that she be seen. But her encounter with the apparatus does not begin and end there. In that encounter, Vitti/Vittoria's ontological status changes, becoming something more than merely Vitti, the actor. By constantly reaching out and attending to the frame and so testing the boundaries of what the apparatus registers, Vitti/Vittoria responds in a mode of non-taking and non-giving that encompasses the newness of the situation in which she finds herself. It is a situation to be clear in which Antonioni pushes the inhuman nature of the apparatus to the extreme, with long takes, different and off center shots, etc. He intensifies tremendously the cinematic apparatus's ability to capture. Vitti/Vittoria names the living form that responds to the apparatus by noting just how impossible the situation is.[91]

Vitti/Vittoria is continually asked to compose herself; to respond to the increasing power of the financial and cinematic apparatus. Two examples display this form of life's ability to respond in the moment by being present to the power and force of the apparatuses in play. The first occurs in a scene I described earlier with Piero. Here, Vittoria plays with and plays off of Piero's advances by feint, by using objects, in particular a window so as to keep him away. She passionately kisses him through a windowpane and then escapes from under his arms to fight another day. For his part, Piero's seduction is direct, linear, and does not involve play. On the contrary, he attempts to grab hold of her and that is what lingers, especially the moment when the seduction appears to be reaching its climax. Then Antonioni, in a visual trope of what separates Vittoria from Piero, focuses on Piero's hand that grips the sheet while he is trying to make love to her (see Figure 5-17). Antonioni sets Vittoria off from Piero in the sequence in two ways: first in close-ups of her hand and the openness with which she holds Piero's pen, and in the repeated framing of her hands as open (see Figure 5-18 and 5-19). Antonioni composes Vittoria as different from Piero to the degree that her grip, her hold, is freer, more open, and without pressure.

Figure 5-17. L'eclisse

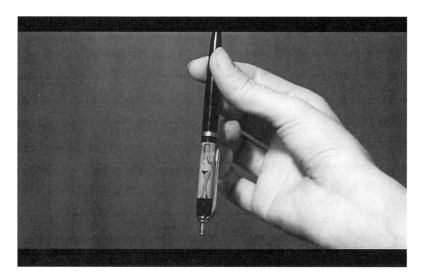

Figure 5-18. L'eclisse

Figure 5-19. L'eclisse

Now let's turn to Vitti. In these same scenes, the actor must fend off an apparatus that is obsessively intent on capturing her from nearly every angle. This is an apparatus that follows Vitti much like Piero follows Vittoria. Both are marked by the hope of a moment of consummation, of perfect capture. But this is more than an *Urtrext* for a slasher film—Antonioni's camera is fantastically powerful in these shots and throughout the film, by which I mean, the apparatus, is able to provide a an extremely well-lit and intensely mobile view of the happenings or actions onscreen (or lack of action, waiting).[92] Such moments reach their zenith in the apartment scenes when Delon and Vitti's response begins to merge with that of Vittoria's. She adopts a number of strategies—slithering out of the frame on occasion or appearing to be more concerned with her immediate surroundings if not with the camera, taking in and playing with objects, walls, and objects. Often, she stays where the camera places her, opening to the power of apparatus that films and frames nearly every inch of her. She offers, however, no mere resistance to the apparatus, but instead something approaching a vulnerability. How does Vitti make herself vulnerable and then why choose to do so?[93]

Her vulnerability concerns a fundamental conflation on her part between her character's position as Vittoria, as the object of desire for the film's protagonists, and Vitti's position as the object of desire and gaze on the part of the apparatus. Both at times seem intent on devouring her; the close-ups of her face, the leering camera, Piero and Roberto's repeated attempts to "have" her. The constant grasping, holding, fixing and fixating of the camera lines up with how all male protagonists in the film interact with her. But something interesting happens. Every moment that Vittoria is made the object of a male gaze, it is as if she begins anew in front of that gaze, as if she doesn't recall or refuses to draw on the past moments of capture by the apparatus or these gazes—the two are often interchangeable—in order to confront them or when engaging with them. Each moment is new, by which I mean the memory of previous moments, of pasts in the film, and with Antonioni do not lead to accumulation of memories or of time. The effect—and here we will want to take issue with some of Deleuze's reading of Antonioni—is that the ontological status for Vittoria is not contained or named in a becoming (of animal, of plant, of woman), but rather is markedly different from that form that becomes. It isn't that Vittoria becomes better or more adept at dealing with Riccardo or Piero or those who wish to make her an object, who do make her an object. The challenge of the moment is precisely that she meets them openly, without memory.

This distinguishes Vittoria from Piero and Vitti from those actors who accept that there is a prior moment of acting that they can draw on. Previous moments and their recollection cannot be drawn upon. Another way of saying this—the effect of the apparatus, that is the feelings of non-belonging, of losing one's life, that one's image is inexorably taken—underpins Vitti's understanding of the moment of capture. No moment is either cause or effect. The figure of Vittoria measures the ontological moment of actuality in *L'eclisse*; she doesn't seek anything: no result, no arriving at something. Instead, there is attention to what is, in ways that others cannot. Hers is not a desire for gain or remembering, but is instead a shedding of debt and of those things given and received so as to reside in the openness of the moment. To do so she must pay attention.

Her openness is not disciplined according to a previous pattern. The impression is of a bodily form that does not put up walls—a form that isn't weighed down by what it has bought, experienced, or thought prior to that moment. Hers is a mode that foregoes acquiring memories or pasts—be they money, property, beliefs about the past—and instead is one that focuses on the present unburdened by previous missteps. In other words, she doesn't receive from the past to anchor the present, but instead is open to what interacting with others brings.

Vitti/Vittoria lets go of previous patterns; she has the capacity to be open without regard to what has happened prior to the moment of capture by the apparatus (or holding and having by Piero). She remains alive to an actuality that does not require other moments in the past or future in order to close that moment down. If a shorthand of that constitutive openness of Vitti/Vittoria in the film exists, it will be found in what amounts to an iconography of the hand—of hands open, closed, touching, and closing.[94] And in this refrain of identifying forms of holding and openness with the protagonists of the film, Antonioni transforms hands themselves nearly into living beings.

OPEN, VULNERABLE, SMILING

Vitti/Vittoria's form of life features an ontological openness found in interactions with objects, things, and others. Her response is to see or touch her way to whatever it is that is on the other side in front of her; capturing her, trying to have her. What is it that sets this form of life apart?

First, Antonioni highlights shots from the back of Vitti's head that make it difficult to recognize her. "Vitti" is not on display, or she is not on display in the typical sense. Often the back of her head is framed in such a way that the spectator assumes that it is actually a face we are seeing. She faces away from the camera, which is key for Antonioni, but also that she doesn't shy away from it.

Second, Vitti's form of life is one that continually attempts to determine the tactile features of the environment. This isn't about the character's psychological profile, which alas has been featured again and again in readings of *Red Desert*, for instance, but instead concerns the use of the senses, especially the tactile to complement the visual. This lines up with Lidia's form of life in *La notte*, namely the attempt to combine the tactile with the visual in such a way as to show the spectator a form of life that could resemble her own. This is a poignant form of life that is curious without seeking—that is not content merely to see, or to see at a distance.

Third, this is a form of life less interested in drawing upon knowledge to engage with the actual, where actuality names not some theoretical space that exists to be thought or to be accounted for in some future already mapped according to an ideal or belief. Vitti/Vittoria performs in the sense of perform as that which carries out the form of life, but also that which completes the form of life by means of addition, because addition concerns the summing of the visual with the tactile.[95] It is this performance of the visual and tactile that allows Vitti/Vittoria to "be" new in every moment—that foregoes and forgets the past and future so as to leave unconditioned the present. This form of life opens to the present so that what is received is not interpreted or held in such a way as to keep the past in thrall to the present or vice versa.

Emblematic of such a constitutive openness to what is given but not taken or made properly one's own is the repeated visual trope of the hand. Truly, Vitti's hands in *Eclipse* are living beings.[96] They have a life of their own, touching, feeling, moving across walls, doors, and objects; this is not some prosthetic god of the Freudian variety, but instead is a form of life placed front and center in terms of the film's narrative and as well as with Vitti's engagement with the apparatus. Her response is to see and touch her way to whatever it is that is on the other side that is trying to have her. In this refusal to hold or grasp, Vitti/Vittoria becomes the *mancus par excellance.*

This may not strike anyone as a strategy worth trying, especially given that the apparatus in question is cinema and not the more powerful apparatuses out to capture us today. Others may respond that, translations of *dispositif* into apparatus notwithstanding, it isn't at all clear how moving to embracing the *mancus* does anything other than shuffle the cards. And as we know only too well, the house always wins. Responses such as these fail, however, to acknowledge the radical potential that inheres in the *mancus* precisely because of the power of grip to encompass all forms of possession, including transitional objects.[97] To reduce ideology to possession and to how tightly we hold on will be seen by some as the epitome of reduction, and so both dangerous and naive. Yet, if possession is nine-tenths of the law as the maxim runs,[98] then it is the one-tenth that deserves more scrutiny. What Vitti/Vittoria, Lidia and Valentina, and Claudia all convey is that foregoing even the slightest amount of holding means to perceive differently in the present and so with it less time is accumulated. For it is ultimately time that an apparatus is accumulating, time through images, time as image, and not just the time-image as Deleuze would have it. And it is accumulated time that conditions responses both in the spectator and the actor.

Furthermore, in these films from Antonioni, the interval between touch and grip, the intermediate area for Winnicott, is also the space between appropriation and dispossession, the space of play for the *mancus*. It is a space that Antonioni and the women protagonists continually try to hold open. In that tension between gripping and gripping less, opportunities can be gleaned for the spectator to practice Adorno's *tatikos*. Where content depends upon a fate held tightly, sequences, parataxis, absence, seduction—form—means opening. That is the final interpretation on which I want to close. Fate: the gratitude that comes unbidden to a form of life that has understood the advantages of holding lightly.

CONCLUSION: ATTENTION, NOT AUTOPSY

Where do the preceding pages lead when it comes to gratitude and the *mancus*? Two places, I think. The first is that the *mancus*, rather than simply being at a loss or identifying with the loss of hands, is transformed into a figure whose lack of hands is precisely what makes the evasion of exchange and gift possible, that what might seem a disability is what allows the development of attention and vulnerability. The *mancus* flits across most of the films' protagonists discussed here to the degree that their vulnerability—to hold, to be held, but not to have—finds an echo in the spectator. An apparatus that has become more powerfully ontological demands lessons in freedom from the hunted, one of which is precisely how to meet the power of the apparatus by lessening the degree to which the object holds the self, other objects, and the apparatus itself. Given the impossibility of negating the apparatus's impropriety, the asymmetry between the actor and the camera often can force the latter into a playful stance vis-à-vis the apparatus by highlighting the actions that draw out how the actor holds and grips. The effect frequently is to transform the actor into a form of life, one characterized principally by grip and the possibility of softening it. This will be the form of life that attends without identifying, receives without possessing, and accepts without acquiescing. Essentially, a drama is being played out between the camera's power to capture actors and in turn to dialectically make visible forms of life that, thanks to the missing edge of their own grip, play with the apparatus as if it were a transitional object among many. In the creative tension between the *mancus* and the apparatus, the spectator witnesses the possibilities afforded the attentive form of life able and willing to forego grips and thus mastery.

In a fragment from Anaxagoras that he quotes in *Parts of Animals*, Aristotle has the former observe that hands are what make men intelligent and wise:

> Now it is the opinion of Anaxagoras that the possession of these hands is the cause of man being of all animals the most intelligent. But it is more rational to suppose that man has hands because of his superior intelligence. For the hands are instruments, and the invariable plan of nature in distributing the organs is to give each to such animal as can make use of it; nature acting in this matter as any prudent man would do. For it is a better plan to take a person who is already a flute-player and give him a flute, than to take one who possesses a flute and teach him the art of flute-playing.[1]

We might modify the terms of the passage along the following lines: Wisdom lies not only in the hands whose grip makes tools possible, but also in the consequences that follow when a grip is released, when hands are not considered as merely possessions. This suggests a further possibility for interpreting the films under discussion here. The spectator is asked to lessen the grip over what she believes is transpiring. In that lessening, the *mancus* onscreen encounters the potential *mancus* of the spectator in the shared commonality of non-identification. Shared wisdom is found in the reaching without grasping that Mara, Edmund, Vittoria, and the spectator share—to attend to what is seen without arriving on the scene constantly ready to perform an autopsy.[2] An ontological space comes into being in which the spectator as form of life and the character onscreen as potential form of life meet. That commonality between them is made possible because of the nature of the cinematic apparatus, whose power in forcing identification with the character onscreen can also be employed in reverse—to create a commonality in the mode of viewing, of seeing, of holding. This is not about seeing per se, or if it is, it is seeing meant to be dispersed into other sensory possibilities.

This explains why I don't believe that these films despair about politics. The films make clear that no ending is ever final. They also make clear that some films more than others laugh at the seriousness with which the spectator is dead set on proposing a tragic perspective on the film's ultimate meaning. The common *mancus* is in this sense deeply comic; a living thing that is unable to accept a gift is thus able to avoid the calculation of exchange, and so is able to interrupt the circuit of exchange and calculation. The *mancus* gives and receives without hands and so foregoes a tight holding of the thing given, of possessing as opposed to merely holding. "The first point to which attention should be called," observes Henri Bergson, "is that the comic does not exist outside the pale of what is strictly HUMAN. A landscape may be beautiful, charming, and sublime, or insignificant and ugly; it will never be laughable."[3]

Second, how do we understand gripping and grasping in relation to the fear that biopower and a mythical violence generate across our lives?[4] Antonioni, Rossellini, and Visconti invite us to observe how a form of life onscreen can withstand the capture of an apparatus and elaborate a cinematic techne, one that the spectator can make out for herself. Such a form of life emerges out of a visual language game that would not have fate as its only possible result. The reason has to do with the relation of attention to the gift: the *mancus* as the form of life that in being unable to accept the gift, is forced to touch, hold, and caress with its eyes. Unable to hold the gift the *mancus* interrupts the circuit of exchange that has come to inflate the gift as well as debt. Can there be any doubt that today less debt accrues when one refuses the improper gifts of neoliberalism, or understands that proper gifts are those that cannot be received with one's hands? Such is the realm of the comic today, namely a mode of giving and taking that is impossible. This is not to say that one doesn't make the effort, but only that with less grip, possession drifts.

Cinema can provide us with an experience in which the form of life that grips less becomes visible thanks to the power of apparatus to capture life. Here, too, the *mancus* emerges as the figure par excellence of a certain kind of spectator and form of life. Cinema is the dream and the magician who hypnotizes, but that is only a part of what the apparatus does. Cinema is no one-way ticket, something that only takes, but also prepares the spectator to give in a certain way. This giving ultimately concerns attention and the ability of the apparatus to instill a refusal of gift-giving. Or better, the gift the cinematic apparatus gives is the one that doesn't always require a gift in return. This isn't the gift that is demanded of us, which is to say that there can be no community of spectators, or if there is, who would willingly choose to be a part of it? Attention doesn't require a tight grip—indeed tight grips are lessened precisely in the light of attention. If we were to relay this in Nietzschean fashion, we might describe an *agon* in which the apparatus as adversary makes noble the form of life onscreen and off.

The Earth Trembles, Germany Year Zero, and Antonioni's trilogy display a visual language meant to convince us to join the ranks of the *mancus*. The irony of this will not be lost on the reader. In a film such as *Eclipse* in which Vitti/Vittoria does nothing *per se* except feel her way in and across the *mise-en-scène*, a form of life comes to her unbidden thanks to what is onscreen, what is shown with her. This form of life is the one that precedes other forms to the degree that it lingers before possessing and being possessed. To be clear, this is not the Heideggerean form of life destined to be mastered by technology, but rather the one who avoids mastery and being mastered because it has opted to grip less—to see less tightly across all the different registers, metaphorical and otherwise, that concern how it holds. It is able to do this because no event precedes the instance of holding or being held; no edge of the self, or of the I becomes available when possession has been forestalled.

The actions and non-actions that make up this form of life's grip we may want to refer to, following Kant, as a kind of schema.[5] And the reason has to do with schema naming a constellation of acts that together create a momentum able to evade fate (at this juncture we might recall that the Greek word for schema originates in the Greek *ékhein*, which counts among its numerous meanings "hold" as well as "to echo").[6] What changes if we emphasize degrees of holding that anchor conceptions of form, self, apparatus, and fear? To practice repeatedly an *ékhein* based on attending to and lessening grip when faced with the power of the proliferation of apparatuses lessens the fatedness of capture and so doing emancipates precisely because one holds less tightly. Such a practice begins with the acknowledgment of a possible gratitude that may result from not gripping so tightly onto causes, objects, masks, and selves.

What does it mean to attend to *ékhein* as holding, gripping, seeing? The first step is located in becoming comfortable with the translation of form of life as holding across different registers, be they the visual or, more broadly, interactions with the other; a willingness to employ holding as a rubric for making sense of our encounters of things and others. By translating our actions in terms of the grip, we allow for greater vulnerability to arise, greater affectivity, greater openness to being affected, and to experiencing not-knowing. For that in some way is what vulnerability in an ontology of holding will mean—being at ease with not knowing. We move closer to such a perspective in acknowledging the commonality we share with the protagonists onscreen. We begin to sense the joy that the form of life with no hands enjoys. At this stage, holding is no longer mere metaphor (if it ever was), but has been translated ethically into a form of life whose very form upends the basis of neoliberal gift-giving. Cinema becomes the site in which that transformation is most readily felt, given the power of the cinematic apparatus to create visual identifications with what is seen onscreen. At the same time, that power can be reversed into techne by which the spectator, by attending, comes to wait for the vicissitudes of identification.

In a famous transcript of an analytic session, Winnicott recounts a number of episodes with a patient suffering from regression. In the last episode recounted, the analyst reports that the patient "had been seriously disturbed because he had had a *headache*, quite different from any that he had had before . . . *It was as if it were situated outside the head*." Winnicott's response arrives as a flash. "The pain being just outside the head represents your need to have your head held as you would naturally have held it if you were in a state of deep emotional distress as a child." Winnicott reaches the following conclusion: "Whenever we understand a patient in a deep way and show that we do so by a correct and well-timed interpretation we are in fact holding the patient."[7] The same practice of holding as interpreting and interpreting as holding underpins many of my attempts in the preceding pages to read the violence of exchange, of gifts that cannot be refused, and apparatuses often hell-bent on seizing. It is all in the holding.

ACKNOWLEDGMENTS

I would not have been able to write this book without the kindnesses of numerous friends. I wish to thank Thomas Lay, Davide Tarizzo, Roberto Esposito, Simona Forti, Jacques Lezra, Richard Morrison, Adriana Cavarero, Rosi Braidotti, Peter Fitzpatrick, Daniela Angelucci, Felice Cimatti, Gregg Lambert, Cary Wolf, Adam Sitze, Mitchell Greenberg, Enzo Traverso, Magali Molini, Karen Pinkus, Ida Dominijanni, Patrick Hanafin, Laura Chiesa and the students in her graduate seminar on film at the University of Buffalo, Premesh Lalu as well as the students at the University of Cape Town, Lorenzo Fabbri, Kevin Attell, Christopher GoGwilt, Annika Thiem, and Julia Chryssostalis. My thanks go as well to the two anonymous reviewers whose comments on the draft manuscript were deeply helpful as I set about revising the book.

Gratitude is fundamentally a touchy subject and so *un'abbracciatona* to Ale, Nico, and Michela.

As I was completing the manuscript, my friend Helen Tartar, Editorial Director of Fordham University Press, perished in an automobile accident. It was Helen to whom I first spoke of the idea of writing a book for the "Commonalities" series. I recall telling her at the 2014 MLA how much I really wanted to write a book on gratitude and cinema. Her wise and generous response put me at ease, and so it is to her that I dedicate this book.

NOTES

PREFACE: UNCOMMON GRIPS

1. D. W. Winnicott, "Transitional Objects and Transitional Phenomena—A Study of the First Not-Me Possession," in *The International Journal of Psychoanalysis* 34 (1953): 89–97.

2. "Knowledge is possession. Its very object is determined by the fact that it must be taken possession of—even if in a transcendental sense—in the consciousness" (Walter Benjamin, *The Origin of German Tragic Drama*, trans. John Osborne [New York: Verso, 2003], 29).

3. Friedrich Nietzsche, *The Gay Science*, trans. Thomas Common (Mineola, N.Y.: Dover Publications, 2006), 75.

4. "The originality of Italian neo-realism as compared with the chief schools of realism that preceded it and with Soviet cinema, lies in never making reality the servant of some *à priori* point of view . . . Neorealism knows only immanence. It is from appearance only, the simple appearance of beings and of the world, that it knows how to deduce the ideas that it unearths. It is phenomenology" (André Bazin, *What Is Cinema? Volume 2*, trans. Timothy Barnard [Berkeley: University of California Press, 2005], 65).

1. FORMS OF LIFE IN A MILIEU OF BIOPOWER

1. A number of recent authors have investigated the enmeshed nature of biology and power that inhere in biopolitics and biopower. For an anthology of some of these readings, see Timothy Campbell and Adam Sitze, eds., *Biopolitics: A Reader* (Durham: Duke University Press, 2013) as well as Nicolae Morar and Vernon Cisney's forthcoming collection of essays for the University of Chicago Press; Patricia Clough and Craig Wilse, eds. *Beyond Biopolitics: Essays on the Governance of Life and Death* (Durham: Duke University Press, 2011); *Biopolitics: An Advanced Introduction*, ed. Thomas Lemke, Monica Casper, and Lisa Moore (New York:

New York University Press, 2011); and the penetrating reading Laura Bazzicalupo provides of biopower in "The Ambivalences of Biopolitics," in *Diacritics* 36.2 (2008): 109–16.

2. *The Foucault Effect: Studies in Governmentality*, ed. Graham Burchell, Colin Gordon, and Peter Miller (Chicago: University of Chicago Press, 1991). For Negri, see in particular his work with Michael Hardt, especially *Commonwealth* (Cambridge: Harvard University Press, 2009). For Esposito, see *Immunitas: The Protection and Negation of Life*, trans. Zakiya Hanafi (Cambridge: Polity Press, 2011) and *Third Person* (Cambridge: Polity, 2012). Agamben continues to add to his life's work on the figure of *homo sacer*. His most recent volume is *The Highest Poverty: Monastic Rules and Form-of-Life*, trans. Adam Kotsko (Stanford: Stanford University Press, 2013); see, too, what is in my view the single best volume on Agamben's thought: Kevin Attell's *Giorgio Agamben: Beyond the Threshold of Deconstruction* (New York: Fordham University Press, 2014). Adriana Cavarero's most recent work is among her most brilliant: *Inclinazioni: Critica della Rettitudine* (Milano: Raffaello Cortina Editore, 2013). For Forti in English see *New Demons: Rethinking Power and Evil Today*, trans. Zakiya Hanafi (Stanford: Stanford University Press, 2014).

3. Giorgio Agamben, *Homo Sacer: Sovereignty and Bare Life* (Palo Alto: Stanford University Press, 1998). Of the numerous volumes dedicated to Agamben that have appeared, see especially: Sergei Prozorov, *Agamben and Politics: A Critical Introduction* (Edinburgh: Edinburgh University Press, 2014); John Lechte and Saul Newman, *Agamben and the Politics of Human Rights: Statelessness, Images, Violence* (Edinburgh: Edinburgh University Press, 2013); Anat Pick, *Creaturely Poetics: Animality and Vulnerability in Literature and Film* (New York: Columbia University Press, 2011); and Matthew Abbott, "No Life is Bare, The Ordinary Is Exceptional: Giorgio Agamben and the Question of Political Ontology," in *Parrhesia* 14 (2012), 23–36.

4. See Giorgio Agamben, "What Is a Paradigm?" in *The Signature of All Things: On Method*, trans. Luca D'Isanto with Kevin Attell (New York: Zone Books, 2009).

5. Walter Benjamin, "Critique of Violence," in *Selected Writings: Volume 1*, ed. Marcus Bullock and Michael W. Jennings (Cambridge: Harvard University Press, 1996): 236–52.

6. Benjamin, 249–50.

7. Ibid., 252.

8. See the German *Duden* entry for the prefix *-ver* (http://www.duden.de/rechtschreibung/ver_; accessed September 11, 2014) as well as B. Roger Maylor, *Lexical Template Morphology: Change of State and the Verbal Prefixes in German* (Amsterdam: John Benjamins), 10–15.

9. Walter Benjamin, "Zur Kritik der Gewalt," can be found in *Gesammelte Schriften* 2, no.1 (Frankfurt a/Main: Suhrkamp, 1977), 200.

10. See Peter Fitzpatrick, "Homo Sacer and the Insistence of Law," in *Politics, Metaphysics, and Death: Essays on Giorgio Agamben's Homo Sacer*, ed. Andrew Norris (Durham: Duke University Press, 2005), 49.

11. Michel Foucault, *The History of Sexuality Volume 1* (New York: Vintage/Random House, 1990). For Agamben's relation to Foucault, see Mika Ojakangas, "Impossible Dialogue on Bio-power: Agamben and Foucault," in *Foucault Studies* 2 (May 2005): 5–28; as well as *Giorgio Agamben: Sovereignty and Life*, ed. Matthew Calarco and Steven DeCaroli (Palo Alto: Stanford University Press, 2007).

12. "The question is thus: Is there an alternative to the blind accumulation of value? Is there an alternative to the chronic trembling in the instant of taking stock? Is there an alternative to the unrelenting compulsion to pay off one's debts? . . . The Nietzsche-inspired critic of the general economy discovers in the heart of common economic life the transformation of moral guilt through monetary debt," Peter Sloterdijk, *Rage and Time: A Psychopolitical Investigation*, trans. Mario Wenning (New York: Columbia University Press, 2013), 29.

13. Walter Benjamin, "Fate and Character," *Selected Writings Volume 1 (1913–1926)*, 204.

14. The phrase comes, of course, from his *Glengarry Glen Ross*. For a brilliant reading of comedy and some of the "losers" of biopolitics, see Alenka Zupančič's *The Odd One In* (Cambridge: MIT Press, 2008).

15. Benjamin, "Fate and Character," 202.

16. Ibid., 204.

17. Ibid.

18. Ibid., 205.

19. "Heiter," in Friedrich Kluge, *An Etymological Dictionary of the German Language*, trans. John Francis David (London: George Bell & Sons, 1891), 142.

20. Benjamin, "Fate and Character," 205.

21. Ibid.

22. Note Agamben's extended reading of genius in *Profanations* where character gives way to the impersonal and the pre-individuated (Giorgio Agamben, *Profanations*, trans. Jeff Fort [Cambridge: MA, Zone Books, 2007], 12).

23. Michael Hardt and Antonio Negri, *Multitude: War and Democracy in the Age of Empire* (New York: Penguin, 2005).

24. Michael Hardt and Antonio Negri, *Commonwealth* (Cambridge: Harvard University Press, 2009), esp. 369–71.

25. "Tragedy removes the fearful emotions of the soul through compassion and terror. And [he says] that it aims at having a due proportion of fear. It has grief for its mother" (*Tractatus Coislinianus*, in Lane Cooper, *An Aristotelian Theory of Comedy with an Adaptation of the Poetics* [New York: Harcourt, Brace and Company, 1922], 224). And comedy's mother? According to the *Tractatus* that would be laughter.

26. Theodor W. Adorno, *Notes to Literature*, vol. 2, trans. Shierry Weber Nicholsen (New York: Columbia University Press, 1992).

27. Though, to be clear, parataxis appears across Benjamin's work. Ernst Bloch's beautiful reading of philosophy as cabaret in Benjamin's *One-Way Street* comes to mind. See Ernst Bloch, "Philosophy as Cabaret," in *New Left Review* 1.116 (July–August 1979), 94.

28. Quoted in Adorno, 113.

29. Ibid.

30. Adorno, 128–29.

31. Roland Barthes *S/Z: An Essay* (New York: Macmillan, 1975), 98.

32. Émile Benveniste, *Indo-European Language and Society*, trans. Elizabeth Palmer (Coral Gables, FL: University of Miami Press, 1973), 161.

33. Ibid., 161–62.

34. Henry Campbell Black, *A Law Dictionary* (St. Paul: West Publishing, 1910), 710; quoted in Susan S. Levine's "To Have and to Hold: On the Experience of Having an Other," in *The Psychoanalytic Quarterly* 73, 940).

35. "Tenere," http://thelawdictionary.org/tenere/#ixzz2DirD1QBb.

36. "Well, we'll use our comparison with possessing and catching pigeons, and say that there are two kinds of catching: one before one has come to possess a thing, in order to get possession of it, and the other when one possesses it, in order to get hold of what one has possessed for some time and have it in one's hands (Plato, *Theaetetus*, trans. John McDowell [Oxford: Oxford University Press, 2014], 198d).

37. A fine place to begin is with Jeffrey Edwards's "Original Community, Possession, and Acquisition in Kant's Metaphysics of Morals," in *Kant and the Concept of Community*, ed. Charlton Payne and Lucas Thorpe (Rochester: University of Rochester Press, 2011): 150–82.

38. "It is because of this difference between the true possession of the master, and all other detention, that we distinguish two sorts of possession, which are expressed by the words of *civil possession*, and *natural possession* . . . The civil or legal possession is that of the master; and the natural or corporeal possession is that of the persons who have only the bare detention of the thing, such as the usufructuary, the farmer, and others. This possession is called natural or corporeal, because it consists only in the bare natural detention without the right of property," Jean Domat, *The Civil Law in its Natural Order*, trans. William Strahan (Boston: Charles C. Little and James Brown, 1850), 843.

39. Gilles Deleuze, *Nietzsche and Philosophy*, trans. Hugh Tomlinson (New York: Columbia University Press, 2006), 63.

40. Ibid. The passage Deleuze cites can be found at Friedrich Nietzsche, *Will to Power: A New Translation*, trans. Walter Kaufmann and R. J. Hollingdale (New York: Random House, 1967), 339.

41. And this accounts for my unwillingness to follow Derrida in making grip and touch homologous. To grip is not to touch. Writing on the significance of the word tender, Derrida comments: "Let us then repeat the question: what is one doing when one is holding out to the other something that must not come from oneself, that must not belong to who is extending it, and saying "Tiens!" in French, and only in French, thus in a language, which is to say something that in principle cannot be touched? Literally, in saying "Tiens!" (as I would like to do here), one proposes that the other touch, that the other grasp, or seize, or get a grip on him- or herself, but also, in receiving and accepting it, that the other /keep/ what one /extends/ to him or her. Saying "Tiens!" signifying "Tiens!" means holding out or extending, and giving to "touch . . . Touch, more than sight or hearing, gives nearness, proximity— it gives nearby" (Jacques Derrida, *On Touching, Jean-Luc Nancy*, trans. Christine Irizarry [Stanford: Stanford University Press, 2005], 94–95).

42. Kenneth Burke, "Terministic Screens," in *Language as Symbolic Action: Essays on Life, Literature and Method* (Berkeley: University of California Press, 1966), 49.

43. Here, of course, we recall Derrida's reading of Mauss and the gift: "'Mauss does not worry enough about this incompatibility between gift and exchange or about the fact that an exchanged gift is only a tit for tat, that is, an annulment of the gift'" (quoted in Christopher Bracken's *The Potlatch Papers: A Colonial Case History* [Chicago: University of Chicago Press, 1997], 155).

44. Carol M. Rose, "Possession as the Origin of Property" (1985). Faculty Scholarship Series. Paper 1830. http://digitalcommons.law.yale.edu/fss_papers/1830 (accessed September 15, 2014).

45. See Esposito's *Immunitas* as well as Chapters 1 and 4 of *Bios*.

46. Jacques Derrida, *Given Time: I. Counterfeit Money*, trans. Peggy Kamuf (Chicago: University of Chicago Press), 13.

47. The problem, as Todd May points out, is accounting: "It is only when one begins to take account of the giving that there is a problem. Gifts are passed to each other or one another in friendship as time passes in an engrossing movie. In each case, the absorption in what is happening precludes any accounting of that passing. When that accounting happens, it is because there is a problem" (Todd May, *Friendship in Age of Economics: Resisting the Forces of Neoliberalism* [Plymouth: Lexington Books, 2012], 113).

48. Interestingly, Derrida had spoken earlier of the self in terms of the gift when noting the circular nature of economy and exchange. "*Oikonomia* would always follow the path of Ulysses. The latter returns to the side of his loved ones or to himself; he goes away only in view of *repatriating* himself, in order to return to the home from which . . . the signal for departure is given and the part assigned, the side chosen, the lot divided, destiny commanded (*moira*). The being-next-to-self of the Idea in Absolute Knowledge would be odyssean in this sense, that of an *economy* and a *nostalgia*, a 'homesickness,' a provisional exile longing for reappropriation"

(Jacques Derrida, "The Time of the King," in *The Logic of the Gift: Toward an Ethic of Generosity*, ed. Alan D. Schrift [New York: Routledge, 1997], 124).

49. In the terms of Derrida's cinders, the role that attention plays there suggests something similar to what I have in mind. "The citations co-appear along with it, they are "sum moned" [*comparaissent*]: an incomplete archive, still burning or already consumed, recalling certain textual sites, the continuous, tormenting, obsessive meditation about what are and are not, what is meant—or silenced by, cinders. These citations are preceded by the word *animadversio*) which in Latin means "observation," "perception," or "call to attention," and which I chose in homage to the journal *Anima* (Jacques Derrida, *Cinders*, trans. Ned Lukacher [Lincoln: University of Nebraska Press, 1987], 26).

50. Georges Bataille, *The Accursed Share: An Essay on General Economy*, trans. Robert Hurley (New York: Zone Books, 1991), 69.

51. Ibid.

52. Bataille, *The Accursed Share*, 70. On laughter and sacrifice, see Lucio Angelo Privitello's "S/laughter Animal-Lēthē," in *Reading Bataille Now*, ed. Shannon Winnubst (Bloomington: Indiana University Press, esp. 170–75).

53. Ibid., 71.

54. Or translated in terms of potlatch: Is all giving to be understood systemically as potlatch? "The potlatch is structured and constrained because no one can refuse to participate or to be a recipient of a gift, which is indicative of the burden that accompanies any gift. If one refuses to participate, this is indicative of one's fear of having to reciprocate and losing in the exchange" (Olson, 40–41).

55. Bataille, *Accursed Share*, 132.

56. "We could not reach the final object of knowledge without the dissolution of knowledge, which aim is to reduce its object to the condition of subordinated and managed things. The ultimate problem of knowledge is the same as that of consumption" (Bataille, *Accursed Share*, 74).

57. Peter Sloterdijk, *You Must Change Your Life*, trans. Wieland Hoban (London: Polity Press, 2013).

58. Michel Foucault, *The Hermeneutics of the Subject: Lectures at the Collège de France 1981–1982*, trans. Graham Burchell (New York: Picador, 2005), 113.

59. A discussion of the significance of form is clearly beyond my means. We can note its etymology, which is frequently linked with the Greek μορθή to mean "appearance," "shape of a thing as essential to the performance of its functions," "any mode . . . or state in which a thing may exist" (*Oxford Latin Dictionary*, ed. P. G. W. Glare (Oxford: Clarendon Press, 1968–82). Liddell and Scott define μορθή as "form, shape," "generally form, fashion, appearance," "a fine or beautiful form," as well as "gesture" (Henry George Liddell and Robert Scott, *A Greek-English Lexicon* [New York: Harper, 1883]). For my purposes, it is important to consider the relation of privation to form, given the interest in holding: "The form indeed is 'nature' rather than the matter; for a thing is more properly said to be what it is when it has at-

tained to fulfillment than when it exists potentially . . . What grows *qua* growing grows from something into something. Into what then does it grow? Not into that from which it arose but into that to which it tends . . . 'Shape' and 'nature,' it should be added, are in two senses. *For the privation too is in a way form* (Aristotle, *Physics* [Digireads, 2004], 18; emphasis mine). The form of life deprived of participation? It is the *idiotés*: "But if the proper precedes the common, it is exclusive, *idion*, which gives *idiotiès*, the person who is private/deprived: deprived of participation, outside the community" (George Faraklas, "Common and Proper: An Attempt to Answer the Question 'What is Philosophy?'" in *Diogenes* 2000 48 [2000]: 44).

60. Ludwig Wittgenstein, *On Certainty*, trans. Denis Paul and G. E. M. Anscombe (Oxford: Basil Blackwell, 1969), 344. *Lebensform* can, as Max Black argues, be compared to "the practice of old map-makers who labeled unexplored areas as 'Terra Incognita" (Max Black, *A Companion to Wittgenstein's Tractatus* [Ithaca: Cornell University Press, 1964], 330). For an attempted mapping, see David Kisik's *Wittgenstein's Form-of-Life* (London: A&C Black, 2008). One of the best readings of Wittgenstein's form of life remains Nicholas F. Gier's "Wittgenstein and Forms of Life," in *Philosophy of the Social Sciences* 10 (1980): 241–58.

61. Ibid., 358–59. On Wittgenstein and animality, see Cary Wolfe, "In the Shadow of Wittgenstein's Lion: Language, Ethics, and the Question of the Animal," in *Zoontologies: The Question of the Animal*," ed. Cary Wolfe (Minneapolis: University of Minnesota Press, 2003).

62. On uncertainty and pain, see Beth Savickey, "Wittgenstein's Use of Examples," in *The Oxford Handbook of Wittgenstein*, ed. Oskari Kuusela and Marie McGinn (Oxford: Oxford University Press, 2011), esp. 677–80.

63. Ludwig Wittgenstein, *Philosophical Investigations*, trans. G. E. M. Anscombe (Oxford: Blackwell, 1997), 19. On the relation of Wittgenstein to Agamben, see Matías Saidel's incisive "Form(s)-of-life. Agamben's Reading of Wittgenstein and the Potential Uses of a Notion," in *Trans/Form/Ação* 37, no. 1 (January/April 2014).

64. Marie McGinn's reading of Wittgenstein's anxiety is apropos: "It is not a question of what occurs in us, but rather of how we use—feel compelled to use—the word 'see.' The second use of the word 'see' reveals a complication in our concept of visual experience; it is connected . . . with the idea of a *comparison* between what is seen and something else." It is the difference between seeing and "seeing as" (Marie McGinn, *The Routledge Guidebook to Wittgenstein's Philosophical Investigations* (London: Routledge, 2013), 315. Badiou agrees: "The limits of my language mean the limits of my world" fill most of Wittgenstein's book. But they are unreadable if we omit the active question that traverses them: what should the world be so that we may silently enact that which brings us in accord with the divine sense of the world? This question alone makes clear that Wittgenstein's ontology is indivisibly a thought of being and a thought of saying" (Alain Badiou, *Wittgenstein's Antiphilosophy*, trans. Bruno Bosteels [London: Verso, 2011], 91).

65. Kenneth Burke, *Rhetoric of Motives* (Berkeley: University of California Press, 1969), 21.

66. On some of these other terms, see Georges Faraklas, "Common and Proper: An Attempt to Answer the Question 'What is Philosophy?' *Diogenes* 2000 48: 41–53.

67. See Chapter 4 of my *Improper Life: Biopolitics from Heidegger to Agamben* (Minneapolis: University of Minnesota Press, 2011).

68. D. W. Winnicott, "Transitional Objects and Transitional Phenomena—A Study of the First Not-Me Possession," *The International Journal of Psychoanalysis* 34 (1953), 89.

69. Winnicott, 90.

70. Ibid., 96.

71. Ibid., 90.

72. Ibid.

73. Ibid., 91.

74. Winnicott, "Transitional Objects," 94.

75. Ibid.

76. Ibid., 95.

77. Ibid.

78. Cf. Roland Barthes's definition of the 'neutral': "My definition of the Neutral remains structural. By which I mean that, for me, the Neutral, doesn't refer to 'impressions' of grayness, of 'neutrality,' of indifference. The Neutral—my Neutral—can refer to intense, strong, unprecedented states. 'To outplay the paradigm' is an ardent, burning activity" (Roland Barthes: *The Neutral: Lecture Course at the College de France (1977–1978)*, trans. Rosalind E. Krauss and Denis Hollier [New York: Columbia University Press, 2005], 7).

79. "Economy is the *nomos*, that is, the regulation of the circulation of forces and information or messages" (Jean-François Lyotard, "Oikos," in *Political Writings*, trans. Bill Readings and Kevin Paul Geiman [Minneapolis: University of Minnesota Press, 2003], 99).

80. "Lack of ambiguity, the repeatability of experience, and fixity of object are the preconditions of calculating and measuring, as they are of thinking in general. This need for unequivocal, repeatable, and fixed is satisfied in the realm of the soul by violence. And a special form of this violence, shockingly flexible, highly developed, and creative in many respects, is capitalism" (Robert Musil, "The German as Symptom," in *Precision and Soul: Essays and Addresses*, ed. and trans. Burton Pike and David S. Luft [Chicago: University of Chicago Press, 1990], 182).

81. Camille Paglia, *Sexual Personae: Art and Decadence from Nefertiti to Emily Dickinson*, Vol. 1 (New Haven: Yale University Press, 1990), 9.

82. Nietzsche, *The Gay Science*, 157. Compare Derrida's perspective on Hegel in *Glas*, trans. John P. Leavey, Jr. and Richard Rand (Lincoln, NE: University of Nebraska Press, 1986).

83. G. W. F. Hegel, *Aesthetics: Volume 2*, trans. T. M. Knox (Oxford: Clarendon Press, 1975), 1220–21.

84. My thanks to Adam Sitze for this concise language.

85. "For the comic must be restricted to showing that which destroys itself is something inherently null, a false and contradictory phenomenon, a whim, e.g., an oddity, a particular caprice in comparison with a mighty passion, or even a *supposedly* tenable principle and firm maxim" (Hegel, *Aesthetics: Volume 1*, 67).

86. Bataille, *The Accursed Share*, vol. 1, 133.

87. Giorgio Agamben, *The Highest Poverty: Monastic Rules and Form-of-Life*, trans. Adam Kotsko (Stanford: Stanford University Press, 2013), 61–62.

88. See Jacques Lacan, "The Circuit," in *The Seminar of Jacques Lacan, vol. 2, The Ego in Freud's Theory and in the Technique of Psychoanalysis, 1954–1955* (New York: Norton, 1991), 83.

89. Bataille, *Accursed Share*, vol. 1, 136.

90. Ibid., 138.

91. My thanks to Michael Jonik for having brought my attention to *manceps* and Lyotard's reading of it.

92. Jean-François Lyotard, *Phenomenology*, trans. Brian Beakley (Albany: SUNY Press, 1991), 130.

93. Ibid., 68.

94. Jean-François Lyotard, *Political Writings*, trans. Bill Readings (Minneapolis: University of Minnesota Press, 1993).

95. Ibid., 148.

96. Roberto Esposito, "The *Dispositif* of the Person," in *Law, Culture, and Humanities*, vol. 8 (February 2012): 17–30.

97. René Descartes, *Discourse on Method and Meditations* (Mineola: Dover Publications, 2003), 41. Lyotard typically will emphasize the seizing implicit in Descartes' mastery: "Master and possessor, as Descartes put it, thus insisting on the act of seizure, an act to be carried out on the set of existing things (called nature). But master and possessor of what *in us*, if we are fully emancipated? (Lyotard, *Political Writings*, 148–49).

98. Lyotard, *Political Writings*, 149.

99. Ibid., 150.

100. Ibid., 152.

2. FREEING THE APPARATUS

1. The etymology of apparatus: "Apparatus, preparation, provision, gear (Lat.) . . . Borrow from Lat. apparatus, preparation.—Lat. apparatus, pp. of *apparare*, to prepare—Lat. ad . . . and parade, to make ready" (Walter Skeat, *An Etymological Dictionary of the English Language* [New York: Macmillan, 1882], 366).

2. For Foucault's reading, see Adam Sitze's and my "Biopolitics: An Encounter," in *Biopolitics: A Reader* (Durham: Duke University Press, 2013): 1–40. For Deleuze's gloss of the term, see "What is a *dispositif?*" in *Michel Foucault Philosopher,* trans. Timothy J. Armstrong (New York: Routledge, 1992), 159–68. For Agamben, see *What Is an Apparatus?* trans. David Kishik and Stefan Pedatella (Stanford: Stanford University Press, 2009).

3. Peter Goodrich, "The Theater of Emblems: On the Optical Apparatus and Investiture of Persons," *Law, Culture, and Humanities* 8, no. 1 (2012), 56.

4. As we do in Samuel Weber's perspective on the onto-theological subject: "At the center of the convergence of theater and media we find precisely the figure that Benjamin described . . . that of 'man' as self-made, as *tyrannos,* in command of others as he seems to be of himself . . . The privileged notion of 'man,' of the 'human,' links Oedipus to the onto-theological subject, the 'personality' that dominates much of Western theater" (Samuel Weber, *Theatricality as Medium* [New York: Fordham University Press, 2004], 113).

5. Goodrich, 56.

6. "The oversight, then, is not to see what one sees, the oversight no longer concerns the object, but the *sight* itself. The oversight is an oversight that concerns vision: non-vision is therefore inside vision, it is a form of vision and hence has a necessary relationship with vision" (Louis Althusser, *Reading Capital,* trans. Ben Brewster [New York: Verso, 1997], 21). Luke Ferretter's summary of Althusser's insight ought to be recalled: "Knowledge can no longer be considered as a form of vision, of given objects, because according to Marx, the major economists have seen certain objects in the field of their analysis, but they have nevertheless failed to come to know them. Knowledge is a process, therefore, in which it is possible not to see what you are looking at" (Luke Ferretter, *Louis Althusser* [New York: Routledge, 2007], 55). See, too, Stephen Heath on Brecht: "The theses on realism, the example of the photograph, can guide us in thinking Brecht and cinema, in thinking the terms of the creation and recreation—there is no one way, no 'form' to be canonically transposed from theatre to film . . . of a Brechtian practice in cinema. They indicate straight away . . . that such a practice is, will be, in direct opposition to the founding ideology of cinema: vision is not knowledge, knowledge being on the contrary the fracturing of vision, the decipherment of the objective contradictions of reality" (Stephen Heath, "From Brecht to Film: Theses, Problems," *Screen* 16, no. 4 [1975], 37).

7. "Classical being was without flaw [*san défault*]; life, on the other hand, is without edges or shading [*sans frange ni dégradé*]. Being was spread out over an immense table; life isolates forms that are bound in upon themselves" (Michel Foucault, *The Order of Things: An Archaeology of the Human Sciences* [New York: Vintage Books, 1973], 273).

8. This, to be clear, Agamben links to desire: "At the root of each apparatus lies an all-too-human desire for happiness. The capture and subjectification of this de-

sire in a separate sphere constitutes the specific power of the apparatus" (Agamben, *What Is an Apparatus?* 17).

9. Vilém Flusser, *Towards a Philosophy of Photography*, trans. Anthony Mathews (London: Reaktion, 1983), 22. My thanks to Patricia Keller for reminding me of Flusser's reading of apparatus.

10. The classic texts: André Bazin, *What Is Cinema?* trans. Timothy Barnard (Montreal: Caboose, 2009); Christian Metz, *The Imaginary Signifier: Psychoanalysis and the Cinema*, trans. Ben Brewster, Alfred Guzzetti, Celia Britton, and Annwyl Williams (Bloomington: Indiana University Press, 1982); Edgar Morin, *Cinema, or the Imaginary Man*, trans. Lorraine Mortimer (Minneapolis: University of Minnesota Press, 2005); Laura Mulvey, "Visual Pleasure and Narrative Cinema," in *Film Theory and Criticism: Introductory Readings*, ed. Leo Braudy and Marshall Cohen (New York: Oxford University Press, 1999): 833–44; Stephen Heath, *Questions of Cinema* (Bloomington: Indiana University Press, 1982); and Kaja Silverman, *The Subject of Semiotics* (New York: Oxford University Press, 1983), esp. Chapter 5.

11. "What determines me, at the most profound level, in the visible, is the gaze outside. It is through the gaze that I enter light and it is from the gaze that I receive its effects. Hence it comes about that the gaze is the instrument through which light is embodied and through which . . . I am *photo-graphed*" (Jacques Lacan, "What Is a Picture?" in *The Seminar of Jacques Lacan: Book XI The Four Fundamental Concepts of Psychoanalysis*, trans. Alan Sheridan [New York: Norton, 1977], 106).

12. Jean-Louis Baudry, "Ideological Effects of the Basic Cinematographic Apparatus," in *Film Quarterly* 28, no. 2 (Winter 1974–75), 45.

13. Ibid.

14. Heath, 191. For a summary of critiques of Heath's position, see Mark Garrett Cooper's "Narrative Spaces," in which he attempts to recuperate and elaborate the consequences of Heath's reading (in *Screen* 43, no. 2 [Summer 2002], esp. 145–47).

15. Ibid., 188.

16. Ibid., 189.

17. This would appear to be the unexpressed assumption of Rancière's reading of the emancipated spectator, especially in the way that the apprentice or spectator inhabits distance with the master: "Intellectual emancipation . . . means the awareness and the enactment of that equal power of translation and counter-translation. Emancipation entails an idea of distance opposed to the stultifying one . . . It is this sense of distance that the 'ignorant master'—the master who ignores inequality—is teaching" (Jacques Rancière, "The Emancipated Spectator," in *Artforum* 45.7 [March 2007], 275).

18. For Rosi Braidotti, see in particular *Nomadic Subjects: Embodiment and Sexual Difference in Contemporary Feminist Theory* (New York: Columbia University Press, 2011) as well as her *Nomadic Theory: The Portable Rosi Braidotti* (New York: Columbia University Press, 2011).

19. Deleuze does hint at such a possibility in his reading of Bresson: "But, even more, it is the tactile which can constitute a pure sensory image, on condition that the hand relinquishes its prehensile and motor functions to content itself with a pure touching . . . The hand doubles its prehensile function (of object) by a connective function (of space); but, from specifically 'grabbing' [*haptique*] one . . ." (Gilles Deleuze, *Cinema II: The Time Image*, trans. Hugh Tomlinson and Robert Galeta [Minneapolis: University of Minnesota Press, 1989], 12–13).

20. The crystal in *Cinema II* often has such a role: "The crystal reveals a direct time-image, and no longer an indirect image of time deriving from movement. It does not abstract time; it does better: it reverses its subordination in relation to movement" (Deleuze, *Cinema II*, 98). Lyotard saw this reversal as the heart of his acinema: "Thus all sorts of gaps, jolts, postponements, losses, and confusions can occur, but they no longer act as real diversions or wasteful drifts . . . It is precisely through the return to the end of identification that cinematographic form, understood as the synthesis of good movement, is articulated following the cyclical organization of capital" (Jean-François Lyotard, "Acinema," in *Narrative, Apparatus, Ideology: A Film Theory Reader*, ed. Philip Rosen [New York: Columbia University Press, 2011], 353).

21. Baudry, 43.

22. Benveniste, 161–62.

23. "Philosophical exegesis will measure the distance that separates myth from real being, and will become conscious of the creative event itself, an event which eludes cognition, which goes from being to being by skipping over the intervals of the meanwhile" (Emmanuel Levinas, *Collected Philosophical Papers*, trans. Alphonso Lingis [Boston: Martinus Nijhoff Publishers, 1987], 13). What is true of philosophical exegesis holds as well for our analysis of film and reciprocity, which begins in acknowledging the "intervals of the meanwhile."

24. Daniel Dayan, "The Tutor-Code of Classical Cinema," in *Movies and Methods*, ed. Bill Nichols (Berkeley: University of California Press, 1976), 448.

25. On cinema as property or part of the commons, see William Brown's terrific "Has Film Ever Been Western," in *Dewesternizing Film Studies*, ed. Saer Maty Ba and Will Higbee (New York: Routledge, 2012). For a different view on possession and belief, see Steven Shaviro's reading of the materiality of cinematic sensation which is "irreducible to, and irrecuperable by, the ideality of signification" (Steven Shaviro, *The Cinematic Body* [Minneapolis: University of Minnesota Press, 1994], 32.3).

26. Here I part ways with Daniel Frampton's reading of cinematic vision. For him, such a vision "holds objects," whereas it is precisely in the practice of montage that objects are held or better are owned at a distance (Daniel Frampton, *Filmosophy* [London: Wallflower Press, 2006], 40). See, too, Dudley Andrew's earlier gloss of the machinery of cinema and belief. "Thus it is that the machinery of cinema, a

machinery composed like all machines of fragments and parts (and in this case one that relies literally on intermittent motion and on the operations of laboratories and chemicals) comes to take on the function of producing reality for its spectators, a seamless, coherent reality both in image and story. This gives to each spectator the *belief* that life itself, no matter how fragmented it may appear, is finally coherent and that his/her own position in it is fully accounted for" (emphasis mine) (Dudley Andrew, *Concepts in Film Theory* [Oxford: Oxford University Press, 1984], 113–14).

27. On the film's hapticity, see in particular Mariam Ross's "The 3-D Aesthetic: Avatar and Hyperhaptic Visuality," *Screen* (Winter 2012) 53 (4): 381–97. Especially illuminating is her suggestion of a line running from the *trompe l'oeil* illusion, to 3D, to hyperhapticity.

28. Maurice Merleau-Ponty, "Eye and Mind," in *The Merleau-Ponty Aesthetics Reader: Philosophy and Painting*, ed. Galen A. Johnson, Michael B. Smith (Evanston, Ill.: Northwestern University Press, 1993), 127; quoted in Frampton, 40.

29. Paul de Man, "Sign and Symbol in Hegel's *Aesthetics*, ed. Andrzej Warminski (Minneapolis: University of Minnesota Press, 1996), 97–98.

30. Winnicott, "Transitional Objects," 91.

31. Ibid., 95.

32. Ibid., 96.

33. Such a perspective on cinema draws us closer to Edgar Morin's theory of film, though we do well to distance ourselves from his image of the spectator who, passive and "in the 'dark room,'" does nothing, and "has nothing to give, even his applause" (Edgar Morin, *Cinema, or the Imaginary Man*, trans. Lorraine Mortimer [Minneapolis: University of Minnesota, 2005], 97).

34. Or historical: "With the return of the current event, the situation changes. For if 'I have seen' the event, *you* have seen it too. Under these circumstances, to be a historian is no longer to say what I have seen, for what would be the point? It is more a matter of pondering what is visible and the conditions of visibility. Not *what* have I seen, but *what is it* that I have seen" (François Hartog, *The Mirror of Herodotus: The Representation of the Other in the Writing of History*, trans. Janet Lloyd [Berkeley: University of California Press, 1988], 267).

35. Writing of Antonioni's *L'avventura*, Bert Cardullo notes: "This reciprocity—a new reality being summoned by a new perceptiveness and in turn compelling that perceptiveness into being—seems to me to be at the heart of the filmmaker's art and of the filmgoer's experience on the level of creative spectatorship" (Bert Cardullo: *Soundings on Cinema: Speaking to Film and Film Artists* [Albany: SUNY Press, 2008], 69).

36. Georg Simmel, "Life as Transcendence," in *The View of Life: Four Metaphysical Essays with Journal Aphorisms*, trans. John A. Y. Andrews and Donald N. Levine (Chicago: University of Chicago Press, 2010), 15. For a survey of contemporary

vitalism along with a critique of Bergson as well as Simmel, see Scott Lash's "Life/ Vitalism," in *Theory Culture Society* (2006) 23: 323–29.

37. See especially Antonio Negri and Michael Hardt's critique of Heidegger and vitalism in *Multitude: War and Democracy in the Age of Empire* (New York: Penguin, 2005), esp. 192–94, as well as Judith Revel's 2008 presentation at the Tate Modern, "The Materiality of the Immaterial: Against the Return of Idealisms and New Vitalisms," available at http://www.uninomade.org/lebensformen /wp-content/uploads/2011/01/Revel-Against-the-return-of-idealisms-and-new -vitalisms.pdf. Cf. Lash's response via Simmel: "Vitalism does not think in terms of a prioris. It does not speak the Kantian language of the condition of possibility , , . It is interested in how human and non-human beings know as they do. This is always connected to interests and power" (Scott Lash, "Lebens- soziologie: Georg Simmel in the Information Age," in *Theory Culture Society* [2005] 22[3], 5).

38. And so in line with Nietzsche's critique of the "idolatry of the actual" (Friedrich Nietzsche, *Thoughts Out of Season, Part II*, trans. Adrien Collins, in *The Complete Works of Nietzsche*, ed. Oscar Levy (New York: Russell and Russell, 1964), volume 5, 72; quoted in Max Horkheimer, *Critical Theory: Selected Essays* (New York: Continuum, 2002), 95.

39. Or better, those elements that strike a balance between giving and taking that are characteristic of a "good object" in the Kleinian sense; between projection and introjection (Melanie Klein, "On Identification," in *Envy and Gratitude* [New York: Simon and Schuster, 2002], esp. 144–45).

40. Paglia, 91.

41. Antonioni's practice of *temps morts* more particularly ought to be understood as just such an invitation, though "the dead time' description is in at least one sense misleading. It is not time, or space, which is dead; these violent primordial forces are never more *alive* and devastating than at such moments" (Hamish Ford, "Antonioni's *L'avventura* and Deleuze's Time-Image, http://sensesofcinema .com/2003/feature-articles/l_avventura_deleuze/).

42. "The senses are apparatus to form concretions of the inexhaustible, to form existent significations—But the thing is not really *observable*; there is always a skipping over in every observation, one is never at the thing itself" (Merleau-Ponty, *The Visible and the Invisible*, 192).

43. Luce Irigaray, *An Ethics of Sexual Difference*, trans. Carolyn Burke and Gillian C. Gill (Ithaca: Cornell University Press, 1993), 161–62.

44. "Lyotard typically precedes us on this score, when he observes that "what is really at stake [is] to reveal what makes one see, and not what is visible . . . what was at stake for that painter was, in effect, to seize perception and render it at birth— perception 'before' perception; the wonder of 'it' happening" (Lyotard, *The Inhuman*, 102; quoted in Irigaray, 135).

45. On craft, see Richard Sennett's wonderful *The Craftsman* (New Haven: Yale University Press, 2008): "Craftwork focuses on objects in themselves and on impersonal practices; craftwork depends on curiosity, it tempers obsession; craftwork turns the craftsman outwards" (288). My thanks to Nathan Moore for introducing me to Sennett's work.

46. On the contemporary inflation surrounding animal studies and the need for more "plant theory," see Jeffrey Nealon's forthcoming *Plant Theory: Vegetal Life and Biopolitics in Foucault, Derrida, and Deleuze & Guattari*.

47. Kenneth Burke, "Comic Correctives," in *Attitudes Toward History* (Berkeley: University of California Press, 1984), 169.

3. "DEAD WEIGHT": VISCONTI AND FORMS OF LIFE

1. "The images of *La terra trema* achieve what is at once a paradox and a *tour de force* in integrating the aesthetic realism of *Citizen Kane* with the documentary realism of Farrebique . . . I would like to emphasize that depth of focus has led Visconti (as it led Welles) not only to reject montage but, in some literal sense, to invent a new kind of shooting script. His 'shots' . . . are unusually long—some lasting three or four minutes. In each, as one might expect, several actions are going on simultaneously. Visconti also seems to have wanted, in some systematic sense, to base the construction of his image on the event itself" (André Bazin, *What Is Cinema?* trans. Hugh Gray [Berkeley: University of California Press, 1968], 42).

2. The critical literature on *The Earth Trembles* is vast, especially its relation to neo-realism. Works dealing with the relation of the aesthetic and ethical in Visconti's films are much less common. See, in particular, the following: Paul Thoams, "Gone Fishin'? Rossellini's *Stromboli*, Visconti's *La terra trema*," in *Film Quarterly* 62, no. 2 (Winter 2008–2009): 20–25; Noa Steimatsky's terrific *Italian Locations: Reinhabiting the Past in Postwar Cinema* (Minneapolis: University of Minnesota Press, 2008); Donatella Spinelli Coleman, *Filming the Nation: Jung, Film, Neorealism and Italian National Identity* (London: Routledge, 2011); Alexander García Düttman, "Luchino Visconti: Insights into Flesh and Blood," in *Cinematic Thinking: Philosophical Approaches to the New Cinema*, ed. James Phillips (Stanford: Stanford University Press, 2008): Guido Aristarco and Luciana Bohne, "Luchino Visconti: Critic or Poet of Decadence?" *Film Criticism* 12, no. 3 (Spring 1988): 58–63; Christopher Wagstaff, *Italian Neorealist Cinema: An Aesthetic Approach* (Toronto: University of Toronto Press, 2007), esp. 30–34; P. Adams Sitney, *Vital Crises in Italian Cinema: Iconography, Stylistics, Politics* (New York: Oxford University Press, 1995).

3. This is not to say that Visconti was inactive. In addition to his work on *Giorni di gloria*, he was, in Micchiché's words, involved in a "theatrical explosion"—a full

twelve of the forty-five treatments he wrote happened between January 20, 1945 and February 28, 1947 (Lino Micciché, *Luchino Visconti: Un profile critico* Venezia: Marsilio, 1996, 12).

4. Andrea Bellavita, *Visconti: Il teatro dell'immagine* (Roma: Ente dello spettacolo, 2006). As Sam Rohdie reminds us, it is impossible to overstate the importance of the journal: "What was remarkable about *Cinema* from its inception, though most evident after 1938, was that every Italian film was treated in the journal as a national event of cultural, artistic, and social-political importance . . . What would become Italian neo-realism critically and in practice was argued out and elaborated in the journal during 1940–1943" (Sam Rohdie, *Intersections: Writings on Cinema* [Manchester: Manchester University Press, 2012], 112).

5. "Visconti requires time for his images to gather up details, objects and gestures that are themselves products of time, that press together in the concreteness memories, histories, cultures, and thereby crystallize and concentrate multiple determinations and directions. Time is required in order to be, to perceive, indeed experience the density" (Rohdie, 117).

6. Luchino Visconti, "Anthropomorphic Cinema," in *Springtime for Italy: A Reader on Neorealism*, ed. David Overbey (Archon Books, 1979), 84. The original can be found in Luchino Visconti, "Il cinema antropomorfico," in *Cinema* no. 173–74 (Sept 25–October 10, 1943). See Düttman's reading of the essay in *Cinematic Thinking*, especially on the power of objects when displayed (38).

7. Here it should be added that the body associated with *peso* is gendered. *Peso* originates in the Latin, *pensu(m)*, "the quantity of silk that the female slave had to weave [*filare*] in one day." See the enlightening entry for *peso* in Manlio Cortelazzo and Paolo Zolli's *Dizionario etimologico della lingua italiana* (Bologna: Zanichelli, 1985), 915.

8. The language I'm using comes from Alphonso Lingis's powerful reading of the phenomenology of things: "On the Greyhound bus, our sensibility sinks into enduring the desolation of the plains . . . The perception of things, the apprehension of their content and the circumscription of their forms, is not an appropriation of them, but an expropriation of our forces into them, and ends in enjoyment" (Alphonso Lingis, *The Imperative* [Bloomington: Indiana University Press, 1998], 70).

9. Francesco Zambaldi, *Etimologico Italiano* (Città di Castello: S. Lapi, 1889), 348.

10. Compare Maurizio Sanzio Viano's reading of passion in Pasolini: "The idea of passion as the semiotic history written on a body that reads signs has momentous implications in film studies, for it alludes to the body of the viewer, the viewer as body. We could even say that cinema made it impossible for us to keep ignoring the bodily aspects of all artistic consumption, because from its inception, film aroused physical reactions in an unprecedented way" (Maurizio Sanzio Viano,

A Certain Realism: Making Use of Pasolini's Film Theory and Practice [Berkeley: University of California Press, 1993], 42).

11. The Greek for *pathos* originally referred, in its Aristotelian usage, to have touched or to have affected: "to have for everything and in everything the characteristic of undergoing, of passivity and that it is ethically neutral: no one can be praised or blamed for his or her *pathe*" (Cortelazzo and Zolli, vol. 4, 889).

12. Or what Paul Virilio refers to as "the administration of fear" (Paul Virilio, *The Administration of Fear* [Los Angeles: Semiotext(e), 2012], 13–14).

13. "Due to the continuous influx of psychophysical correspondences thus aroused, they [films] suggest a reality which may fittingly be called 'life.' This term as used here denotes a kind of life which is still intimately connected, as if by an umbilical cord, with the material phenomena from which its emotional and intellectual contents emerge . . . The concept, 'flow of life,' then covers the stream of material situations and happenings with all that they intimate in terms of emotions, values, thoughts" (Siegfried Kraucauer, *Theory of Film: The Redemption of Physical Reality* [Princeton: Princeton University Press, 1997], 71).

14. "Affect as immanent evaluation, instead of judgment as transcendent value . . . But the good is outpouring, ascending life, the kind which knows how to transform itself, to metamorphose itself according to the forces it encounters, and which forms a constantly larger force with them, always increasing the power to live, always opening new 'possibilities'" (Gilles Deleuze, *Cinema 2: Time-Image*, trans. Hugh Tomlinson and Robert Galeta [New York: Continuum, 2005], 137).

15. "Why not Hegel? Well, somebody has to play the role of traitor. What is philosophically incarnated in Hegel is the enterprise to 'burden' life, to overwhelm it with every burden, to reconcile life with the State and religion, to inscribe death in life—the monstrous enterprise to submit life to negativity, the enterprise of resentment and unhappy consciousness. Naturally, with this dialectic of negativity and contradiction, Hegel has inspired every language of betrayal, on the right as well as on the left (theology, spiritualism, technocracy, bureaucracy, etc." (Gilles Deleuze, *Desert Islands and Other Text (1953 1974)* [Los Angeles: Semiotext(e), 2004], 144).

16. Kenneth Burke, "Comic Correctives," in *Attitudes Toward History* (Berkeley: University of California Press, 1984), 169. My thanks to Cary Wolfe for pointing me in the direction of Burke on the comic.

17. Speaking of fascism and comic frames, Burke writes: "With so many instrumentalities now on the side of privilege, we hold a comic frame must detect the lure of such incentives, must make people conscious of their operation, if they are not to be victimized by such magic. It is because people must respect themselves, that the cult of Kings is always in the offing" (Burke, 168).

18. "A photograph, whether portrait or action picture, is in character only if it precludes the notion of completeness. Its frame marks a provisional limit; its content refers to other contents outside that frame; and its structure denotes something

that cannot be encompassed—physical existence" (Kraucauer, *Theory of Film*, 19–20).

19. See Steimatsky's elegant reading of the landscape of Acitrezza in *Italian Landscapes*.

20. Visconti imagined the opening this way: "It's dawn in the port of a small town near Catania. The fishermen are returning home with their boats after a difficult night. The rough life of the fishermen and their difficulties are seen through a family and one of its members the young Antonio. How unjust, restricted and fated there is the meager work of the fisherman; how much desire there is in the young protagonist to escape from all that" ("*La terra trema*—Appunti per un film documentario sulla Sicilia (1948)," Luchino Visconti, http://www.luchinovisconti .org/pagine/documenti_vis/documenti_scheda.asp?id_opera=14&id_genere=22.

21. Not only the exotic but the political too: "The emphasis on dialect is itself a political gesture. Again, Gramsci had addressed the problem of dialects in his extensive writings on the Italian language (also published after the film was made), arguing that '[e]very time the question of language surfaces, in one way or another, it means that a series of other problems are [sic] coming to the fore: the formation and enlargement of the governing class, the need to establish more intimate and secure relationships between the governing groups and the national-popular mass, in other words to reorganize the cultural hegemony'" (P. Adams Sitney, 88).

22. Roland Barthes, *Camera Lucida: Reflections on Photography*, trans. Richard Howard (New York: Farrar, Straus and Giroux, 1981), 91. Barthes continues: "Death must be somewhere in society; if it is no longer (or less intensely) in religion, it must be elsewhere; perhaps in the image which produces Death while trying to preserve Life . . . a kind of abrupt dive into Literal Death." See, too, Bazin's reading of the photograph in *La terra trema*: "The shots are fixed-frame, so people and things may enter the frame and take up position; but Visconti is also in the habit of using a special kind of panning shot which moves very slowly over a very wide arc: this is the only camera movement which he allows himself, for he excludes all tracking shots and, of course, every unusual camera angle." Bazin will call this a "remarkable plastic balance—a balance which only a photograph could absolutely render here" (Bazin, 42). See Laura Mulvey's important reading of Barthes, photography, and Rossellini's *Voyage to Italy* in her *Death 24x a Second: Stillness and the Moving Image* (London: Reaktion, 2006): "Rossellini used this terrain to extend into cinema the blurred boundaries between the material and the spiritual, reality and magic, and between life and death that Bazin and Barthes associated with photography. In both films, however, death forms a central thematic element and both films enable the cinema's paradoxical relation between movement and stillness to achieve a degree of visibility" (104). Nowell-Smith senses a relation as well: "Only when a storm whips up and the storm bell is rung and the women huddle on the steps does the church become real. But its reality is like that of the rocks that guard the en-

trance to the harbor, a symbol of permanence, but suggesting unlike the rocks, permanent fear" (Nowell-Smith, 39).

23. On the importance of collective individuation, see how Visconti ended his treatment of Verga's *Malavoglia*: "Antonio returns to the sea. He is one of the defeated [*vinti*], he is alone; and perhaps only now is he able to understand that he lost because he was alone" (Gianni Rondolino, *Luchino Visconti* [Turin: UTET, 2003], 205).

24. "He [the Cylcops] prayed, and the blue-manned sea-god heard him. / Then he broke off an even larger chunk of rock, / Pivoted, and threw it with incredible force. / it came down just behind our dark-hulled ship, / Barely missing the end of the rudder. The sea / Billowed up where the rock hit the water" (IX, 534–40) (Homer, *Odyssey*, trans. Stanley Lombardo [Indianapolis: Hackett Publishing, 2000]).

25. Luchino Visconti, "Tradizione ed invenzione," in Lino Micciché, *Luchino Visconti: Un profile critico* (Venezia: Marsilio, 1996), 96. Unless otherwise noted, all translations are my own.

26. In the following pages, I am consciously reading Visconti's film against Franco Cassano's perspective on the sea: "The sea prevents the closing of the circle, even the polished, reflexive one of philosophy. The polis is unthinkable without the restlessness and the complex loyalty embedded in the double nature of those who live by the coast. Without the sea, power quickly runs the risk of falling into the hands of a despot or of the philosophers; the opening in the horizon caused by the sea ensures, at the same time, that no knowledge can be condensed in one final thought, and no power can become fixed in the immobility of personal ownership" (Franco Cassano, *Southern Thought and Other Essays on the Mediterranean* [New York: Fordham University Press, 2012], 19). I want to thank Lucia Re and Claudio Fogu for having invited me to engage with Cassano's work.

27. Michel Foucault, *Security, Territory, Population: Lectures at the Collège de France 1977–1978*, trans. Graham Burchell (New York: Picador, 2009).

28. Leo Spitzer, "Milieu and Ambiance: An Essay in Historical Semantics," in *Philosophy and Phenomenological Research* 3, no. 1 (1942): 1–42. The second part follows in *Philosophy and Phenomenological Research* 3, no. 2 (1942): 169–218.

29. Spitzer, "Milieu and Ambiance," 170. The passage from Pascal continues in interesting fashion: "This is our natural condition, and yet most contrary to our inclination; we burn with desire to find solid ground and an ultimate sure foundation whereon to build a tower reaching to the Infinite. But our whole groundwork cracks, and the earth opens to abysses" (Blaise Pascal, *Pensees (Thoughts)*, vol. 3 [New York: Digireads.com Publishing, 2004], 14).

30. On chorality in Italian cinema, see Joseph Luzzi's *A Cinema of Poetry: Aesthetics of the Italian Art Film* (Baltimore: Johns Hopkins University Press, 2014) and Noa Steimatsky's "Photographic *Verismo*, Cinematic Adaptation, and the Staging of a Neorealist Landscape," in *A Companion to Literature and Film*, ed. Robert Stam and Alessandra Raengo (Oxford: Blackwell, 2004): 205–28.

31. Visconti, "Anthropomorphic Cinema."

32. Sartre, *Notebooks for an Ethics*, 129. That Visconti was deeply familiar with Sartre's thought is well-known. Micchiché reminds us that in 1945 Visconti chose to stage Sartre's *Huis clos* as well (Micchiché, 12).

33. "These things, these objects, this nature, gain not only a body, which, at the studio they lack, but a 'soul', a 'life', that is subjective presence. Certainly in real life, glass menageries, knickknacks, handkerchiefs, pieces of furniture charged with memories, are already like little presences watching over us, and we admire landscapes sprinkled with soul. The cinema goes further still: it takes hold of things scorned in everyday life, handled as tools, used out of habit, and it kindles new life in them: 'Things were real, they now become present'" (Edgar Morin, *The Cinema, or The Imaginary Man*, trans. Lorraine Mortimer [Minneapolis: University of Minnesota Press, 2005], 65).

34. This relation between thing and human being in the frame recalls the relation of the visible and the invisible and to what Merleau-Ponty referred to as flesh: "The flesh is not matter, is not mind, is not substance. To designate it, we should need the old term 'element,' in the sense it was used to speak of water, air, earth, and fire, that is in the sense of a *general thing*, midway between the spatio-temporal individual and the idea. . . . The flesh is in this sense an 'element' of Being" (Merleau-Ponty, *The Visible and the Invisible*, 139; quoted in *Merleau-Ponty and Environmental Philosophy*, ed. Sue L. Cataldi and William S. Hamrick [Albany: SUNY Press, 2007], 4).

35. This seems a necessary corollary to Kraucauer's perspective on "camera-reality": "The railway noises in *Brief Encounter* are not intended to denote mental agitation; the streets in *Umberto D.* lead a life of their own; and the furniture, staircases, and cars in slapstick comedy behave exactly like actors in the flesh" (Kraucauer, *Theory of Film*, 266).

36. *Dizionario di retorica e stilistica: arte e artificio nell'uso delle parole*, ed. Angelo Marchese (Milano: Mondadori, 1991).

37. "Modern idolatry, in short, is laboring under the superstition that it has overcome superstition, left it behind in the misty past, or in less developed places . . . It has rationalised the idol as a mere technology, a mechanical or cybernetic reproduction subject to the will of the producer . . . The deep magic of the modern image is precisely in the denial of its magic, the affirmation of its scientificity, and the uneasy, intermittent acknowledgment of its unpredictability and autonomy" (W. J. T. Mitchell, "What Do Pictures Want?" in *In Visible Touch: Modernism and Masculinity*, ed. Terry Smith [Chicago: University of Chicago Press, 1997], 225).

38. Here Micciché is right to remind us of the importance, historically, of the defeated: "There is no space whatsoever for liberation; there is no authentic trace of hope; all of his stories are systematically ones of clear, absolute, unchanging and nearly all, *historical*, defeats. History is seen and represented by Visconti as a mech-

anism from which his protagonists are excluded; their defeat is never (or nearly never) the result of a process that belongs to their individual existence, but seems determined by the pressure of what is 'other than the self'" (Micchiché, 79).

39. The key term here is use: "Every sign *by itself* seems dead. What gives it life?—In use it is *alive*. Is life breathed into there?—Or is the *use* its life?" (Ludwig Wittgenstein, *Philosophical Investigations*, 432). "Wittgenstein is continually reminding us that the phenomena in which he is interested—e.g. providing interpretations, ostensively defining, reading, making a move in a game of chess, feeling pain—make sense only when 'surrounded by certain normal manifestations of life'" (David H. Finkelstein, Wittgenstein on Rules and Platonism," in *The New Wittgenstein*, ed. Alice Crary, Rupert Read [New York: Routledge, 2002], 66).

40. Nowell-Smith pinpoints the commonality between the apparatus and the camera: "It [the camera] records the presence of strangers . . . but it does not say where they come from or who they are. It shares the viewpoint of the fishermen, for whom all visitors are strangers and, by implication, not merely strangers but strange" (Nowell-Smith, 39).

41. Renzo Renzi, *Cinema*, 35, 67.

42. Ibid., 67.

43. Ibid.

44. Ibid., 66.

45. Ibid., 67.

46. Micciché, 88.

47. Ibid.

48. Luce Irigaray, *Ethics of Sexual Difference*, trans. Carolyn Burke and Gillian C. Gill (New York: A&C Black, 2005), 60.

49. Ibid., 61.

50. Charles Peirce, "Prolegomena to an Apology for Pragmaticism," in *Peirce on Signs*, ed. James Hoopes (Chapel Hill: University of North Carolina Press, 1991), 252.

51. Aristotle, *Poetics*, trans. S. H. Butcher (New York: Macmillan 1961), 74.

52. On the role of the Mediterranean in Italian film, see the first volume of California Italian Studies dedicated to the theme (*California Italian Studies* 1, no. 1 [2010], at http://escholarship.org/uc/ismrg_cisj?volume=1;issue=1). On the plan to film a trilogy, see Renzo Renzi, *Visconti segreto* (Roma: Laterza, 1994), 60–61. The final episode was to recount how peasants came to "occupy" the land.

53. Lest we congratulate ourselves as spectator too quickly, consider the etymology of the word *autopsy*, which is from the Greek *auto* (self) + *opsis* (seen). Autopsy becomes a form of personal observation. Thus, we may be able ultimately to see ourselves, but as someone once said, it will always be too late.

54. This might explain the sense of aliveness that characterizes the women in the film as they are less subject to a Fate that impoverishes the brothers. See Kracauer's reading of Thomas Hardy and fate (*Theory of Film*, 233–34).

55. "What life and society require of each of us is a constantly alert attention that discerns the outlines of the present situation, together with a certain elasticity of mind and body to enable us to adapt ourselves in consequence. TENSION and ELASTICITY are two forces, mutually complementary, which life brings into play" (Henri Bergson, *Laughter: An Essay on the Meaning of the Comic*, trans. Cloudesley Brereton and Fred Rothwell [New York: MacMillan, 1914], 44).

56. Giorgio Agamben, "Notes on Gesture," in *Means without End: Notes on Politics*, trans. Vincenzo Binetti and Cesare Casarino (Minneapolis: University of Minnesota Press, 2000), 55.

57. Emmanuel Levinas's gloss of identification and home comes to mind: "The *way* of the I against the 'other' of the world consists in *sojourning*, in *identifying oneself* by existing here *at home with oneself* . . . Dwelling is the very mode of *maintaining oneself* [*se tient*] and *can*. The 'at home' is not a container but a site where *I can* . . ." (Emmanuel Levinas, *Totality and Infinity*, trans. Alphonso Lingis [New York: Martinus Nijhoff, 1979], 37).

58. Agamben, "Notes on Gesture," 56.

59. "The caress consists in seizing upon nothing, in soliciting what ceaselessly escapes its form toward a future never future enough, in soliciting what slips away as though it were not yet. It searches, it forages. It is not an intentionality of disclosure but of search: a movement unto the invisible. In a certain sense it expresses love, but suffers from an inability to tell it. It is hungry for this very expression, in an unremitting increase of hunger" (Levinas, *Totality and Infinity*, 256–57).

60. In how the cinematic apparatus "holds objects," it may be seen as comic. See Daniel Frampton's *Filmosophy: A Manifesto for a Radically New Way of Understanding Cinema* (London: Wallflower Press, 2006), especially 40–42.

61. Friedrich Nietzsche, *The Birth of Tragedy and Other Writings*, trans. Ronald Speirs (Cambridge: Cambridge University Press, 1999), 51–52.

62. Here as elsewhere, Kraucauer precedes us. Writing of Chaplin, he observes an affinity with Italian neo-realism: "Perhaps the most impressive trait of his Tramp is a truly unquenchable capacity for survival in the face of the Goliaths of this world; the life force which he embodies brings to mind films on plant growth . . . Here is where a link can be established between the old Chaplin comedies and certain neorealistic films: *Cabiria* and *Umberto D.* resemble the Tramp in that they are as vulnerable as they are indestructible" (*Theory of Film*, 281).

63. Bergson, 26.

64. Ibid.

65. This emphasis on attention and gesture goes missing in Rodhie's account: "With Visconti, who creates melodramas, there is a necessity and inevitability to events . . . In Visconti, nothing is spontaneous or improvised in his preparation of his films . . . or in the final results . . . Viscontian reality is overwrought, exceedingly construed, and passionately dramatised" (Rohdie, 124).

66. Visconti's choice to juxtapose 'Ntoni's grip with Mara's touch of the photograph is not happenstance: "And if dialectic is that thought which masters the corruptible and converts the negation of death into the power to work, then the photograph is undialectical: it is a denatured theater where death cannot 'be contemplated,' reflected and interiorized; or again, the dead theater of Death, the foreclosure of the Tragic, excludes all purification, all *catharsis*" (Roland Barthes, *Camera Lucida: Reflections on Photography*, trans. Richard Howard [New York: Vintage, 1993], 90).

67. Burke, *Permanence and Change*, 49. Cf. Merleau-Ponty's reading of *Umwelt*: "All the *Umwelten* are carried in a unique being that is always closed to them. Behind all the produced worlds is hidden the nature-subject . . . We must simply see that we are surrounded by higher realities that we cannot bring to intuition" (Maurice Merleau-Ponty, *Nature: Course Notes from the Collège de France* [Evanston, Ill.: Northwestern University Press, 2003], 177).

68. This suggests an update to Foucault's earlier injunction on politicization: "If to politicize means to return to standard choices, then it is not worth it. To new power techniques one must oppose *new forms of politicization*" (Michel Foucault, *Foucault Live: Collected Interviews, 1961–1984*, ed. Sylvere Lotringer (Los Angeles: Semiotexte 1996), 209). New forms of politicization are less needed than is a diagnosis of precisely where mythic violence operates today.

69. This, according to Aristotle, would not be about conflict, though it does concern "events": "To say that a story can only take place if it is connected to a central conflict forces us to eliminate all stories which do not include confrontation and to leave aside all those events which require only indifference or detached curiosity, like a landscape, a distant storm, or dinner with friends" (Aristotle, *Poetics*, 11).

70. Levinas, *Totality and Infinity*, 124. Levinas speaks of giving and signification in terms that are helpful in the current context: "Signification or expression thus contrasts with every intuitive datum precisely because *to signify is not to give*. Signification is not an ideal essence or a relation open to intellectual intuition, thus still analogous to the sensation presented to the eye. It is preeminently the presence of exteriority" (emphasis mine).

4. PLAYFUL FALLS IN A MILIEU OF CONTAGION

1. As illuminating as Karl Schoonover's musings are on *Germany Year Zero* and Rossellini's "obscene cinema," I think it important not to inflate the mystery of Edmund's face. The corporeality of Edmund's body—his stride, his height, his unflappability—are precisely what allows him to stand in for Germany in year zero in lieu of juxtaposed shots. Karl Schoonover, *Brutal Vision: The Neorealist Body in Postwar Italian Cinema* (Minneapolis: University of Minnesota Press, 2012), 27–29.

2. This is true even if the impression remains one of marginalization with respect both to *Paisà* and *Rome, Open City*. On *Germany Year Zero* and neo-realism, the best accounts in English remain Peter Brunette, *Roberto Rossellini* (Berkeley: University of California Press, 1987); Tag Gallagher, *The Adventures of Roberto Rossellini* (New York: Da Capo Press, 1998); Luca Caminati, *Roberto Rossellini Documentarista: Una Cultura della Realtà* (Roma: Carocci, 2012); Christopher Wagstaff, *Italian Neorealist Cinema: An Aesthetic Approach* (Toronto: University of Toronto Press, 2007); David Bruni, *Roberto Rossellini: Roma, Città Aperta* (Torino: Lindau, 2006); *Roberto Rossellini: Magician of the Real*, ed. David Forgacs, Sarah Lutton, and Geoffrey Nowell-Smith (London: British Film Institute, 2000); Peter E. Bondanella, *The Films of Roberto Rossellini* (Cambridge: Cambridge University Press, 1993); and Roberto Rossellini and Stefano Roncoroni, *Roberto Rossellini: The War Trilogy* (New York: Grossman, 1973). For the initial critical reaction as well as Rossellini's responses ("*Germany Year Zero* is a cold movie, as cold as a sheet of glass"), see Gianni Rondolino's *Roberto Rossellini* (Turin: UTET, 1989), 135–39.

3. Rancière's remarkable reading appears in *Film Fables*, trans. Emiliano Battista (Oxford: Berg, 2006). I am indebted to Rancière's insights, for the chapter would have been unthinkable without them. As the reader will soon see, I do part ways with him around the notion of play and gratitude.

4. Rancière's argument recalls a point that many have made concerning a number of Rossellini's films. See David Forgacs's reading of blankness in *Rome Open City: Roma Città Aperta* (London: BFI Pub., 2000) for the most acute.

5. Rancière, 131.

6. Ibid., 132.

7. One of the most judicious and insightful readings of Rancière and cinema is Abraham Geil's "The Spectator without Qualities" in *Rancière and Film*, ed. Paul Bowman (Edinburgh: Edinburgh University Press, 2013): 53–82.

8. One might well wonder if such a perspective ignores something like a "trained incapacity," to borrow again a term dear to Kenneth Burke, which in the context of the film would mean an incapacity to hold both love and hate together. For the term, see Burke's *Permanence and Change: An Anatomy of Purpose* (Berkeley: University of California Press, 1984): "One adopts measures in keeping with his past training—and the very soundness of this training may lead him to adopt the wrong measures. People may be unfitted by being fit in an unfit fitness" (10).

9. Or more simply, as Fellini claimed, that Rossellini during this period had "an enormous trust in the things photographed" (Fellini, *Fare un film*; quoted in David Forgacs, "Rossellini's Pictorial Histories," *Film Quarterly* 64, No. 3 [Spring 2011], 26).

10. See Tag Gallagher's account of the ending: "We realize that Edmund has sensed the horror of himself and his world—has like the Italians in *Paisà*, confronted shame and leapt from an impulsive longing for liberty." His conclusion is that

"Edmund's other crime, then—his suicide—is an impulse for freedom" (Tag Gallagher, *The Adventures of Roberto Rossellini* [New York: Da Capo Press, 1998], 246, 247).

11. There is another feature of Rossellini's cinema that requires our attention, namely the connection between impassivity and what we might call the impolitical. In an interview with *Cahiers du Cinéma*, Rossellini's interviewers—Eric Rohmer and François Truffaut—call his attention to the absence of "cinematic effects" in his films—that he often opts *not* to draw the public's attention to important scenes. Rossellini's answer is intriguing: "I always try to remain impassive. What I find most surprising, extraordinary, and moving in men is precisely that great actions and great events take place in the same way and with exactly the same resonance as normal everyday occurrences. I try to transcribe both with the same humility. There is a source of dramatic interest in that" (quoted in Peter Bondanella, *A History of Italian Cinema* (London: Continuum, 2009), 130. This suggests another reading of neo-realism based on a flattening of the notion of event. Cf. Emerson's perspective on event: "Although no diligence can rebuild the universe in a model by the best accumulation or disposition of details, yet does the world reappear in miniature in every event, so that all the laws of nature may be read in the smallest fact" (Ralph Waldo Emerson, "Intellect," in *The Essential Writings of Ralph Waldo Emerson* [New York: Modern Library, 2000], 270).

12. Simone Weil's *Gravity and Grace*, trans. Arthur Wills (New York: Putnam, 1952). Lee Russell gets as close anyone to the importance of Weil's thought for Rossellini's film-making. See his "Roberto Rossellini" in *New Left Review* (I/42, March–April 1967): 69–71.

13. Ibid., 47.

14. Ibid., 49.

15. Ibid.

16. Simone Weil, "Human Personality," in *Simone Weil: An Anthology*, ed. Siân Miles (New York: Grove Press, 1986): 49–78.

17. On the notion of "drink-present" in German as poison, see Marcel Mauss, "Gift, Gift," in *The Logic of the Gift: Toward an Ethic of Generosity*, ed. Alan D. Schrift (New York: Routledge, 1997): 28–31. See, too, of course Jacques Derrida's reading of *pharmakon* in *Dissemination*, trans. Barbara Johnson (Chicago: University of Chicago Press 1981), 95–117; and Roberto Esposito's consideration of it in the light of community and immunity in the first chapter of *Communitas*.

18. In this we owe a debt to Slavoj Žižek who was among the first, along with Rancière, to propose a non-linear reading of cause and effect between Enning and Edmund. See his classic "Rossellini: Woman as Symptom of Man," in *October*, Vol. 54 (Autumn, 1990): 18–44. Rancière's reading can be found in "La Chute des corps" in *Roberto Rossellini* (Paris: Cahiers du Cinema, 1989).

19. Melanie Klein, *Envy and Gratitude* (New York: Simon and Schuster, 2002), 187.

20. Ibid., 188.

21. Ibid., 192.

22. "Man transfers his libido not only to animate but also to inanimate objects. He has a personal relation to almost all the objects of his environment, and this relation originates in his sexuality" (Karl Abraham, "Hysteria and Dementia Praecox," in *Selected Papers of Karl Abraham* [New York: Hogarth Press, 1973], 66). Megalomania isn't far behind: "The mental patient transfers on to himself alone as his only sexual object the whole of the libido which the healthy person turns upon all living and inanimate objects in his environment, and accordingly his sexual over-estimation is directed towards himself alone and assumes enormous dimensions. For he is his whole world" (75).

23. In the script, Rossellini describes the final sequence this way. "Edmund stares out the window, then closes his eyes and throws himself out." Interestingly, Rossellini feels it necessary to add: "Edmund is falling through the air" (Roberto Rossellini, *The War Trilogy: Open City, Paisan, Germany-Year-Zero*, trans. Judith Green [New York: Grossman, 1973], 466).

24. "Excessive idealization denotes that persecution is the main driving force. As I discovered many years ago in my work with young children, idealization is a corollary of persecutory anxiety—a defense against it—and the ideal breast is the counterpart of the devouring breast" (Klein, 193).

25. On the use of non-diegetic music in Italian neo-realism see M. Thomas Van Order, *Listening to Fellini: Music and Meaning in Black and White*; Richard Dyer's "Music, People and Reality in Italian Neo-Realism," in *European Film Music*, ed. Miguel Mera and David Burnand (London: Ashgate, 2006); and David Forgacs's comparison of soundtracks in Rossellini's other films in *Rome Open City* (London: British Film Institute), 55. The point for all is that "neorealism revolutionizes almost everything in filmmaking except the conventions of the sound track" (Van Order, 15).

26. The film recalls nothing so much as that most neo-realist *Star Trek* episode of them all, "Miri." Banned in the United Kingdom for years, the episode recounts the story of how the crew of the *Enterprise* discover a world in which children live until adolescence at which point their immunity to the disease no longer protects them.

27. Abraham, 75.

28. Certainly, Rossellini remained dubious throughout his life when it came to the virtues of education. See, in particular, his "Il mondo in cui viviamo," especially those pages dedicated to the etymology of *educare* in the Latin *educere*, which among its many meanings meant castration, too (Roberto Rossellini, *Utopia Autopsia 10* [Rome: Armando, 1974]).

29. Consider the role that vaudeville plays in the film according to Millicent Marcus (*Italian Film in the Light of Neorealism* [Princeton: Princeton University Press, 1987], 41–44).

30. George Crabb, *English Synonymes: Explained in Alphabetical Order* (New York: Harper, 1897), 789.

31. Weil, *Gravity and Grace*, 156.

32. Ibid.

33. "The finale of *Germany Year Zero* seemed clear: it was a true light of hope . . . And the gesture of the child in killing himself is a gesture of abandonment, a gesture of exhaustion with which he puts behind him all the horror he has lived and believed because he acted according to a precise set of morals. He feels the vanity of all this and the light goes on inside him and he has this moment of abandonment" (*L'avventurosa storia del cinema italiano raccontato dai suoi protagonist, 1935–1959*, ed. Franca Faldini and Goffredo Fofi [Milano: Feltrinelli, 1979]; quoted in Brunette, 86).

34. Klein, 203. The word that comes to mind in such a context is serenity: "Serenity does not always require passive acceptance. Of course, that a situation is undesirable or tragic need not in itself be sufficient grounds for acting against it. The point is that adopting a general outlook does not compel one to adopt particular evaluations for specific situations or to act towards them in specific ways" (Charles Crittenden, "Serenity," in *Journal of Indian Philosophy* 12, no. 3 [September 1984], 209). See Kraucauer's boring reflections on boredom: "If, however, one has the sort of patience specific to legitimate boredom, then one experiences a kind of bliss that is almost unearthly. A landscape appears in which colorful peacocks strut about . . . And look—your own soul is likewise swelling, and in ecstasy you name what you have always lacked: the great passion" (Sigfried Kraucauer, "Boredom," in The *Mass Ornament: Weimar Essays*, trans. Thomas Y. Levin [Cambridge: Harvard University Press, 1995], 334).

35. This raises important parallels with contemporary life today in the absence of community: "The attention economy has became an important subject during the first years of the new century. Virtual workers have less and less time for attention, they are involved in a growing number of intellectual tasks, and they have no more time to devote to their own life, to love, tenderness, and affection . . . The scenario of the first years of the new millennium seems to be dominated by a veritable wave of psychopathic behaviour. The suicidal phenomenon is spreading well beyond the borders of Islamic fanatic martyrdom. Since WTC/911 suicide has become the crucial political act on the global political scene. Aggressive suicide should not be seen as a mere phenomenon of despair and aggression, but has to be seen as the declaration of the end" (Francesco "Bifo" Berardi, "What Is the Meaning of Autonomy Today?" (http://republicart.net/disc/realpublicspaces/berardi01_en.htm).

36. "Hate, as a relation to objects is older than love. It derives from the narcissistic ego's primordial repudiation of the external world with its outpouring of stimuli. As an expression of the reaction of unpleasure evoked by objects, it always

remains in an intimate relation with the self-preservative instincts; so that sexual and ego-instincts can readily develop an antithesis which repeats that of love and hate" (Sigmund Freud, "Instinct and Its Vicissitudes," *Standard Edition of the Complete Psychological Works of Sigmund Freud*, vol. 14, trans. James Strachey [London: Hogarth Press, 1953–74], 139).

37. "According to Rossellini, the modern camera had equipped the human eye 'with a gaze that allows it, for the first time in the history of the world, to surpass its own finitude to meet up with reality in all its aspects'—a claim that has affinities with theological notions of revelation as much as with philosophical ideas of enlightenment. Despite his self-proclaimed atheism, Rossellini continually cast his projected informational utopia in theological terms. Knowledge, put into visible form, broadcast across the continent or organized into an easily accessible video database, would bring about not only widespread peace and cooperation, but also a kind of metaphysical clarity, a return to a prelapsarian 'Eden of information'" (Michael Cramer, "Rossellini's History Lessons," in New Left Review 78 [November–December 2012], 122). Enzo Ungari recognized just this feature of Rossellini's camera many years earlier: "Rossellini has no shame in *Germany, Year Zero* . . . This is his profound lesson for modern film: the implacable camera" (Enzo Ungari, "Quando il 'decoupage' sembrava una prigione: Conversazione con Carlo Lizzani," in *Cult Movie* II, no. 3 [aprile-maggio, 1981; quoted in Brunette, 83]).

38. On the figure of the *flâneur*, see Giuliana Bruno's now seminal account in *Streetwalking on a Ruined Map: Cultural Theory and the City Films of Elvira Notari* (Princeton: Princeton University Press, 1993). See, too, Wheeler Dixon's opposing perspective in *It Looks at You: The Returned Gaze of Cinema* (Albany: State University of New York Press, 1995), 64–65.

39. Or more simply, observation. On the notion of "observation cinema," see the opening chapter of Anna Grimshaw and Amanda Ravetz's *Observational Cinema: Anthropology, Film, and the Exploration of Social Life* (Bloomington: Indiana University Press, 2009).

40. Deleuze certainly understood this: "To describe the relationship of the eye and the hand, and the values through which this relation passes, it is obviously not enough to say that the eye judges and the hands execute. The relationship between the hand and the eye is infinitely richer, passing through dynamic tensions, logical reversals, and organic exchanges and substitutions." Later he adds: "Finally, we will speak of the haptic whenever there is no longer a strict subordination in either direction, either a relaxed subordination or a virtual connection, but when sight discovers in itself a specific function of touch that is uniquely its own, distinct from its optical function" (Gilles Deleuze, *Francis Bacon*, trans. Daniel W. Smith [London: Continuum, 2005], 154; 155). On their relation to hapticity in cinema, see Barbara Kennedy, *Deleuze and Cinema* (Edinburgh: Edinburgh University Press, 2002): "This hapticity is simultaneously optic and tactile. The visual becomes felt. The felt

connection between eye and hand is felt, in coagulation, an evolution of hand into eye" (117).

41. Jacques Derrida, *On Touching–Jean-Luc Nancy*, trans. Christine Irizarry (Stanford: Stanford University Press, 2005), 124.

42. Walter Benjamin, *The Arcades Project*, trans. Howard Eiland and Kevin McLaughlin (Cambridge: The Belknap Press of Harvard University Press, 1999), 206–7.

43. Rossellini saw the ending similarly: "And the gesture of the child in killing himself is a gesture of abandonment, a gesture of exhaustion with which he puts behind him all the horror he has lived and believed because he acted exactly according to a precise set of morals . . . he abandons himself to the great sleep of death, and from there is born a new way of living and of seeing . . ." (Faldini and Fofi, *L'avventurosa storia del cinema italiano* [Bologna: Cineteca Bologna, 2009], 112; quoted in Brunette, 86).

44. André Bazin, *What Is Cinema?* (Berkeley: University of California Press, 2005), 62.

45. Ibid.

46. Ibid., 63.

47. Stanley Cavell's response to isolation comes to mind in this regard: "I am not to give myself explanations that divide me from myself, that take sides against myself, that would exact my consent, not attract it. That would cede my voice to my isolation. That I might never be found" (Stanley Cavell, *Conditions Handsome and Unhandsome: The Constitution of Emersonian Perfectionism* (Chicago: The University of Chicago Press, 1990, 100).

48. Wilfred Bion, "A Theory of Thinking," in *Second Thoughts: Selected Papers on Psychoanalysis* (London: William Heinemann Medical Books, 1967), 111. The follow-up merits attention: "This initiates the state, described by Freud in his 'Two Principles of Mental Functioning,' in which dominance by the reality principle is synchronous with the development of an ability to think and so to bridge the gulf of frustration between when a want is felt and the moment when action is appropriate to satisfying the want culminates in its satisfaction" (112).

49. Certainly, other views on thought and tolerance are equally possible: "Is there not something catastrophic in the very nature of thought? Thought is driven by an excessive compulsion, and is itself an excess over and beyond perception. Thinking is looking for what exceeds the powers of sight, what is unbearable to look at, what exceeds the possibilities of thought" (Alphonso Lingis, *Dangerous Emotions* [Berkeley: University of California Press, 2000], 134).

50. "Man no longer finds himself confronted by a world of ideas in which he can choose his own truth on the basis of a sovereign decision made by his free reason. He is already linked to a certain number of these ideas, just as he is linked by birth to all those who are of his blood. He can no longer play with the idea [*jouer avec*

l'idee], for coming from his concrete being, anchored in his flesh and blood, the idea remains serious" (Emmanuel Levinas, "Reflections on the Philosophy of Hitlerism," *Critical Inquiry* 17, No. 1 [Autumn, 1990], 70).

51. Ibid., 114.

52. "Bion formulated the notion that 'thinking' is dependent on the successful outcome of two main mental developments. One is the development of thoughts; the second is the development of the apparatus necessary to deal with the thoughts (Ronald Britton, "Keeping Things in Mind," *Clinical Lectures on Klein and Bion*, ed. Robin Anderson [London: Routledge, 2014], 106). Compare this with Rossellini's interview with Mario Verdone in which he says that "in my way of seeing, the waiting: every solution is born of the wait. It is the wait that brings things to life, that unleashes the reality, the wait which—after a building up yields the liberation" (Mario Verdone, "Colloquio sul neorealismo," in Roberto Rossellini, *Il mio metodo: Scritti e interviste*, ed. Adriano Aprà [Venice: Marsilio, 1987], 13). Inga M. Pierson offers an insightful reading of *Germany Year Zero* in her 2008 dissertation, *Towards a Poetics of Neorealism: Tragedy in Italian Cinema 1942–1948*.

53. In a terrific essay on Winnicott and masochism, Emmanuel Ghent notes the relation between healing, making whole, and holy, all of which are etymological cognates. He goes on to observe Winnicott's description in *Playing and Reality* of false self as "missing the boat," or at times simply as "missing, " "being absent." In the Old Testament the Hebrew word designating sin has as its literal meaning to miss as in "missing the boat," "missing an opportunity to be present, alive" (Fromm, 1966, p. 132). The cure for missing is to become whole through surrender; the cure for sinning, in this sense, is to come alive, to be present in full awareness, authentic, centered in true self, holy" (Emanuel Ghent, "Masochism, Submission, Surrender—Masochism as a Perversion of Surrender," in *Contemporary Psychoanalysis* 26, no. 1 [1990], 109).

54. We might choose to call such a perspective "impolitical": "But it is also the case that what appears as a choice is only the awareness of a reality to which we belong without ever wholly belonging to it. What else would the impolitical be, if not this imperceptible disjuncture?" (Roberto Esposito, "Preface to *Categories of the Impolitical*," in *Diacritics* 39.2 [Summer 2009], 113).

5. THE TENDER LIVES OF VITTI/VITTORIA

1. For Antonioni, the Marxist, see "The Cinema of Poetry," a reading of Antonioni's "obsessive framing" as well as John David Rhodes's incisive gloss: Pier Paolo Pasolini, "The Cinema of Poetry," in *Movies and Methods Vol. 1*, ed. Bill Nichols (Berkeley: University of California Press, 1976): 542–58, as well as his "Pasolini's Exquisite Flowers: The 'Cinema of Poetry' and a Theory of Art Cinema," in *Global Art Cinema: New Theories and Histories*, ed. Rosalind Galt and Karl Schoonover

(New York: Oxford University Press, 2010), 142–63); Frank Tomasulo, "The Bourgeoisie Is Also a Class: Class as Character in Michelangelo Antonioni's *L'avventura*," in *Jump Cut: A Review of Contemporary Media*, n. 49 (Spring 2007), http://www.ejumpcut.org/archive/jc49.2007/Tomasulo/text.html. For the geographer, see Manuela Mariani and Patrick Barron's "Cinematic Space in Rome's *Disabitato*: Between Metropolis and Terrain Vague in the Films of Fellini, Antonioni, and Pasolini," in *Modernism/modernity* 18, no. 2 (April 2011): 309–33; and *Taking Place: Location and the Moving Image*, ed. John David Rhodes and Elena Gorfinkel (Minneapolis: University of Minnesota Press, 2011). On climate change as well as biopolitics, see Karen Pinkus's breathtaking "Antonioni's Cinematic Poetics of Climate Change," in *Antonioni: Centenary Essays*, ed. Laura Rascaroli and John David Rhodes (New York: Palgrave, 2011).

2. Here I remain indebted to Seymour Chatman's singular insight: "Antonioni's most valuable contribution to the cinema can already be seen—his unrelenting insistence on the value of the pure visual given" (Seymour Benjamin Chatman, *Antonioni, Or, The Surface of the World* [Berkeley: University of California Press, 1985], 7). So, too, John David Rhodes: "Antonioni's vision is, in fact, abstract and abstracting. But it is the abstract (oblique, formally belabored, defamiliarizing) mode of looking that makes us really see things, people, and places in the first place. The abstracting gaze is already competing and coming to terms with a landscape that has become, itself, increasingly abstract" ("Rethinking Michelangelo's Modernism: A Conversation Between Karl Schoonover and John David Rhodes," University of Minnesota Press, http://www.upress.umn.edu/book-division/theme/rethinking-antonioni). For a classic reading of Antonioni and alienation, see Umberto Eco's *The Open Work*, trans. Anna Cancogni (Cambridge: Harvard University Press, 1989), especially the chapter "Form as Social Commitment."

3. Is *L'avventura* an *Urtext* for all Scandinavian films and television series in which a woman or girl goes missing? *The Girl with the Dragon Tattoo* and the Danish *Forbrydelsen*? Seemingly, where there's an island, a woman is sure to disappear.

4. The difference between touch and holding goes missing in Chatman's account, which reduces touch from three dimensions to two and so creates the collusion between the eye and the hand (Chatman, 120–22).

5. "Because beings in fact do not *give themselves*, but appear at the same time as something in them resists (their matter, but also their very presence, where they are), because they remain in the completed enclosure of their shape only by withdrawing their very existence, the sense that will not so much open access to them but reveal their presence will in fact be touch, the sense of surface and boundary, which encloses as much as it opens, and conceals as much as it displays" (Frank Kausch, "The Greek View as Political Experience," *Diogenes* 49 [2002]: 37).

6. Lyotard, "The Grip (*Mainmise*), 148. Cf. Deleuze's reading of Francis Bacon: "The words Leiris uses to describe Bacon—hand, touch, seizure, capture—evoke

this direct manual activity that traces the possibility of fact: we will capture the fact, just as well will 'seize hold of life'" (Deleuze, *Francis Bacon*, 161).

7. Or a repetition that is not a possession:

> "To be &
> be the present.   Would it be a
>
> repetition? Only if we thought we
> owned it, but since we don't, it
> is free & so are we . . ." (John Cage, *Silence*, 184)

8. Viktor Shklovsky, "Art as Technique," in *Russian Formalist Criticism*, trans. Lee T. Lemon and Marion J. Reis (Lincoln: University of Nebraska Press, 1965), 12 See also Carlo Ginzburg's lovely reading of defamiliarization: "To understand less, to be ingenuous, to remain stupefied: these are reactions that may lead us to see more, and to take account of what lies deeper, what is closer to nature" (Carlo Ginzburg, *Wooden Eyes: Nine Reflections on Distance* [New York: Columbia University Press, 2001], 13).

9. Consider Kenneth Burke's definition of form as the "the creation of an appetite in the mind of the auditor, and the adequate satisfying of that appetite" (Kenneth Burke, *Counter-Statement* [Berkeley: University of California Press, 1968], 31).

10. Antonioni speaks of the screenplay in just these terms: "Screenplays are on the way to becoming actually sheets of notes for those who, at the camera, will write the film themselves. The turn being taken by other arts as well, such as music and painting, inexorably headed toward freer forms, authorizes us to think so" (Michelangelo Antonioni, *Screenplays of Michelangelo Antonioni* [New York: The Orion Press, 1963], xviii).

11. It would at a minimum be far removed from Levinas's hand that acquires: "The hand *comprehends* the thing not because it touches it on all sides at the same time . . . but because it is no longer a sense-organ, pure enjoyment, pure sensibility, but is mastery, domination, disposition—which do not belong to the order of sensibility. An organ for taking, for acquisition, it gathers the fruit, but holds it far from the lips, puts it in reserve, possesses it in a home" (Levinas, *Totality and Infinity*, 161).

12. On the uncanny and its relation to figure-ground inversion, see El Hadi Jazairy, "Cinematic Landscapes in Antonioni's *L'avventura*," *Journal of Cultural Geography* 26 (2009): 349–67. On the uncanny in *L'avventura* and *La notte*, see Laura Rascaroli and John David Rhodes "Antonioni and the Place of Modernity: A Tribute," in *Framework* 49, no. 1 (Spring 2008): 44–47.

13. There is in the scene all of the various etymologies of grip, gripe, and grasp: "From *greifen* in German and then from the Sanskrit–GRAH, grih-na, "seize, take (also of leeches), hold, catch, stop; grasp, gain possession of, capture, captivate (the heart); attack; eclipse, rob, deprive of, receive from, assume, acquire, purchase, and

then grahaya, cause to seize, take or grasp, be about to seize; desire to grasp; cherish." *A Sanskrit English Dictionary*, 87 (http://openlibrary.org).

14. Nicholas Royle, *The Uncanny* (Manchester: Manchester University Press, 2003), 88.

15. Such a reading dovetails nicely with Alessia Ricciardi's rich insights into Antonioni's film-making as well as her reminder of the importance of drives via Lacan. "In the essay, 'Position of the Unconscious' (1964), Lacan decisively concluded that "every drive is virtually a death drive" after making the observation that "the signifier as such, whose first purpose is to bar the subject, has brought into him the meaning of death" (Jacques Lacan, *Écrits*, 719; quoted in Alessia Ricciardi, "Becoming Woman: From Antonioni to Anne Carson and Cindy Sherman, *The Yearbook of Comparative Literature* 56 [2010], 8).

16. Or an accident. Consider the extended sequence in the screenplay, cut to a few seconds in the film, in which "another care draws up alongside Sandro's and is about to pass him. But Sandro steps on the accelerator and pulls ahead with a tremendous burst of speed." Interestingly, it is only when Sandro very nearly crashes into a wall that Anna becomes "attentive" (Antonioni, *Screenplays*, 102).

17. Cf. Domietta Torlasco's reading of the death drive in Cavani's *The Night Porter* and its relation to "suspended play": "The time of the death drive is here a time out of joint, in which death will have always taken place—a circular time that offers no escape but also no instantaneous release" (Domietta Torlasco, *The Time of the Crime: Phenomenology, Psychoanalysis, Italian Film* [Palo Alto: Stanford University Press, 2008], 55). In *L'avventura*, however, with no catastrophic violence to inflect death, the ego is anything but consolidated or bound. This suggests a form of life constitutively different from the ego or self.

18. "Life is form and form is the modal of life. The relationships that bind forms together in nature cannot be by pure chance, and what we call natural life is in effect a relationship between forms, so inexorable that without this, natural life could not exist" (Henri Focillon, *The Life of Forms in Art*, trans. Charles Beecher Hogan and George Kubler [New York: Zone Books, 1989], 2).

19. "In that the camera on the one hand pierces quotidian surfaces with its peculiar technologies of representation, yet on the other tends to make its own work invisible, film is capable of ushering the spectator into the realms of profane illumination, into an arena of flash-like, nonintentional, and sensuous cognition similar to the one Benjamin unearthed in the works of the surrealists, of Baudelaire, and in the context of his own experiments with drugs and intoxication. Cinema may after all allow for forms of reciprocity reminiscent of the experience of auratic phenomena" (Lutz Peter Koepnick, *Walter Benjamin and the Aesthetics of Power* [Lincoln: University of Nebraska Press, 1999], 224–25).

20. Charles Rockwell Lanman, *A Sanskrit Reader: With Vocabulary and Notes* (Boston: Ginn & Co., 1912), 162.

21. Here Levinas precedes us: "Anticipation grasps possibilities; what the caress seeks is not situated in a perspective and in the light of the graspable. The carnal, the tender par excellence correlative of the caress, the beloved is identified either with the body-thing or the physiologist, nor with the lived body [*corps propre* of the 'I can' . . . In the caress, . . . the body already denudes itself of its very form, offering itself as erotic nudity" (Levinas, *Totality*, 258).

22. We might also note that degrees of holding—be it a musical note, holding on to a boat, holding oneself—can only be known when one has held and let go. It is this return to holding and then letting go that profoundly links the forms of life we see on the screen to form of living on the other side of the screen in our lives.

23. "In short, the animal merely uses its environment, and brings about changes in it simply by its presence; man by his changes makes it serve his ends, masters it. This is the final, essential distinction between man and other animals, and once again it is labour that brings about this distinction" ("The Part played by Labour in the Transition from Ape to Man," Friedrich Engels, http://www.marxists.org/archive/marx/works/1876/part-played-labour/).

24. One answer? "The camera eye refuses to simplify, to reduce the heterogeneous complexity of the world to a few motifs merely in order to validate some ideology" (Chatman, 7).

25. "It is the fact of dying that includes a radical reversal, through which the death that was the extreme form of my power not only becomes what loosens my hold upon myself by casting me out of my power to begin and even to finish, but also becomes that which is without any relation to me, without power over me—that which is stripped of all possibility—the unreality of the indefinite" (Blanchot, *Space of Literature* [Lincoln: University of Nebraska Press, 1982], 154–55; quoted in Gilles Deleuze, *Difference and Repetition* [London: Continuum, 2004], 138).

26. "For truth is neither in seeing nor in grasping, which are modes of enjoyment, sensibility, and possession; it is in transcendence, in which absolute exteriority presents itself in expressing itself, in a movement at each instant recovering and deciphering the very signs it emits" (Levinas, *Totality and Infinity*, 172).

27. Throughout my reading of hold and grip in *L'avventura*, I am deeply indebted to the writing of David Sudnow and his brilliant memoir of learning to play jazz on the piano. "Looking's workload progressively lightens for finding distances, the gaze at the keyboard progressively diffuses in function, as places gradually become places toward which the appreciative fingers, hand, and arm are aimed." The experience is one of sensing "a rate of movement and distance required at varying tempos and developing, thereby, an embodied way of accomplishing distances." What we might ask in such a perspective does "there" refer to? "How to go from place to place as an accomplishment" (David Sudnow, *Ways of the Hand: The Organization of Improvised Conduct* [Cambridge: MIT Press, 1978], 12).

28. Winnicott, "Transitional Objects and Transitional Phenomena," in *Playing with Reality* (London: Routledge, 2012), 15. "Come to think of it, do any of us grow right up out of a need for an intermediate area between ourselves, with our personal inner world, and external or shared reality? The strain that the baby feels in sorting out the two is never altogether lost, and we allow ourselves a cultural life, something that can be shared, yet something that is personal (D. W. Winnicott, *Talking to Parents* [New York: The Winnicott Trust, 1993], 19).

29. What also comes to mind, surprisingly, is veneration. Writing almost thirty years ago, Mario Perniola focuses on *veneratio*, which he defines as saying "yes to oneself. Not, of course, to one's own desires, dreams, and ideals: all these things are too imbued with negation and absence, too abstract and inconsistent to be truly retained elements or aspects of oneself. Seduction may be rightly defined as the magic of absence, but 'venus' is quite to the contrary, inseparable from presence from one's own situation, from that which is given to us. To venerate means to be at peace with oneself, to know how to will backward, to want that which has happened . . . to want the present without being conditioned by its contents" (Mario Perniola, "Venusean Charme," in *Recoding Metaphysics: The New Italian Philosophy*, ed. Giovanna Borradori [Evanston: Northwestern University Press, 1989], 96).

30. Walter Benjamin's reading of experience and narration in "The Storyteller" might be read differently in this light. In Winnicott's reading of transitional objects, the development Benjamin describes would result from the lack of transitional phenomena through which creativity and reality testing are possible. Today, the running amok of apparatuses in neo-liberalism would appear in such a light as the proliferation of toys but not playthings. For their part, counter-*dispositifs* would name those transitional objects that do not move to possession all at once because the objects do not in any sense "belong" to the individual.

31. It is, in other words, a place in which gravity dominates: "Energy, freed by the disappearance of the objects which provide motives, always tends to go downwards" (Simone Weil, *Gravity and Grace*, 8).

32. Christian Metz. "Photography and Fetish," in *October* 34 (Autumn 1985), 87.

33. Ibid., 88.

34. Ibid.

35. Writing of Georges Méliès and infinitely repeatable *trucage* (special effects), Linda Williams notes how *trucage* "offers two related forms of mastery over the threat of castration posed by the illusory presence of the woman's body made possible by cinema: on the one hand, the drama of dismemberment and reintegration performed on all bodies, and on the other hand the celebration of the fetish function of the apparatus itself, particularly in its ability to reproduce an image of the woman's body" (Linda Williams, "An Implantation of Perversions," in *Narrative, Apparatus, Ideology: A Film Reader Theory*, ed. Philip Rosen [New York: Columbia University Press, 1986], 526). See as well Metz's reading of *trucage*: "It is in fact

essential to know that the cinema in its entirety is, in a sense, a vast *trucage*" (Christian Metz, "*Trucage* and the Film," in *The Language of Images*, ed. W. I. T. Mitchell [Chicago: University of Chicago Press, 1980], 154).

36. As well as possession. "How one possesses oneself is tied to how one possesses things and persons. To be free with regard to one's own existence, the loss of everything and everyone" (Emmanuel Levinas, *Quaderni*, 107).

37. Consider in this regard Metz's views on the difference between the indexical and the iconic. "The photographic *take* is immediate and definitive, like death and like the constitution of the fetish in the unconscious, fixed by a glance in childhood, unchanged and always active later . . . I will add that in life, and to some extent in film, one piece of time is indefinitely pushed backwards by the next: This is what we call 'forgetting'" (Metz, "Photography and Fetish," 84).

38. In terms Levinas employs, we might choose to speak of vertigo in the spectator: "The negation of every qualifiable thing allows the impersonal there is to arise again, returning intact behind every negation, whatever be the degree of negation. The silence of infinite spaces is terrifying. The invasion of this *there is* does not correspond to any representation. We have described elsewhere its vertigo. And the elemental essence of the element, with the mythical facelessness from which it comes, participates in the same vertigo. In driving out darkness the light does not arrest the incessant play of the *there is*" (Levinas, *Totality and Infinity*, 190).

39. Antonioni considers just such a possibility in "Screen Test," though here he is clearly preceded by Rossellini's short film, *Una voce umana*.

40. Proposing a philosophy of sexual difference, Adriana Cavarero observes: "Such a thought could not simply unmask the false neutrality of philosophy. It would have to become the representative potency of and for a female subject able to name and think herself, having as her starting point the originary and irreducible sexual difference: sexual difference as the foundation of thought for the female subject, neither absorbable in and by the other sex, nor mere accident" (Adriana Cavarero, "The Need for Sexed Thought," in *Italian Feminist Thought: A Reader*, ed. Paolo Bono and Sandra Kemp [Oxford: Basil Blackwell, 1991], 183).

41. For recent discussions of *La notte*, see Torunn Haaland, "*Flanerie*, Spatial Practices and Nomadic Thought in Antonioni's *La notte*," *Italica* 90.4 (2013): 596–619; Jeremy Carr, "People and Their Places in Antonioni's *La notte*," *CineAction* 93 (January 2014): 50–55; the enlightening discussion conducted by Enzo Paci with his students on Antonioni in *Annali d'Italianisitica* 29 (2011): 33–58; Alessia Ricciardi's wonderful reading of women in Antonioni's films, "Becoming Woman: From Antonioni to Anne Carson and Cindy Sherman," in *Yearbook of Comparative and General Literature* 56 (January 2010): 6–23; and Frank Tomasulo and Jason McKahan, "'Sick Eros': The Sexual Politics of Antonioni's Trilogy," in *Projections: The Journal of Movies and Mind* 3 (January 2009): 1–23.

42. On Antonioni's existentialist *bona fides*, see Kevin Aho, *Existentialism: An Introduction* (Cambridge: Polity, 2014); Manuela Gieri, *Contemporary Italian Filmmaking: Strategies of Subversion* (Toronto: University of Toronto Press, 1995); and of course Chatman's *Antonioni*, especially 55–60.

43. "A social relationship will be called 'communal' if and so far as the orientation of social action—whether in the individual case, on the average, or in the pure type—is based on a subjective feeling of the parties, whether affectual or traditional, that they belong together" (Max Weber, *Economy and Society: An Outline of Interpretive Sociology* [Berkeley: University of California Press, 1968], 40).

44. Describing *L'eclisse*, Chatman writes: "The contingency of incidental objects photographed with loving care opens a world that we must contemplate, not categorize . . . The semantic burden is shifted to the viewer's shoulders: that is Antonioni's gift to cinema" (Chatman, 100; 101).

45. And, according to Levinas, feminine: "The feminine has been encountered in this analysis as one of the cardinal points of the horizon in which the inner life takes place-and the empirical absence of the human being of 'feminine sex' in a dwelling nowise affects the dimension of femininity which remains open there, as the very welcome of the dwelling" (Levinas, *Totality and Infinity*, 158).

46. The larger debt that *Eyes Wide Shut* owes to *La notte* remains to be acknowledged. Lee Siegel, "*Eyes Wide Shut*: What the Critics Failed to See in Kubrick's Last Film," in *Harper's Magazine* 76 (October 1999): 150.

47. Maurizio Lazzarato does. "Like machines, humans are hybrids of 'dead' and 'living labor'. Machinic enslavement (or processes) precedes the subject and object and surpasses the personological distinctions of social subjection. The latter, between the living and dead, subject and object, are the result of the reterritorialization process centered on 'man' and 'labor'"(Maurizio Lazzarato, *Signs and Machines* [Los Angeles: Semiotext(e), 2014], 120).

48. Simone Weil, *First and Last Notebooks* (Oxford: Oxford University Press, 1970), 335; quoted in Sharon Cameron, *Impersonality: Seven Essays* (Chicago: University of Chicago Press, 2009), 141.

49. On sound in Antonioni's films, see Chapter 5 in Antonella C. Sisto's *Film Sound in Italy: Listening to the Screen* (New York: Palgrave, 2014). The classic account remains Carlo Di Carlo's *Michelangelo Antonioni* (Roma: Bianco e Nero, 1964).

50. Hermann Broch, *Geist and Zeitgeist*, trans. John Hargraves (New York: Counterpoint, 2002), 42.

51. "We shall neither be the first upon those heights / nor the last; no, a few of our kind / will join us continually, and one fine day / we shall say We, we shall / forget the I. And then perhaps / we shall speak thus: . . ." (Hermann Broch, *The Guiltless*, trans. Ralph Manheim [Boston: Little, Brown and Company, 1974], 237).

52. "The thing that repels me the most about philosophers is the emptying process of their thinking. The more often and more skillfully they use their basic terms,

the less remains of the world around them. They are like barbarians in a high, spacious mansion of wonderful works. They stand there in their shirt sleeves and throw everything out the window, methodically and steadfastly, chairs, pictures, plates, animals, children, until there's nothing left but whole empty rooms. Sometimes the doors and windows come flying last. The naked house remains. They imagine that these devastations make it *better*" (Elias Canetti, *The Human Province*, trans. Joachim Neugroschel [London: André Deutsche, 1985], 126).

53. "To ask *what is* to ask *as what*: it is not to take the manifestation for itself" (Levinas, *Totality and Infinity*, 177).

54. We might describe Antonioni's Milan as a kind of picturesque park: "What does Smithson say? That the picturesque park is not the transcription on the land of a compositional pattern previously fixed in the mind, that its effects cannot be determined, *a priori*, that presupposes a stroller, someone who trusts more in the real movement of his gaze than in the fictive movement of his gaze" (Yve-Alain Bois and John Shepley, "A Picturesque Stroll around 'Clara-Clara,'" *October* 29 [Summer 1984], 36). Interestingly, Antonioni's own method mimics this: "One thing I can say: Until I edit a film of mine, I have no idea myself what it will be about. And perhaps not even then. Perhaps it will only be a reflection of a mood . . . I depart from my shooting script constantly" (Cardullo, 84).

55. Antonioni, *Screenplays*, x.

56. Kenneth Burke suggests a milieu of "maybe": "Pleasure and pain can no longer be exactly what they would be to us sheerly as animals, and similarly with love and hate (or fear), once we approach problems of 'acceptance' and 'rejection' through the genius of that specifically linguistic pair, 'Yes' and 'No' (to which we should add the strategic midway stage of 'Maybe')" (Kenneth Burke, *Attitudes*, 373–74).

57. "The aptitudes of hands are written in their curves and structure . . . The hand means action: it grasps, it creates, at times it would seem even to think" (Focillon, 65).

58. What Chatman writes of Vittoria in *L'eclisse* holds true for Lidia as well: "Vittoria sees the world with rare clarity. She can take pleasure in life's simpler beauties" (59). See Antonioni's interview from 1962 in *Postif* on this score: "Under her layer of anxiety she is serene enough . . . She is resigned but eventually she is smiling: love isn't everything. And up to now eclipses haven't been final" (quoted in Chatman, 251).

59. Peter Brunette, *The Films of Michelangelo Antonioni* (Cambridge: Cambridge University Press, 1998), 117–18.

60. "I am positive that the world today is filled more with dead feelings than with live ones. I would like to know more about these residues. Perhaps we have to go back to the beginning and ask what is a feeling. And to identify it almost as an effect . . . in relation to not only its protagonist but also its observer" (Antonioni, xii).

61. "The comic will come into being, it appears, whenever a group of men concentrate their attention on one of their number, imposing silence on their emotions and calling into play nothing but their intelligence" (Bergson, *Laughter*, 5).

62. "Film is the first art capable of demonstrating how matter plays tricks on man [*wie die Materie dem Menschen mitspielt*]" (Walter Benjamin, "The Work of Art in the Age of Mechanical Reproduction," in *Illuminations*, ed. Hannah Arendt [1968], 247). For a terrific reading of Benjamin's relation to Hegel, the end of symbolic art, and the role of the hand, see Eva Geulen's *The End of Art: Readings in a Rumor After Hegel* (Stanford: Stanford University Press, 2006): "Terms drawn from the German root *Hand*—'grasp' (*Handgriff*), 'manipulation' (*Handhabe*), 'manifest' (*handgrieflich*)—constitute their own semantic field in his text" (83).

63. Umberto Eco's emphasis on forms in Antonioni's films is rightly placed if not the emphasis on alienation alone: "Antonioni lets his forms express the alienation he wants to communicate to his public" (Eco, 149).

64. Which is not to say, as Umberto Eco does, that all are "useless" in the film: "This movie about a useless and unlikely love affair between useless and unlikely characters tells us more about contemporary man and his world than a panoramic melodrama involving workers in overalls and countless social conditions" (149).

65. "Mimetism is a source of continual conflict. By making one man's desire into a replica of another man's desire, it invariably leads to rivalry; and rivalry in turn transforms desire into violence" (René Girard, *Violence and the Sacred* [London: Continuum, 2005], 179).

66. See, for example, Richard Peña's audio commentary for the Criterion Collection DVD of *L'eclisse* (*L'eclisse*, directed by Michelangelo Antonioni [1962; Italy: The Criterion Collection, 2014], DVD).

67. Or to an impression of ineptness: "Antonioni is a master of the medium—but in a highly individualistic and peculiar way. He has none of the conventional director's tricks of the trade, perhaps not even ordinary syntax, and he is painfully inept and obvious when has to fall back on a simple action sequence (like the street fight in *La Notte* . . . He uses a seemingly random, peripheral course of development, apparently merely following the characters through inconsistencies and inadvertences; and without all the usual plot cues and paraphernalia)" (Pauline Kael, "The Sick-Soul-of-Europe Parties, 'La Notte,' 'La Dolce Vita,' 'Marienbad,'" in *The Massachusetts Review* 4, no. 2 [Winter, 1963], 378). See, too, Eric Rhode, *A History of Cinema from Its Origins to 1970* (London: A. Lane, 1976), 589–91.

68. Roland Barthes, "Appendix: 'Dear Antonioni . . .'" in Geoffrey Nowell-Smith, *L'avventura* (London: British Film Institute, 2008), 63–64.

69. Antonioni, for his part, preferred not to speak of alienation: "I never think in terms of alienation; it's the others who do. Alienation means one thing to Hegel, another to Marx, and yet another to Freud; so it is not possible to give a single definition . . . It is a question bordering on philosophy, and I'm not a philosopher or a

sociologist. My business is to tell stories, to narrate with images—nothing else. If I do make films about alienation . . . they are about characters, not about me" (*Michelangelo Antonioni: Interviews*, ed. Bert Cardullo [Jackson: University Press of Mississippi, 2008], 56).

70. "The opposition between the movement of the figure and the immobility of the screen acts . . . as an agent of segregation and frees the object from the shot in which it was integrated. It becomes substantial in some way . . . It becomes a corporeal thing" (A. Michotte van den Berck, "La participation émotionalle du spectateur à l'action représentée à l'écran"; quoted in Edgar Morin, *The Cinema, or the Imaginary Man*, trans. Lorraine Mortimer [Minneapolis: University of Minnesota Press, 2005], 118).

71. The effect here as elsewhere is physical. "All Antonioni's works may thus be regarded as essays on the relation between reality and perception . . . Haunted by the forces and after-effects of the Real, each original framing and spatial disposition of figures, each exquisitely textured composition, constitutes a physical provocation . . . Antonioni continually makes us a witness to the processes of trans-formation" (James S. Williams, "The Rhythms of Life: An Appreciation of Michelangelo Antonioni, Extreme Aesthete of the Real," in *Film Quarterly* 62 [Fall 2008], 52).

72. "A form can assume a new and revolutionary character without being an event in and of itself; it can also assume this character from the simple fact of being transported from a rapidly moving environment into a slowly moving one, or inversely" (Focillon, 63).

73. "There is thus a hierarchy of speeds to be found in the history of societies, for to possess the earth, to hold terrain, is also to possess the best means to scan it in order to protect and defend it" (Paul Virilio, *Bunker Archeology*, trans. G. Collins [Princeton: Princeton Archeology Press, 1994], 19).

74. This piece dovetails with Angelo Restivo's reading of *L'eclisse* and the Italian economic miracle: "Antonioni has created an *analgon* to the economic miracle itself: that is, the paradoxical 'event' that is only visible through its traumatic effects" (Angelo Restivo, *The Cinema of Economic Miracles: Visuality and Modernization in the Italian Art Film* [Durham: Duke University Press, 2002], 120).

75. For an incisive reading of the concluding sequence, see Mirella Jona Affron's essay, "Text and Memory in *Eclipse*," in *Literature/Film Quarterly* 9, no. 3 (1981): "Antonioni's rejection of significance is ultimately the viewer's; there is no other choice. Abstraction breaks away from the narrative altogether as befits this conclusion: that whereas place may be either friendly or hostile to the memory of sentiment, non-sentiment is . . . located in a setting which, fragmented by the nature of montage, is further fragmented by compositions whose form is recognizable only as form" (150–51).

76. "Can't you see that Antonioni's films are films made for directors and not for actors? How can you not have see that there's really no one key scene in any of

Antonioni's films? Haven't you ever noticed how sick people are of seeing my face on screen? Do you have any idea what Marlon Brando wants in the script in order for him to do the film? He wants the audience to be sick and tired of the other actors in the film, and so when the audience is fed up, he arrives with his crucial scene, with close-ups and he's amazing. Do you really think that always having to be on screen, which is what happens in Antonioni's films, is really an advantage for the actor?" (Oriana Fallaci, "Alienata con riserva," in *Intervista con il mito* [Milan: Rizzoli, 2011], 67).

77. "In the scopic field, the gaze is outside, I am looked at, that is to say, I am a picture . . . What determines me, at the most profound level, in the visible, is the gaze that is outside. It is through the gaze that I enter light and it is from the gaze that I receive its effects" (Jacques Lacan, "What Is a Picture?" in *The Four Fundamental Concepts of Psychoanalysis*, ed. Jacques-Alain Miller, trans. Alan Sheridan [New York: Norton, 1977], 106). Kaja Silverman completes the insight for cinema: "Lacan metaphorizes the gaze as a camera so as to characterize it as an 'apparatus' whose only function is to put us 'in the picture'" (Kaja Silverman, *The Threshold of the Visible World* [London: Routledge, 2013], 132). On sexuality in Antonioni, see David Forgacs's "Antonioni: Space, Place, Sexuality," in *Spaces in European Cinema*, ed. Myrto Konstantarakos (London: Intellect Books, 2000): 101–11.

78. "'Acceptance of'—not necessarily 'acquiescence to.' By acceptance is meant an openness to the factors involved. One may accept a situation in thundering against it. Voltaire accepted. Acceptance is exposure" (Kenneth Burke, *Counter-Statement* [Berkeley: University of California Press, 1968], 108). In what remains perhaps the most insightful reading of all of Antonioni's films, Richard Gilman locates the place of acceptance in *L'avventura*'s closing image: "And here the search . . . comes to the same end, or a fractional distance beyond. The acceptance is made of what we are like; it is impossible not to accept it as this film dies out on its couple shatteringly united in the dust, because everything we are not like, but which we have found other means of shedding, has been stripped away" (Richard Gilman, "About Nothing—With Precision," in *Theater Arts* 47, no. 7 [1962]: 11).

79. Few have given Vitti her due in this regard. An important exception is Gilberto Perez, who in a film essay accompanying the Criterion edition, recognizes some of Vitti's heroic acting: "But just as Antonioni's films enact a special way of looking, so Vitti's special quality as a performer arises from the way she looks at things and the way she is looked at and is aware of being looked at, from the interplay between her as the subject and as the object of the gaze. Just as Antonioni is, more than a director of dramatic scenes, a director of attention, so Vitti is a performer of attention, which she pays to her surroundings and receives from Antonioni's camera with much the same inquiring, responsive intentness" (Gilberto Perez, "*L'eclisse*: Antonioni and Vitti," in *L'eclisse*, Criterion, DVD).

80. This suggests that we must view Vitti herself with "attentive suspicion: "Appearances in Antonioni as in Murnau are viewed with attentive suspicion," not because appearances are deceptive but because they are unclear and incomplete, ambiguous fragments of a whole beyond our purview, glimpses fraught with the invisible" (where focus etymologically refers in Latin to the hearth, to home, to the light that makes visible)" (Gilberto Perez, *The Material Ghost: Films and Their Medium* [Baltimore: Johns Hopkins Press, 1998], 144). On fragmentation in *L'eclisse*, see David Gianetti, *Invito al cinema di Michelangelo Antonioni* [Milan: Mursia, 1999], 94–100).

81. See again Vitti and Antonioni's interview with Oriana Fallaci, in particular Vitti's recollection of her name change. When told that Maria Luisa Ceciarelli was no name for an actress, Vitti "sat down at a table in a bar and began studying the question of my name. I wanted to take half of my mother's last name—she was named Vittiglia—and Vitti worked really well. Monica went well with Vitti and so after writing it two or three times, and pronouncing it five or six, I had my debut as Monica Vitti. I am so completely Monica Vitti that my mother and father call me Monica and not Maria Luisa" (Fallaci, 63). On Vitti's importance for Italian cinema more generally, see Lydia Blanc, "Searching for Monica Vitti," in *Positif—Revue Mensuelle De Cinéma* 11 (2004): 73–74.

82. Or a new grammar of life: "The last sequences of *L'eclisse* are baffling because they introduce a new tone, a new narrative into the usual narrative of day-to-day life. In being so unexpected, so unusual, this language jolts the viewer because it provides a new grammar of life. Indeed, it presents a new—renewed—life" (Paolo Bartoloni, "Blanchot and Ambiguity," in *CLCWeb: Comparative Literature and Culture* 12, no. 4 [2010], http://docs.lib.purdue.edu/clcweb/vol12/iss4/7).

83. See Noa Steimatsky's forthcoming essay, "Pass/Fail: The Antonioni Screen Test," in *Framework* 55, no. 2: 191–219.

84. When asked to explain what else changed when she became Monica Vitti, her voice perhaps, her face, her writing, Vitti responds: "Not the voice. Not the way I write. My face [*volto*], that yes. I made myself physically this way because I wanted to be this way physically. You should have seen photographs of me from seven years ago to appreciate how much I have changed" (Fallaci, 63).

85. On Antonioni's non-use of montage, see Mark Rudman, *Realm of Unknowing: Meditations on Art, Suicide and Other Transformations* (Middletown, Conn.: Wesleyan University Press, 1995): 55–79.

86. "Actuality is when the lighthouse is dark between flashes: it is the instant between the ticks of the watch: it is a void interval slipping forever through time: the rupture between past and future: the gap at the poles of the revolving magnetic field, infinitesimally small but ultimately real. It is the interchronic pause when nothing is happening. It is the void between events" (George Kublier, *The Shape of Time: Remarks on the History of Things* [New Haven: Yale University Press, 1962],

17). We may choose to call this actuality *temp mort*, though we ought to recall Levinas's reading of dead time in relation to the notion of interval: "The interval is not to life what potency is to act. Its originality consists in being between two times. We propose to call this dimension dead time" (Levinas, *Totality and Infinity*, 58).

87. Or the apparatus as toy, which calls to mind Jeffrey Mehlman's penetrating gloss of Benjamin's notion of play: "Toys, even when not imitative of adult utensils, are a coming to terms [*Auseinandersetzung*], and doubtless less of the child with adults than of adults with him. A precarious coming to terms that is marked by a tearing apart, it is shot through with unmastered 'traces' of the other" (Jeffrey Mehlman, *Walter Benjamin: An Essay on His Radio Years* [Chicago: University of Chicago Press, 1993], 4).

88. They may, of course, line up more simply as operators for fetishizing: "For the cinematic effects I am evoking here (playing on the framing and its displacements), the properly fetishistic element seems to me to be the '*bar*', the edge of the screen, the separation between the seen and the unseen, the 'arrestation' of the look. Once the seen or the unseen are envisaged rather than their intersection (their edge), we are dealing with scopic perversion itself, which goes beyond the strict province of the fetish" (Metz, *The Imaginary Signifier*, 87).

89. For this reason Vitti's performance has been called mannerist. Speaking of the initial sequences of *L'eclisse*, Penelope Houston writes: "Intellectually, one is aware of what Antonioni is doing and why he has chosen to do it in this dehumanising way. But at the same time, in its deliberate echoing of the more sombre moods of *La Notte*, the scene pushes style towards the thin edge of mannerism" ("Film Reviews: *The Eclipse*," in *Sight and Sound* 32, no. 2 [Spring 1963]: 90).

90. As the spectator must. In the screenplay for *L'eclisse*, Antonioni, in detailing the final sequence, recognizes the sense of expectation he is creating around Vittoria and Piero: "The bus stops. Several passengers descend. Neither Vittoria nor Piero are among them. The people who got off the bus disappear into the background" (Antonioni, 361).

91. Here I take issue with Angelo dalle Vacche's reading of ventriloquism in *Red Desert*. It seems to me less the case that Antonioni gains "representational freedom" through Vitti thanks to the "images he assigns to his actress" (Angelo dalle Vacche, *Cinema and Painting: How Art Is Used in Film* [Austin: University of Texas Press, 1996], 49). And so rather than adopting the term "convalescent," "neurotic," or "artist," a more apt term is precisely the form of life that is missing a hand and so is unable to seize and to be seized by the apparatus.

92. On this note, see Antonioni's *mise-en-scène* in the third part of *I tre volti* ("Tre Volti [1965]: Soraya Screen Test Clip," YouTube video, 4:00, posted by belogtoob, December 5, 2014, https://www.youtube.com/watch?v=4hfBD2Gwnaw).

93. "*The Second*: According to you the great actor is everything and nothing. First: Perhaps it is just because he is nothing that he is before all everything. His

own special shape never interferes with the shapes he assumes" (Denis Diderot, *The Paradox of Acting* [New York: Hill and Wang, 1957], 41).

94. It is much along the lines of a great power that "promulgates a necessary actuality which had long been seeking with feeble rudimentary movement to define itself" (Focillon, 155).

95. One of the obsolete meanings of "perform" is precisely "to complete or make up by means of an addition" (*Oxford English Dictionary*. 2nd ed., 20 vols. Oxford: Oxford University Press, 1989. Also available at http://www.oed.com/).

96. "After all, the hand touches the world itself, feels it, lays hold of it, and transforms it. The hand contrives astonishing adventures in matter. It not only grasps what exists, but it has to work does not exist; it adds yet another realm to the realms of nature" (Focillon, 71).

97. Winnicott himself explains the emphasis on transitional object and not Klein's "internal object": "The transitional object is not an internal object (which is a mental concept)—it is a possession" (Winnicott, "Transitional Objects," 94).

98. "But in law our maxim [nine-tenths of the law], as I have said, had really no special significance. It is but another way of saying "beati possidentes" or "melior est conditio possidentis" or other similar maxims expressing *commoda possessionis*" ("Legal Possession: Two Maxims," Henry Goudon, Heinonline, Citation: 13 Ill. L. R. 293 1918–19).

CONCLUSION: ATTENTION, NOT AUTOPSY

1. Aristotle, *Parts of Animals*, 687a2–687a23. See John Burnet's gloss of Anaxagoras's fragment in his *Early Greek Philosophers*: "The Nous in living creatures is the same in all (fr. 12), and from this it followed that the different grades of intelligence we observe in the animal and vegetable worlds depend entirely on the structure of the body . . . Man was the wisest of animals, not because he had a better sort of Nous, but because he had hands" (http://www.classicpersuasion.org/pw/burnet /egp.htm?chapter=6#N_70_).

2. Attention, not autopsy, is required: "The eye or, rather, autopsy: by this I mean the eye used as an indicator as to who is speaking, the 'I have seen' as an intervention in his narrative on the part of the narrator, as a way of providing proof" (Hartog, 261).

3. Bergson, *Laughter*, 4.

4. Consider the etymology of gripe, grip, grasp from the German *greifen* and then from the Sanskrit: "GRAH, *grih-na*," seize, take (also of leeches), hold, catch, stop; grasp, gain possession of, capture, captivate (the heart); attack; eclipse, rob, deprive of, receive from, assume, acquire, purchase . . . *Grahaya*, cause to seize, take or grasp, be about to seize; desire to grasp; cherish (*A Sanskrit English Dictionary*, available at http://www.openlibrary.org).

5. See Jean-Luc Nancy's helpful gloss of *Bild* and schema in the first *Critique*: "Kant calls the free *Bild* that precedes all images, all representations, and all figurations . . . a *schema* in the first *Critique*. He says in the third *Critique* that aesthetic judgment is nothing other than the reflexive play of the imagination when it 'schematizes without concepts': that is, when the world that forms itself, that manifests itself, is not a universe of objects but merely a schema (*skema*, 'form,' or 'figure')" (Jean-Luc Nancy, "The Sublime Offering," in *Of the Sublime: Presence in Question*, ed. Jeffrey S. Librett [Albany: SUNY Press, 1993], 29). On the rhetorical difference between schema and figure, see Hayden White's masterful discussion in *Metahistory: The Historical Imagination in Nineteenth-Century Europe* (Baltimore: Johns Hopkins University Press, 1973), 32–33.

6. See the entry for *ΣEX* in *A Greek-English Lexicon*, ed. Henry George Liddell and Roberto Scott (Oxford: Oxford University Press, 1819), 629.

7. D. W. Winnicott, *Holding and Interpretation: Fragment of an Analysis* (London: The Hogarth Press and the Institute of Psycho-analysis, 1986), 191–92.

INDEX

Abraham, Karl, 100–1, 194n22
Adorno, Theodor W., xi, 12, 14–16, 24, 89, 99; gratitude and invariability, 8–11; parataxis, 9–11
Agamben, Giorgio: biopolitics, 1–3; desire, 178n8; genius, 171n22; "homeland of gesture," 83–84; *homo sacer*, 2; monastic form of life, 35–36; *oikonomia*, 1
alienation, 71–72, 144, 207n69
Althusser, Louis, 178n6
Anaxgoras, 162, 212n1
animal, 34–35, 45–46, 58–59
Antonioni, Michelangelo, 117–60; existentialist, 117, 132, 205n42; on dead feelings, 206n60; on editing, 206n54; on screenplays, 200n10
apparatus: and alienation, 150–51; cinematic, 118, 133, 146–48, 163–64; etymology, 177n1; liberation, 131; ontology, 150–52, 154; transitional object, 52
Aristotle, 31, 80, 162, 175n59; pathos, 185n111; story and conflict, 191n69
attention: community and, 17–18; frame and, 81–83; generous, 53–56; observation and, 74; primitive affectivity and, 14; and reciprocal aliveness, 58; relation to grip, 163. *See also* form of life
autopsy, 189n53, 212n2
Avatar, 50
L'avventura, 118–31

Badiou, Alain, 175n64
Barthes, Roland, 10, 144; "neutral," 176n78; photography and death, 185n22; photography and nature, 191n66; photography and violence, 67, 72

Bataille, Georges, 19–23, 36, 58; "surrender to capitalism," 36–37
Baudry, Jean-Louis, 45–48
Bazin, André, 184n1; "event itself," 61; landscape, 64; seeing and knowing, 110–11
Benjamin, Walter, 82; aura, 201n19; *blosses Leben*, 74; "Critique of Violence," 27; divine violence, 67; "Fate and Character," 6–7; *Heiterkeit* and *Verurteilung*, 7–8; play, 207n63; possession and having, 109; "The Storyteller," 203n30; tactility, 109–10; toys, 210n86
Benveniste, Émile, 11–14, 36; gratitude, 48–49
Berardi, Franco, 195n35
Bergson, Henri: the comic, 163, 207n61; elasticity, 190n55; freedom and seriousness, 85–87
Bion, Wilfred, 112–15, 197n48, 198n52
biopolitics: cinema and, vii–viii; milieu and, 69–70; negative, 3; as thanatopolitics, 3, 10; tragic readings, 10
biopower: biology; 169–70; bodily existence, 1; comedy; 7–8; fear, 2–4, 9; mythical violence, 24, 38, 42, 163–64; possession, viii, ix, 24. *See also* form of life
Blanchot, Maurice, 202n25
Bloch, Ernst, 172n27
Blow-Up, 140
Broch, Hermann, 135–37, 205n51
Brunette, Peter, 141
Burke, Kenneth: acceptance as exposure, 209n78; comedy, 59, 185n17; "comic corrective," 64–65; definition of form, 200n9; milieu of "maybe," 206n56; symbolic, 26–27; terministic screen, 15;

Burke, Kenneth (cont.)
  trained incapacity, 192n8; ways of
  seeing, 87

Cage, John, 200n7
Canetti, Elias, 206n52
Cardullo, Bert, 53, 181n35
Cassano, Franco, 187n26
Cavarero, Adriana, 170n2, 204n40
Cavell, Stanley, 197n47
Chaplin, Charlie, 190n62
Chatman, Seymour, 199n2, 205n44,
  206n58
cinema. *See* form of life
Cinema (journal), 61, 181n4
Citizen Kane, 184n1
comedy: grip, 83–84; laughter and, 171n25;
  Nietzsche's perspective on, 32–33;
  parataxis and, 59; serenity and, 7–8;
  slapstick, 188n35; and vitality, 64
community, 17, 88–89, 105, 116
creativity, 72–74

Dayan, David, 49
death drive, 125
defamiliarization, 119, 144, 149, 199n2,
  200n8. *See also* form of life
Deleuze, Gilles, 58, 157; affect, 185n14; eye
  and hand, 196n40; haptic, 109–10;
  primitive affective form, 14–16; seizure
  and grip, 199n6; time-image, 64, 159
Delon, Alain, 152, 157
De Man, Paul, 50–52
dementia praecox, 100–1
Derrida, Jacques: *Cinders*, 174n49; gift
  annulled, 173n43; gift-giving as
  interruption, 114–15; *Given Time*, 17–18;
  grip, 173n41; *oikonomia*, 173n48;
  proximity, 109
Descartes, René, 177n9
De Sica, Vittorio, 61
Diderot, Denis 211n93
dispositif. *See* apparatus
dispossession. *See* possession; spectator

The Earth Trembles, 61–90. *See also* icon
L'eclisse, 116–17, 141–60, 205n44, 206n58,
  208n74, 211n90
Eco, Umberto 64, 207nn62,63
ékhein, 164–65
Emerson, Ralph Waldo, 193n11
Engels, Friedrich, 202n23
envy. *See* Klein, Melanie
Esposito, Roberto 19, 38
The Exorcist, 106

Fallaci, Oriana, 208n76
fate. *See* Benjamin, Walter; fear
fear: and biopower, 10; and desire, 129; of
  falling, 120; of fate, 9, 82; gratitude and,
  7, 99; milieu of, 117, 206n56; mythical
  violence and, 2–3, 8–10, 163; and
  nothing, 35; permanent, 186n22;
  potlatch and 174n54; tragedy and, 64, 84,
  171n25
Fellini, Federico, 192n9
fetish, 129, 133, 211n88. *See also* mastery
film: continuity editing, 50; montage, 50–51;
  reality effect, 48
flâneur, 108–10
flesh, 73, 90
Flusser, Vilém, 45–46
Focillon, Henri, 201n18, 206n57, 208n72,
  212n96
Forbrydelsen, 199n3
form of life: attention in, 117; capitalist,
  145–46; care of the self in, 24–25;
  defamiliarization and, 149–50;
  evasion of apparatus in, 148–49;
  Heideggerean, 164; as *manceps* and
  mancus, 37–41; militant, 35; neoliberal
  gift-giving and, 165; privation as,
  174n59; relation to common, 27–28;
  relation to mastery, 140–41; response to
  biopower, viii–ix; response to mythic
  violence, 38–39; spectator as, 116–17.
  See also generosity
Foucault, Michel: classical being, 178n7;
  genealogy, 33; *The Hermeneutics of the
  Subject*, 24–25; politicization, 191n68;
  Security, Territory, Population, 69
Frampton, Daniel, 180n26
Freud, Sigmund, 159, 195n36, 197n48,
  207n69

generosity: capitalism and, 64–65; circuit
  of, viii–ix, 11–12; of comedy, 33–37, 59, 92;
  and envy in *Germany Year Zero*, 108;
  form of life and, 15–16, 25, 132; and
  impropriety of image, 50; intimacy and,
  23–24; non-possession and, 3, 33;
  as a passion, 72; relation to life, ix.
  See also Nietzsche, Friedrich
Germany Year Zero, 91–116
gesture: and exhaustion, 197n43; relation to
  hand, 82–85; and Monica Vitti, 152
gift: absorption and, 173n47; etymology,
  200n13; gift, counter-gift and, 18; relation
  to *Gift* (poison), 104, 107–8; relation to
  mythic violence, 88–89; and transitional
  object, 159

Ginzburg, Carlo, 200n8
Girard, René, 142, 207n65
The Girl with the Dragon Tattoo, 199n3
Goodrich, Peter, 43–44, 52
Gramsci, Antonio, 185n21
gratitude, 127–28
grip: i, 118; as form of seeing, 36–37;
etymology, 212n4; in *L'avventura*, 126–27;
and transitional object, 159; uncanny,
120–26

hand: as living beings, 159; bodies with, viii;
comprehension and, 200n11; mastery
and, 89–90; missing, 40–41
haptic. *See* Deleuze, Gilles
Hardt, Michael, 1, 7, 170n2, 182n37
Heath, Stephen: appropriation of image, 50;
on Brecht, 178n6; documentary, 51–52;
property of image, 46–48
Hegel, Georg Wilhelm, 51, 176n82, 177n85;
alienation, 207n69; burden of life, 185n15;
"subjective caprice," 7–9, 33–35, 42;
tragedy and comedy, 33–34
Heidegger, Martin, 1, 35–36. *See also* form
of life
Hölderlin, Friedrich, 8–10
holding: death drive, 125–26; as form of
ékhein, 164; grasping and, 15–16, 118;
and having, x
hypostasis, 10–11

icon: attending to, 90; contemplation of,
77–78; definition, 79–80; difference with
fetish, 73; in *The Earth Trembles*, 73–75;
and index, 204n37
idolatry, 56, 188n37
impolitical, 198n54
intermediate area. *See* Winnicott, D. W.
intimacy: and finite world, 56–57; and
holding, 131, 137; with objects, 152
Irigaray, Luce: caress, 57; women and
tangible invisible, 57–58
I tre volti, 149

Kael, Pauline, 207n67
Kant, Immanuel, 164, 213n5
Klein, Melanie, 30, 51; envy and gratitude,
97–99; good object, 97, 106–7; idealization, 194n24
Kraucauer, Siegfried: boredom, 195n34; flow
of life, 64, 185nn13,18; Italian neorealism,
190n62; slapstick, 188n35

Lacan, Jacques: 36, 179n11, 201n15, 209n77
lack, 40–41

landscape: attention to, viii; and boredom,
195n34; interiority and, 111; as relation to
objects held, 127
Lazzarato, Maurizo, 205n47
Levinas, Emmanuel: caress, 190n59, 201n21;
concrete being, 197n50; on feminine,
205n45; grasping, 202n26; identification
and dwelling, 190n57; intervals of
"meanwhile," 180n23; possession, 204n36;
signfication as giving, 191n70; "there is,"
204n38; "to ask as what," 206n53. *See also*
hand
Lingis, Alphonso, 184n8, 197n49
Lyotard, Jean-François: dispossession, 39,
49; "The Grip (*Mainmise*)," 37–41, 118;
seeing and the visible, 182n44

La macchina ammazzacattivi, 61
macchina da presa, 150, 152
Mainmise. See Lyotard, Jean-François
Mamet, David, 5
mancus, 118; in *The Earth Trembles*, 62–64;
in *Germany Year Zero*, 103–4; in *L'eclisse*,
159–60; vulnerability and, 161–63. *See
also* form of life
mastery: and fetish, 130; and financial
capitalism, 147; and strolling, 138; of
unfamiliar, 120
Mauss, Marcel, 173n43, 193n17
Mediterranean, 80, 131, 189n52
Merleau-Ponty, Maurice: delirium
as vision, 50; flesh as element of
Being, 57–58, 182n42, 188n34; *Umwelt*,
191n67
Metz, Christian, 129–30, 204n37
milieu: biopower and, 69; dead, 71–72; of
envy in *Germany Year Zero*, 97–98,
100–2; and individuation, 81–82; relation
to reciprocity in *La notte*, 137
Miracolo a Milano, 61
Morin, Edgar, 181n33, 188n33
Mulvey, Laura, 185n22
Musil, Robert, 176n80
Mussolini, Benito, 74

Nancy, Jean-Luc, 213n5
Negri, Antonio, 1, 7, 170n2, 182n37
neoliberalism, 16
neorealism: Italian, 70, 93, 190n62
Nietzsche, Friedrich, 6, 33, 171; and agon,
163; *The Birth of Tragedy*, 32, 84–85;
generosity, ix; un-tragic individual,
85–86; will-to-power and affect, 14–15
nomos, 31, 35, 175n79
La notte, 132–42, 144, 147

object: distinction from thing, 36–37; dispossession of, x; engaging with, 86–87; as gift, 22–23; giving away of, 19–20; "good," 97–99, 105, 107, 112–15; in frame, 72–73; partial, 129–31; possession of, 12–16, 152; transitional, viii, 26, 28–32, 51–59
Odyssey, 68
Oliver Twist, 93

Paglia, Camille, 32, 56
parataxis: in *La notte*, 139–42; practice of, 32; as suspension of inevitability, 15–16. *See also* Adorno, Theodor W.
Pascal, Blaise, 69, 187n29
Pasolini, Pier Paolo, 184n10
Peirce, Charles, 79
Perniola, Mario, 203n29
Plato, 85, 172n36
possession, 16, 128, 147, 171n38, 212n98. *See also* object
potlatch, 174n54
praeparatus, 45–48, 87, 116, 119

Rancière, Jacques, 92–96; dissensus, 98, 100; "emancipated spectator," 179n17; freedom and grace, 93–94
reciprocity, 181n35; and gift, 30, 34–36; anti-, 67, 110; apparatus and, 44–45; circuit of, 13–14, 89; comedy and, 7; failed reciprocity in *Germany Year Zero*, 98, 114; forms of, ix, 11, 22, 27, 35, 48–49, 91, 105–6, 126, 134, 137, 146, 201n19; holding, having, and 126, 152; montage and, 50; relation to gratitude, xi, 38, 40, 73, 96–97; spectator and, 85–87
Renzi, Renzo, 77–80
Ricciardi, Alessia, 201n15
Rohmer, Eric, 193n11
Rome Open City, 104–6
Rose, Carol, 16
Rossellini, Renzo, 100
Rossellini, Roberto, vii, 7, 57, 91–116, 198n52

Sartre, Jean-Paul, 73, 95, 188n32
Scarface (1932), 44
Schmitt, Carl, viii, 52
Screentest, 149, 204n39
Sennett, Richard, 183n45
serenity, 7–8, 195n34
Shapiro, Steven, 180n25
Shklovsky, Victor. *See* defamiliarization
Silverman, Kaja, 209n77
Simmel, Georg, 53–55, 181n36, 182n37
sleepwalking, in *La notte*, 133–38

Sloterdijk, Peter, 171n12
The Sopranos, 44
spectator: apparatus and, 45–57; and attention, ix, 81, 140–44; belief and, 50, 180n26; body of, 47; cinematic techne and, 7, 146–50; and comedy, 59, 65–66; elasticity and, 86–87; emancipated, 39–41, 47, 179n17; exposure and, 85, 127–34; frustration of, 113–19; gaze of, 49–50; as improper form of life, 46–47; lack and, 41–42; milieu and, 69–72; and mythic violence, 82; non-possession and, x, 48–51, 60, 64–65, 161–63; and waiting, 45–46, 77–80
Spitzer, Leo, 69–70, 187n29
Star Trek, 194n26
Sudnow, David, 202n27

tactility, 158–59, 199n5
techne: cinematic, 56, 64–65, 125–26; as practice of attention, 53, 59; relation to anthropos, 70. *See also* spectator
temp mort, 182n41, 210n86
La terra trema. See *The Earth Trembles*
thing: holding and, vii; intimacy and, 37. *See also* Bataille, Georges
tragedy: catharsis and, 191n66; relation to fear, 171n25; power of exchange and, 33–34; relation to grip, 83–84
transitional object. *See* Winnicott, D. W.
trucage, 203n35
Truffaut, François, 193n11

uncanny. *See* grip
unconscious, 125

veneration. *See* Perniola, Mario
Verga, Giovanni, 68–69, 187n23
violence, divine, 2–4, 6–7
violence, mythic: biopower and, 31, 38, 42; care of self and, 25; and holding, 39; as intensification of the political, 52, 191n68; *mancus* and, 45; milieu of, 61, 65–71, 85–90, 108; and tragedy, 34, 84, 163. *See also* Barthes, Roland
Virilio, Paul, 147, 185n12, 208n73
Visconti, Luchino, 125, 144; "Anthropomorphic Cinema," 62–64, 68; creativity and, 71–72; relation to Antonioni, 131
Vitti, Monica, 118, 120, 144, 208n76; and alienation, 154; as *mancus*, 159; conflation with Vittoria in *L'eclisse*, 146–48; doubled in *La notte*, 132; face 210n84; as generous form of life, 158–59; hands, 123; invisible appearance, 210n80; and name change,

210n81; and ontological play, 150–52, 154; response to apparatus, 156–57; as subject and object of gaze, 209n79

Weber, Max, 205n43

Weber, Samuel, 178n4

Weil, Simone, 134; good and evil, 106; gravity, 95–96, 203n31; impersonal, 96; void, 96

Winnicott, D. W., 128, 150, 160; creativity and play, 30–31; "first not-me possession," 51–52; holding as interpretation, 165; intermediate area, 128–29, 203n28; missing self, 198n53; play and attention, 28–30; transitional object, 30, 51, 128–29, 212n97

Wittgenstein, Ludwig: certainty, 25–26; form-of-life as language, 26–27; and seeing, 175n64; sign and life, 189n39

Žižek, Slavoj, 193n18

COMMONALITIES
Timothy C. Campbell, series editor

Roberto Esposito, *Terms of the Political: Community, Immunity, Biopolitics.* Translated by Rhiannon Noel Welch. Introduction by Vanessa Lemm.

Maurizio Ferraris, *Documentality: Why It Is Necessary to Leave Traces.* Translated by Richard Davies.

Dimitris Vardoulakis, *Sovereignty and Its Other: Toward the Dejustification of Violence.*

Anne Emmanuelle Berger, *The Queer Turn in Feminism: Identities, Sexualities, and the Theater of Gender.* Translated by Catherine Porter.

James D. Lilley, *Common Things: Romance and the Aesthetics of Belonging in Atlantic Modernity.*

Jean-Luc Nancy, *Identity: Fragments, Frankness.* Translated by François Raffoul.

Miguel Vatter, *Between Form and Event: Machiavelli's Theory of Political Freedom.*

Miguel Vatter, *The Republic of the Living: Biopolitics and the Critique of Civil Society.*

Maurizio Ferraris, *Where Are You? An Ontology of the Cell Phone.* Translated by Sarah De Sanctis.

Irving Goh, *The Reject: Community, Politics, and Religion after the Subject.*

Kevin Attell, *Giorgio Agamben: Beyond the Threshold of Deconstruction.*

J. Hillis Miller, *Communities in Fiction.*

Remo Bodei, *The Life of Things, the Love of Things*. Translated by Murtha Baca.

Gabriela Basterra, *The Subject of Freedom: Kant, Levinas*.

Roberto Esposito, *Categories of the Impolitical*. Translated by Connal Parsley.

Roberto Esposito, *Two: The Machine of Political Theology and the Place of Thought*. Translated by Zakiya Hanafi.

Akiba Lerner, *Redemptive Hope: From the Age of Enlightenment to the Age of Obama*.

Adriana Cavarero and Angelo Scola, *Thou Shalt Not Kill: A Political and Theological Dialogue*. Translated by Margaret Adams Groesbeck and Adam Sitze.

Massimo Cacciari, *Europe and Empire: On the Political Forms of Globalization*. Edited by Alessandro Carrera, Translated by Massimo Verdicchio.

Emanuele Coccia, *Sensible Life: A Micro-ontology of the Image*. Translated by Scott Stuart, Introduction by Kevin Attell.

Timothy C. Campbell, *The Techne of Giving: Cinema and the Generous Forms of Life*.

Étienne Balibar, *Citizen Subject: Foundations for Philosophical Anthropology*. Translated by Steven Miller, Foreword by Emily Apter.

Ashon Crawley, *Blackpentecostal Breath: The Aesthetics of Possibility*.

Terrion L. Williamson, *Scandalize My Name: Black Feminist Practice and the Making of Black Social Life*.

Jean-Luc Nancy, *The Disavowed Community*. Translated by Philip Armstrong.